One Right Reading?

With affection
and a prayer for
God's blessing
on your many services
to the Church,

Mary Ann Donovan, SC

One Right Reading?

A GUIDE TO IRENAEUS

Mary Ann Donovan, s.c.

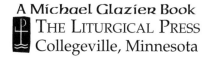
A Michael Glazier Book
THE LITURGICAL PRESS
Collegeville, Minnesota

Cover design by Ann Blattner. Icon: Saint Irenaeus of Lyons.

A Michael Glazier Book published by The Liturgical Press.

1	2	3	4	5	6	7	8

Library of Congress Cataloging-in-Publication Data

Donovan, Mary Ann.
    One right reading? : a guide to Irenaeus / Mary Ann Donovan.
        p.   cm.
    "A Michael Glazier book."
    Includes bibliographical references and index.
    ISBN 0-8146-5875-X (alk. paper)
    1. Irenaeus, Saint, Bishop of Lyon.   Adversus haereses.
I. Title.
BR1720.I7D66   1997
239'.3—dc21   97-37792
                                                                                    CIP

In memory of
Professor Walter H. Principe, C.S.B.
Scholar, Teacher, and Friend

Contents

Acknowledgments

This project has continued over some years, and I owe a large debt of gratitude. A grant from the Association of Theological Schools helped fund a year of research at Oxford University. The Jesuit School of Theology at Berkeley, under the leadership of Thomas F. Gleeson, S.J., George Griener, S.J., T. Howland Sanks, S.J., and David Stagaman, S.J. provided the support of a good working environment, made research and writing leaves possible, and offered consistent encouragement. I owe particular thanks to my colleagues and students both at JSTB and in the Graduate Theological Union, as well as the staff at JSTB. Those who read and commented on various drafts were Professors John Endres, S.J. and Frank Houdek, S.J. of the Jesuit School of Theology, Professor Rebecca Lyman of the Church Divinity School of the Pacific, Professors Elizabeth Liebert and Antoinette Wire of San Francisco Theological Seminary, and Professor Virginia Burrus of Drew University Theological School (then a doctoral candidate at the GTU). Invaluable help came from my research assistants and doctoral students: Lizette Larson-Miller, Joseph Thometz, Peter Togni, S.J., and Ann Roberts Winsor. Peter McGrath, S.J. guided me into computer literacy. The talent and training of these men and women made possible a task, much of whose worth is due to their input. The responsibility for the outcome is, of course, mine.

Finally, I want to acknowledge the loving support of my family, especially my father, Joseph Donovan, my brother Jerry and his wife Elizabeth Donovan, my sister Mary Lou and her husband Paul Wood, and my sister Suzanne Donovan, S.C.; of my friends, especially Anne Brotherton, S.F.C.C., Maureen Hester, S.N.J.M., Mary Margaret Pazdan, O.P., and Sandra Schneiders, I.H.M.; and of my Sister of Charity community, especially the members of my small group.

Abbreviations

AB	Anchor Bible
ABD	*Anchor Bible Dictionary*
AEPHE	*Annuaire de l'École Pratique des Hautes Études*
AH	*Adversus haereses*
ANF	Ante-Nicene Fathers
Anton.	*Antonianum*
BTB	*Biblical Theological Bulletin*
EHPhR	*Etude d'histoire et de philosophie religieuses*
FRLANT	Forschungen zur Religion und Literatur des Alten und Neuen Testaments
Gr.	*Gregorianum*
HThR	*Harvard Theological Review*
JThS	*Journal of Theological Studies*
LCC	Library of Christian Classics
LingBibl	*Linguistica biblica*
LXX	Septuagint
NRSV	New Revised Standard Version
PG	Patrologia Graeca
PL	Patrologia Latina
REG	*Revue des études grecques*
RSPhTh	*Revue des sciences philosophiques et théologiques*
RSR	*Recherches de science religieuse*
RStR	*Religious Studies Review*
RSV	Revised Standard Version
RThAM	*Recherches de théologie ancienne et médiévale*
SC	Sources chrétiennes
SecCen	*The Second Century*
SM	*Sacramentum Mundi*
StMiss	*Studia missionalia*
TC	*Traditio Christiana*
TS	*Theological Studies*
VigChr	*Vigiliae Christianae*
ZThK	*Zeitschrift für Theologie und Kirche*

PART ONE

Introduction

Who is a Christian? Is there a hallmark of Christianity, a clear and recognizable Christian identity? Such questions, frequently posed near the close of the second "Christian" millennium, were equally pressing near the opening of the first millennium. The second century was *the* century for the construction of Christian identity. One of the principal architects of that identity was Irenaeus of Lyons. His work shaped the Scriptures, the exegesis, the theology, the institutions, and the spirituality of nascent Christianity to such an extent that his imprint is discernible almost two thousand years later. In his writings the Christian Bible takes recognizable shape as composed of the two testaments. He employs a definite style of exegesis, using the techniques of his day to read Christian texts and to claim for Christianity the texts of Judaism. He understands the Rule of Faith to be in a dialogical relationship with the Scriptures in such a way that each serves to amplify and correct the other. He describes the dynamism of the Rule of Faith in the vocabulary of tradition, thus entering into a discussion of offices within the Church, a discussion invoked as authoritative by many western Christians to this day. By contrast, his distinctive spirituality, a spirituality marked by an appreciation of creation and a unique insight into the interplay between the Spirit of God and the human spirit, has been influential primarily in eastern Christianity.

Granted the immense importance of the Irenaean contribution, it may be surprising to realize that his work is little known. The reason is evident to those engaged with that work: access to his texts is extremely difficult. Not until 1982 did there appear a critical edition of his major extant work, *Adversus haereses*. Not until 1992 did we see the first volume of a good, readable English translation. But the presence of a good edition and a good translation alone does not resolve the problem; if anything, difficulty of access is sharpened as the text is more available. The work continues to present the contemporary reader with serious challenges in content and style. The style (and so the internal organization of the work) functions with assumptions alien to contemporary readers; the content, in part because it is deeply engaged with second-century Gnosticism, is esoteric. Such are the problems that render the great Irenaean contribution inaccessible to many. Because this major work is both so significant and so difficult of access scholars have either focused on one aspect or another of Irenaeus's thought or have synthesized it. In either case they have largely avoided following the organization Irenaeus himself imposed on his work as the present book does.

The intent of this book is to serve as a companion to the reader of *Adversus haereses*. It is not a commentary but a reader's guide. As such it offers an introduction to the intricacies of the Irenaean style, explains the content of his thought with attention to his major contributions, and points out areas that have been the focus of scholarly interest. The aim is to present clearly and concisely what Irenaeus says, following the order of his argument. I critique his position when such critique is appropriate, but my first intention is to present his thought on its own terms. In doing so it is of course inevitable that I give my own reading. My hope is that my reading will lead others back to the text of Irenaeus himself. If this work draws others to that reading, if it enables others to read Irenaeus more easily, it will have accomplished its goal. It is, after all, through engagement with Irenaeus that readers will shape an informed opinion about his continuing contribution to the Christian Church.

The reader who grapples with the Irenaean text struggles to find an authentic interpretation, that is, to hear Irenaeus speaking in a way that is integrally himself yet understandable in the reader's own context. Anyone who seriously engages the text in this way will find Irenaeus himself struggling to defend what he considers to be the authentic interpretation of the Christian faith. The issue of interpretation is thus two-edged, and is a recurring theme of the book.

Another concern facing the reader of the Irenaean text is to recognize the voice of the Gnostics against whom he is writing. Their voices, or perhaps better their faces, lie hidden from view in the text, but careful reading does discern their lineaments. The issue of recognition of the genuine face of the Gnostics with whom Irenaeus is engaged is another concern around authenticity, and a second recurring theme of this book.

The first chapter introduces Irenaeus in his world and discusses the methodology that provides unity to *Adversus haereses*. That methodology is first and foremost a method of scriptural interpretation, precritical and rhetorical in form. Within its own canons it is a method that provides a tight unity.

The remaining chapters fall into four parts that serve as guides to the content of *Adversus haereses*. Part One, "The Face of the Foe," looks at the Gnostics through the eyes of Irenaeus. The conflict between them is a conflict of interpretation centering both on the right interpretation of the Christian Scriptures and the right to interpret them. Chapter Two presents the view of the Valentinians found in *AH* I. 1–9, then reflects on the appeal of the Valentinian mythology as well as on the problems involved in the quasi-canonical acceptance of the division of humanity into three groups with corresponding destinies as part of the Valentinian system. Chapter Three examines the Irenaean contrast between the unity of the Church's faith and the diversity of Gnostic doctrines, practices, rites, and exegeses that forms the bulk of *AH* I. 10–22. As he prepares to close this book Irenaeus places *AH* I. 23–31 as a "bookend" with *AH* I. 1–9, pairing the opening section on Valentinian mythology with a closing section on Valentinian origins in which he attends to the link between belief and life. In Chapter Four, which corresponds to *AH* II, we see Irenaeus taking the stance of the theologian, working from the Rule of Faith to refute the five major positions of his opponents. A brief review of the situation of the Valentinians vis-à-vis the Christian Church concludes Part Two.

Parts Three, Four, and Five correspond to Books III, IV, and V of *Adversus haereses*. The underlying issue between Irenaeus and the Gnostics concerns the content and transmission of Christian faith. An adequate response to them requires him to present an authoritative interpretation of that faith. Because he is convinced that the Scriptures belong to the Christian community in such a way that any valid interpretation must be consistent with the faith of the community, an authoritative interpretation of the faith for him includes authoritative interpretation of the Scriptures. All of this material will thus stress scriptural interpretation, although with differing emphases.

Part Three, "One God, One Christ," reviews the content of *AH* III and thus a second-century Christian understanding of one God and one Christ. Irenaeus frames his presentation between discussions of the Church: the Church as place of Truth (*AH* III. 1–5) and the Church as place of the Spirit (*AH* III. 24, 1–III. 25, 7.) Having set this context, he organizes treatment of each of his two major topics in typically threefold fashion. Chapter Five follows his examination of the witness to the one God in three levels of Scripture writing: the "global witness" of the Scriptures, the witness of the evangelists, and that of the other apostles, while Chapter Six accompanies him as he turns to the content of faith in the one Son of God, looking at it under these three headings: the Son of God was really a *man;* Jesus was truly the Son of *God;* Christ the Savior is the *antitype* of Adam. His use of chiasm is evident throughout, and receives explicit treatment.

Part Four, "The One Story of Salvation," deals with the unity of the Old and New Testaments, the subject of *AH* IV. Here Irenaeus teaches that the one God, together with God's Word and Spirit, acts continuously in history for the salvation of humanity. There is only one history of salvation and it runs from the Old Testament through the New. He organizes his thought in three stages, which correspond to Chapters Seven, Eight, and Nine. The first and third stages of his thought depend respectively on the words of Christ and the parables of Christ; these two frame the central stage, which presents the Old Testament as prophecy of the New. Key exegetical insights are his relationship of prophecy to vision and his appeal to the authority of the post-resurrection teaching of Jesus Christ.

Part Five, "The Salvation of the Flesh," focuses on *AH* V. The emphasis falls throughout on the flesh common to the Incarnate One and to humanity. As is his custom, Irenaeus employs a threefold organization. Discussions of the resurrection of the flesh, with attention to Paul's epistles (Chapter Ten) and of the events of the end time, based primarily on Daniel and Revelation (Chapter Twelve), frame the central part (Chapter Eleven) in which three events from the life of Christ capsulize the story of salvation and at the same time establish the identity between the Father and the Creator. The exegesis continues the antignostic bent of the earlier books in both form and purpose.

CHAPTER ONE

Irenaeus, the Man and the Book

"Living among the Celts . . . lacking the writer's skill"
(*AH* I. preface, 3)

Keen detective work is required to know a man for whom no biography exists, of whom there is no portrait, whose letters have been reduced to scraps, whose sermons were neither taped nor—so far as anyone knows—transcribed. In fact, his major extant work has survived only thanks to the services of a translator (Rufinus) whose concern to render it "orthodox" exceeded his desire to render it accurately. Yet to initiate study of just such a man and his work is the purpose of this chapter. Clearly Irenaeus presents his students with a challenge! He is a typical instance of an author known primarily through his works, none of which is directly autobiographical. In his case this situation poses an interesting and complex problem. Some little personal information can be gleaned from the fragments of his writings preserved by Eusebius. To that material can be added the indirectly personal information any author betrays through factors like style, subject matter, and organization of material. It is the last factor that complicates the issue with regard to Irenaeus. Because he is accessible primarily through his own works and because until recently his principal work, *Adversus haereses,* has been criticized as lacking cohesion if not coherence, he has been regarded (or disregarded!) as a fuzzy thinker.

There is an alternative view. I concur with more recent scholars who recognize in Irenaeus a clear and subtle thinker whose work has a sophisticated unity.[1] I further recognize that he employs his remarkable skill to support a teaching (or magisterial) model of organization for the Christian Church as well as an understanding of Christian living deeply respectful of the complex unity of the individual.

The two sections of this chapter are intended to allow Irenaeus to show himself as a clear thinker whose work has a complex unity. I begin with a review of what can be known directly about the man from the extant material. Then I turn to his work, examining the principle he uses to organize and provide unity in his major work, *Adversus haereses,* and the method he uses to develop that work.

A FIRST GLIMPSE OF THE MAN

Irenaeus lived and worked in the Mediterranean world of the late second century, the era of the Antonines at the apogee of the Roman empire. Although his world was a vast one, the amazing uniformity of the ruling classes provided it with the kind of social cohesion reminiscent of late Victorian England. Peter Brown aptly remarks:

> [The empire] was held together by the illusion that it was still a very small world. Seldom has a state been so dependent on so delicate a sleight of hand. By 200, the empire was ruled by an aristocracy of amazingly uniform culture, taste and language. In the West, the senatorial class had remained a tenacious and absorptive elite that dominated Italy, Africa, the Midi of France and the valleys of the Ebro and the Guadalquivir; in the East, all culture and all local power had remained concentrated in the hands of the proud oligarchies of the Greek cities. Throughout the Greek world no difference in vocabulary or pronunciation would betray the birthplace of any well-educated speaker. In the West, bilingual aristocrats passed unselfconsciously from Latin to Greek; an African landowner, for instance, found himself quite at home in a literary salon of well-to-do Greeks at Smyrna.[2]

Conformity was the price of inclusivity: conformity of lifestyle, traditions, education, and language. Nonconformists were excluded from this world whether, like the "barbarians," they could not conform or whether, like the Jews, they would not. By the end of the second century converted Christians found themselves identified as nonconforming "dissenters" and excluded from participation.[3]

Irenaeus's native city was Smyrna in Asia Minor and the link with Asia Minor is a recurring motif in his life and work.[4] He moved to southern Gaul, whose churches were associated with his home church. It is not surprising that Lyons and Smyrna should be the end points of a second-century journey or that at another time the same traveler should visit Rome. Irenaeus himself remarks, "The world is at peace because of the Romans, and we walk the roads without fear, and sail where we will" (*AH* IV. 30, 3). This same peace was a factor in the spread both of Christianity and of Gnosticism.

The site of ancient Smyrna today is marked by huge architectural remains built between the times of Hadrian (117–138) and Septimus Severus (193–211).[5] Irenaeus was a city man. He was brought up in one bustling Asiatic city and spent the years of his maturity in yet another thriving metropolis, a commercial town that was the Roman administrative capital of the province of Lugdunensis: Lyons (ancient Lugdunum) on the Rhone river.[6] There Irenaeus became the leader of the Christian community, and engaged in written controversy to defend the teaching of that Church.

While tradition has identified Irenaeus as bishop of Lyons the designation may not be apt. Frank D. Gilliard notes that Irenaeus "is not entitled *episkopos* by any extant contemporary source, including his own work," but continues that "his background in Asia Minor in the circle of Polycarp and (probably) in Rome is enough to make reasonably certain that he was a titled, monarchic bishop."[7] Whether or not one agrees that "his background in Asia Minor" makes "reasonably certain that he was a titled, monarchic bishop" it seems beyond dispute that both Irenaeus and Pothinus served as heads of the Lyonese Christian community. Irenaeus functioned as a bishop but he was chary in the use of the title. In his day the office seems to have been more clearly developed than the terminology. The better to communicate his sense of himself as well as to avoid anachronisms that use of the title may imply, I follow his practice and do not use the title for Irenaeus.

It is to the fragments of Irenaeus's own writings preserved in Eusebius's *Ecclesiastical History* that one must turn for the slender amount of biographical data available.[8] The church historian preserves part of a letter to Florinus in which Irenaeus describes his early years spent in Smyrna as a pupil of Polycarp, who himself had talked "with John and with others who had seen the Lord" (*Hist. eccl.* V. 20, 6). Irenaeus had in Polycarp a mentor who provided a living link with the first Christian generation. Knowledge of the date of Polycarp's martyrdom[9] is used to fix the date of Irenaeus's birth, usually given as ca. 140.

It is certain that Irenaeus was a presbyter and the emissary of the Church of Lyons to Eleutherius, bishop of Rome, after the martyrdoms of 177 (*Hist. eccl.* V. 4, 1-2).[10] The letter describing the martyrdoms that "the distinguished churches of this country" addressed to "the churches in Asia and Phrygia" (*Hist. eccl.* V. 1, 2) affirms the links between the churches of Asia Minor and those in the Rhone Valley.[11] The letter names among the martyrs two with ties to Asia Minor, namely "Attalus, a Pergamene by race who had always been a pillar and support of the Christians there" (*Hist. eccl.* V. 1, 17) and "a certain Alexander, a Phrygian by race and a physician by profession, who had lived in Gaul for many years" (*Hist. eccl.* V. 1, 49). Apparently Irenaeus was already a recognized leader in the community when he carried the letter to Rome. Eusebius affirms that when Pothinus, head of the church of Lyons, died in prison, Irenaeus succeeded him (*Hist. eccl.* V. 5, 8)

Within three years of the martyrdoms the rising influence of Gnosticism was a grave concern to Irenaeus; he was well into the writing of *Adversus haereses* by 180. (One can infer the dating from the list of bishops of Rome

Irenaeus gives in *AH* III; there he names Eleutherius [ca. 174–ca. 189] as the one in Rome who "now has the episcopacy from the apostles" [*AH* III. 3, 3 (SC 211:37)].)

Just as a pastoral concern spurred Irenaeus to write early in his career as a Church leader, so another pastoral concern moved him to take up his pen again in the last glimpse available in Eusebius, who preserves portions of the Irenaean letter to Victor of Rome (ca. 188–ca. 198). This letter (*Hist. eccl.* V. 24, 9-18) concerns the date of Easter. In it Irenaeus supports the right of the churches of Asia Minor to their traditional date and practices where these differed from those kept in the West. His defense of Asia Minor is no surprise; that his position was against imposing Roman practice moderates his insistence elsewhere on agreement with the church of Rome.[12] The date of Irenaeus's death is unknown; the tradition of his martyrdom is late and unreliable.[13]

IRENAEUS'S WORK

The Complete Works

Knowledge of the ancient world together with the minimal biographical data available cast some light on the shadowy figure of Irenaeus, but the mirror in which we best view him is the one held up by his own works. Two survive in their entirety; of these the *Epideixis* (known to English readers as *Proof of the Apostolic Preaching* or *The Demonstration*) was only recovered in 1904.[14] It is a brief apologetic work couched in catechetical form. However, it has neither had as much influence on the Christian tradition nor generated such a quality of scholarly activity as has Irenaeus' major extant work, the object of this study, *Adversus haereses*.

When we delve into *Adversus haereses* to clarify the picture of Irenaeus, however, we are almost immediately brought up short. In its opening lines the author remarks that, living as he does among the Celts, one should not expect of him the art of discourse, which he never learned, or the power of writing, to which he had never aspired, or elegance of words or persuasiveness, of which he is ignorant (*AH* I. preface, 3). Over the last one hundred fifty years numerous critics have given the "amen" to his properly modest self-disclaimer. Much of the difficulty has stemmed from the tendency to judge Irenaeus by modern standards and so to expect a recognizably "systematic" treatise. Absence of readily recognizable canons of unity encouraged the search for evidence of sources. Both the formal and the theological unity of *AH* were rendered suspect by the work of the source critics, especially Harnack, Bousset, and Loofs, whose viewpoint was shared to some extent by Widmann and Benoît.[15] The effect, if not the intent, of the work of these critics was to reduce *AH* IV in particular to a pastiche of ill-related parts; concurrently Irenaeus became a well-intentioned if inept editor. More recently Phillipe Bacq's studies of *AH* IV have made it apparent that Irenaeus is indeed a systematic thinker, although the canons of his system differ markedly from ours.[16]

The Rule of Faith

What, then, are the canons by which Irenaeus organizes his thought? He recognizes one canon or rule, the Rule of Faith (also called the Rule of Truth) that serves as the interpretive principle for his reading of the Scriptures. In turn, the Scriptures supply the explanation of the Rule of Faith understood as a kind of "narrative creed" telling the theological story of Christ the Word.

Irenaeus is the first to use the term "Rule of Faith," which also has a prominent place in his *Proof* (for example, in no. 3). The earliest credal patterns differed in complexity, from the early confessions including "Jesus is Lord" (Rom 10:9) through "the gospel" outlined by Paul to the Corinthians (1 Cor 15:3-9) to the more theological affirmation in the opening verses of Romans (Rom 1:3-4). By the mid-second century one finds related patterns in Justin's description of baptism (*Apol. 1,* 61). However, credal development should not be conceived of as moving in a straight line from simple to complex. As J.N.D. Kelly comments:

> The second-century conviction that the "rule of faith" believed and taught in the Catholic Church had been inherited from the Apostles contains more than a germ of truth. Not only was the content of that rule, in all essentials, foreshadowed by the "pattern of teaching" accepted in the apostolic Church, but its characteristic lineaments and outline found their prototypes in the confessions and credal summaries contained in the New Testament documents.[17]

The Rule of Faith governs right exegesis, and the Scriptures (the object of the exegesis) explain the Rule of Faith. Logically this is a circular argument, but in practice the relationship Irenaeus understands between the Rule of Faith and the Scriptures is not so much circular as dialogical. In the happy formulation of Rowan A. Greer, "text and interpretation are like twin brothers; one can scarcely tell the one from the other. What emerges is an unbroken dialogue between Scripture and tradition, between the letter and the spirit, and between the word and the experience of those hearing it."[18] The two are less mirror images of one another than conversation partners, each of whom amplifies and corrects the insights of the other.

Content, Dynamism, and Function of Rule of Faith

The middle section of *AH* I (I. 10 through I. 22) treats the variations of Gnostic systems. Irenaeus begins with discussion of the Rule of Faith, here called "the solid truth" (*AH* I. 9, 5 [SC 264:152]). He summarizes the content of the Rule of Faith under the names of the Three: the one God Father almighty, who made heaven and earth and all that is in them; the one Christ Jesus Son of God, incarnate for human salvation; and the Holy Spirit. It is the Spirit who through the prophets proclaimed the *oikonomia*, the plan of God for salvation. Under the third heading the Spirit proclaims the birth, life, death, and resurrection of Jesus (unlike the later Nicene-Constantinopolitan creed, which elaborates faith in Jesus Christ as the one who was born, lived, died, and rose, and so lists all of this under the second heading). Such is the content of the Rule of Faith, which is the heart of what is handed on through a dynamic process (*AH* I. 10, 1 [SC 264:154–158]).

The dynamism of the Rule of Faith cannot, for Irenaeus, be expressed in a vocabulary of development. The very possibility of development is excluded *a priori* from the second-century horizon of consciousness.[19] Instead, to deal with the transmission of the Rule of Faith Irenaeus invokes the vocabulary of tradition.[20] Here, too, are specific role assignments: the cast includes prophets, apostles, their disciples, and "the Church." The faith *belongs* to the universal Church; having been *proclaimed* by the prophets it was *received* by the Church from the apostles and their disciples. The Church that *accepted* the faith *guards, preaches,* and *teaches* it, *transmitting* it as if possessing a single mouth (*AH* I. 10, 1-2 [SC 264:154–160]). In this way Irenaeus outlines a clear dynamism around the rule of faith, although it is only later that he will return to the question "who speaks for the Church?"

It is important, finally, that the truth *is* the doctrine that is proclaimed, accepted, guarded, preached, taught, transmitted. There is not a separable principle of truth beyond it. How Irenaeus understands truth affects both the proclamation and reception of doctrine in all phases. As a second-century writer he assumes the objective, unchanging nature of truth, independent of the interpreter, a truth that is contained in the Rule of Faith and yet at the same time exceeds the grasp of human reason. Hence he will develop a methodology that embraces both supreme confidence in the truth proclaimed by the Church and a rather full awareness of the limits of human speech about God. It is as if he says: "The Lord has trusted himself to the Church in the Spirit. The truth may be found in the Scriptures entrusted to the Church; her rulers teach the truth. But the truth they teach is limited by our poor human capacity. God, who *is* truth, far outstrips the capacity of our grasp." The consequence is that one is asked to accept the Church's interpretation of the Scriptures, and so Church teaching, as the closest approximation to truth available to the human condition.

Granted this position, the heretic is one who distorts truth, reading the Scriptures falsely and without the authority of a genuine teacher. An authentic teacher has priority over a false teacher. The priority in question is a matter of authority and not a matter of the chronological priority of orthodoxy over heresy. Since the work of Walter Bauer it is no longer possible to assert uncritically the chronological priority of orthodoxy.[21] To do so leads to an unwarranted retrojection of the fourth-century situation into the second century. As Frederik Wisse has pointed out, in the earlier period "sound doctrine" was basically the teaching of sound people, such as the apostles of old and the official Church leadership of that time.[22] He assumes the absence of a comprehensive and widely accepted Rule of Faith and so finds that soundness came to depend on the reputation of the author. Wisse holds that "this means that 'orthodoxy' must have begun as orthocracy, i.e., the truth claim of a teaching depended on the accepted authority of the person who taught it."[23] It is true that there was not a *comprehensive* Rule of Faith, but there was indeed a *widely accepted* one. What was at work was not the unbridled exercise of authority, but the exercise of authority within a believing community whose norms were in the living faith proclaimed in the word and celebrated in sacrament.

In Irenaeus's opinion the Valentinians distort the truth, reading the Scriptures falsely and without the authority of a genuine teacher. They are heretics. How important it is in his eyes, then, for the true teacher to refute heresy not only for the sake of those being led astray (*AH* I. preface, 1 and 2) but also for the salvation of the false teachers themselves! (See *AH* I. 31, 3; III. 25, 7; IV. preface 1 and 2.) They are doing a disservice to truth, and so they deceive themselves. Such is the conviction impelling Irenaeus.

Closely related to the *content* and *dynamism* of the Rule of Faith is its *function:* to unify the Church wherever in the world it is found. Although languages may vary there is one and the same tradition in Irenaeus's view. In fact neither the richness nor the poverty of the words used by the Church's leaders will improve or diminish the tradition (*AH* I. 10, 2 [SC 164:158]). The historically critical reader senses a naïveté here that can subvert Irenaeus's credibility. It would be a mistake, however, to allow such sensibility to distract from the point at issue: Irenaeus understands the Rule of Faith to function to create unity in such a way that human limitations will not impede it. Dissident interpretations are to be rejected.

The Relation of the Rule of Faith to the Scriptures

Granted what we have just seen, it is not surprising to find Irenaeus asserting that the Scriptures belong to the Church in such a way that *any valid reading must be congruent with the faith of that community.* In his review of Valentinian Gnosticism Irenaeus notes repeatedly that its exegesis presents an interpretation of the Christian Scriptures incompatible with the Rule of Faith. He writes: "Refusing the truth, some introduce lying words . . . falsifying the word of the Lord, making themselves evil interpreters of what had been well said" (*AH* I. preface, 1 [SC 264:18]). He points out that such people substitute glass for the emerald of the word, and mix the brass of falsehood with the gold of its truth (*AH* I. preface, 2 [SC 264:20]). Gnostic understanding of the exegetical task was correlative to their understanding of the Scriptures. In their opinion, according to Irenaeus, the truth about the Pleroma "has not been said clearly [in the Scriptures] because all are not capable of this knowledge,

mysteriously shown by the Savior to those who are able to understand it" (*AH*
I. 3, 1 [SC 264:50]). From this perspective one task of exegesis is to explain
to the initiate the full but hidden meaning of the Scriptures. In one of his
strongest passages on the topic Irenaeus argues:

> They say such things about their Pleroma and the formation of the universe,
> *forcing those things which were well said to adapt to these which are evilly in-*
> *vented.* And not only do they try to make such proofs from the gospels and the
> apostles, *changing the exegeses and adulterating the expositions,* but also from
> the law and the prophets, as there are many parables and allegories able to be
> interpreted in many ways, *deceitfully adapting [these] through their weighty ex-*
> *position* to their own fiction they lead in captivity from the truth those who do
> not conserve a firm faith in the one God the Father almighty and in the one Jesus
> Christ Son of God (*AH* I. 3,6 [SC 264:60–62]).

The difficulty is false interpretation.[24] The assumption behind Irenaeus's insistence on right interpretation is that what is of prior importance is the community's faith in Jesus Christ; the New Testament is the written precipitate of
that faith.

With Irenaeus one is still in the formative period of the Christian Scriptures.
It is in his writings that the Bible takes recognizable shape as constituted of
the two testaments. In Christianity's earliest years its Scriptures had been the
Jewish Scriptures, cited frequently and alluded to extensively by the writers of
its own documents,[25] used directly by the Apostolic Fathers,[26] and proclaimed
liturgically (together with the "apostolic memoirs") as Justin witnesses.[27] By
the end of the first century the composition of most of the documents today
comprising the New Testament was completed.[28] Already some of these writings were recognized as Scripture (*Barn.* 4.14; *2 Clem.* 2.4; 14.1). Justin (in
the passage cited above) gives evidence that by the mid-second century the
worshiping community used the gospels liturgically (thus as Scripture). The
Bible known to Irenaeus included the Jewish Scriptures, the four gospels, a
collection of Paul's letters, Acts, Revelation, 1 Peter, and 1 and 2 John.[29]

Not only does Irenaeus first name the collection of Christian documents the
"New Testament" (*AH* IV. 9, 1), but it is also he who first reflects thematically
on biblical interpretation. In a prior step Christians had already effected a
transformation of the sacred writings of the Jews by reading them as witnesses
to Christ.[30] At each stage what is involved is a theological reading of the Scriptures.[31] The Church's Rule of Faith determines its reading of the Bible.

The Rule of Faith and the Organization of *Adversus haereses*

Irenaeus employs the Rule of Faith throughout *Adversus haereses,* but he
uses it in various ways. The whole work is an exercise organized toward exegesis under the Rule of Faith. In Book One, designed to expose or denounce

Gnostic teaching, the organization of the material is itself revelatory. The book falls into three parts with a preface and conclusion: (1) exposition of the Valentinian teaching (*AH* I. 1–9);[32] (2) unity of the faith of the Church and diversity of the heretical systems (*AH* I. 10–22); (3) origin of Valentinianism (*AH* I. 23–31.2). Part 1 subdivides into four sections, each of which concludes with a reprise of the related exegesis. Part 2 serves as a centerpiece, contrasting orthodox unity with heterodox diversity. Its first and third subdivisions focus on the unity of the Church's faith and the Rule of Faith respectively. The middle subdivision presents the contrasting Gnostic pluriformity of doctrines, practices, exegeses, and rites. Part 3 falls into two sections, one treating the multiple remote ancestors of the Valentinians and the other describing their immediate ancestors. Each section is concluded with a summary of related material. The movement is from one Gnostic system and its exegesis (always criticized, as we have seen, by contrast to the "right" exegesis) through comparison with orthodox unity to multiplicity of Valentinian Gnostic ancestors, remote and immediate. Analysis thus reveals a dominant role for the Rule of Faith, immediately apparent when Irenaeus contrasts the Gnostic positions to the Rule of Faith (*AH* I. 10 and also later at *AH* I. 22) supported by right exegesis of the Scriptures.

The picture is different in Book Two, which Irenaeus planned as a definitive "overthrow" of Gnostic teaching. Here the Rule of Faith serves to supply Irenaeus with the understanding of God against which he measures the Gnostic understanding of the Deity, which he finds wanting and rebuts. As he attacks Gnostic exegesis Irenaeus presents what he views as the conditions for the right use of the Scriptures, in which he also explores the role of theology.

In Books Three through Five, his "proof from the Scriptures," Irenaeus interprets the Scriptures according to the Rule of Faith in order to complete the destruction of the Gnostics. The method of exegesis he uses also offers him a way to provide internal unity to the remaining three books. Because the unity of Book Four has been both severely criticized and thoroughly analyzed for the Irenaean method of exegesis in action, I will use it now to introduce that method, following Bacq.

In the preface to Book Four Irenaeus points out that the distinctive feature of his argument to follow is that it rests on "the words of Christ," as by contrast *AH* III is based on the witness of the apostles. The internal unity of *AH* IV, then, depends on the use Irenaeus makes of "the words of the Lord." In each case he announces a word, cites it, and finally comments on it. In the following brief example of this procedure the scriptural verses are boldfaced and the three steps italicized:

> *(Announcement)* Again the Lord himself showed Abraham saying to the rich man about people still alive: *(Citation)* **If they will not listen to Moses and the prophets neither, if anyone should return to them from the dead, will they believe him.** *(Commentary)* It is not a question of a story about a rich man and

a poor man. First the Lord teaches us to flee delights lest in living in worldly pleasures and many festivities we should become slaves of our passions and forget God (*AH* IV. 2, 3-4 [SC 100:402]).

Bacq has shown that the three major divisions of the book are governed by this process, as are the subdivisions into sections and articles. The pattern recurs regularly while allowing for a greater or lesser expansion of each step. For example, the single article *AH* IV. 2, 4 contains Irenaeus's commentary on Luke 16:31, while an entire chapter (IV. 26) is devoted to the commentary on Matt 13:44; the commentary on John 4:35-38 extends through three chapters (IV. 23–25). The literary process in each case includes the same three steps: announcement of the word, citation of the word, and commentary on it.

In addition, the words of the Lord serve as the conducting thread of the argument and unify it internally. Thus Irenaeus joins the words that buttress his argument by means of a series of "linking words" and additional scriptural citations. What at first reading seems to be a totally arbitrary connection among texts becomes a sensitive and intelligent interlinking. The following passage, Bacq notes, can stand as an example:

> Those who fear God and are concerned to keep his law will run to Christ and they will all be saved: "Go," he said to his disciples, "to the lost sheep of the house of Israel" (Matt 10:6). Of the Samaritans also, it says, when the Lord had remained among them two days, "many more believed because of his word and they said to the woman: 'now we no longer believe because of your word, for we have heard him ourselves, and we know that he is truly the Savior of the world'" (John 4:41-42). Paul also says: "Thus all Israel will be saved" (Rom 11:26) (*AH* IV. 2, 7 [SC 100:410]).

The Johannine text about the conversion of the Samaritans may have been called to mind by the complete Matthew text, which reads: "These twelve Jesus sent out with the following instructions: 'Go nowhere among the Gentiles, and enter no town of the Samaritans, but go rather to the lost sheep of the house of Israel'" (Matt 10:5-6). Taken alone, the Matthew text would suggest that the Samaritans were to be excluded from the gospel. Seeing this, Irenaeus introduces the passage from John. A theological reason accounts for the connection between these two passages. The linking word "Israel" joins the Romans passage to the Matthew passage and completes the theological idea: all of Israel, Jews and Samaritans, will be saved if faithful to the law.[33]

As Bacq has pointed out, there are two literary processes that Irenaeus uses correlatively to structure his thought in *AH* IV, both dependent on the words of the Lord. The first consists of the three steps named: announcement of a word, citation of it, and commentary on it. This supplies external unity to his work. The second process consists in joining the words of the Lord to one another, so supplying internal unity to his developing argument. Used together these two processes supply the formal unity of *AH* IV. In Bacq's opinion the resultant structure takes the form of "concentric circles."[34] In fact the Irenaean structure is chiastic. I will develop this idea in Part Two, especially ch. 5.

Irenaeus's exegesis offers a reading steeped in an intimate knowledge of the text that allows allusions to carry the weight of an extended direct quotation. His style of announcement, citation, and explanation, with abundant use of linking words, seems geared to aural understanding; such orientation is not surprising, granted the low level of literacy and a culture attuned to verbal rather than written communication.[35] Equally important, his custom of allusive linkage, drawing on an intimate knowledge of the Scriptures, allows him to bring a depth and scope of related passages to bear on the theme at hand.

The formal unity supplied by this method supports a unified content: the explanation of the Rule of Faith or the meaning of belief in the One God, Father, Son, and Spirit with, as we shall see, implications for the understanding of Church, human person, and human destiny. To proclaim this content is Irenaeus's task as leader of the Church, a task shaped by the context in which his work is carried out, as well as by the specific context of each section of his writing.

Clearly this second-century Christian is a man of intelligent faith who clings passionately to the Rule of Faith as a principle guarding him in controversy. He appears fearless in the face of complexities, handling them adroitly while breathing passion even into abstruse argument. Equally he allows the Rule of Faith and the Scriptures mutually to breathe life into one another, developing a rich and evocative exegesis.

CONCLUSION

Irenaeus, who organized and wrote this careful, balanced study, betrays a supple and educated intelligence as well as a spirit thoroughly informed by Christian faith and touched by the controversy around the developing canon of the Scriptures. Furthermore he is convinced that Gnostic exegesis betrays Christian faith. It remains to be considered why that betrayal is so intensely important to Irenaeus. It is time to turn to the context that evoked his work, the struggle with Gnosticism.

NOTES

[1]Among them are Ysabel de Andía, *Homo Vivens. Incorruptibilité et divinisation de l'homme selon Irénée de Lyon* (Paris: Etudes Augustiniennes, 1986); Philippe Bacq, *De l'ancienne à la nouvelle alliance selon S. Irénée. Unité du livre IV de l'Adversus Haereses* (Paris: Lethielleux, 1978); Jacques Fantino, *L'homme image de Dieu: Chez Saint Irénée de Lyon* (Paris: Cerf, 1986); Antonio Orbe, *Teología de San Ireneo, I. Comentario al Libro V del "Adversus Haereses"* 1–3, Biblioteca de Autores Cristianos, serie maier, 25, 29, 33 (Madrid: La Editorial Católica, 1985, 1987, 1989); Real Tremblay, *La manifestation et la vision de Dieu selon S. Irénée de Lyon,* Münsterische Beiträge z. Theologie 41 (Münster: Aschendorff, 1978.)

²Peter Brown, *The World of Late Antiquity: AD 150–750* (London: Harcourt, Brace, Jovanovich, reprint 1978) 14.

³See Brown, *World* 16–17.

⁴The epigraphal evidence for the association was studied by Amable Audin, "Sur les origines de l'église de Lyon," in Faculté de Théologie s.j. de Lyon-Fourvière, eds., *L'Homme devant Dieu: Mélanges offerts au Père Henri de Lubac 1: Exégèse et patristique* (Lyons: Aubier, 1963) 223–234.

⁵See Brown, *World* 17.

⁶See Amable Audin, "Sur la géographie du Lyon-Romain: la population, les voies et les quartiers d'après les documents épigraphiques," *Revue de géographie de Lyon* 27 (1952) 133–139; idem, "Sur les origines de l'église de Lyon"; Jean Comby, *177–1977: Aux origenes de l'église de Lyon: Irénée* (Lyon: Faculté de théologie, 1977); idem, *L'évangile au confluent. Dix-huit siècles de christianisme à Lyon* (Lyon: Chalet, 1977).

⁷Frank D. Gilliard, "The Apostolicity of Gallic Churches," *HThR* 68 (1975) 27. Gilliard further notes that "only twice in *Adversus haereses* (and nowhere in his other extant writings) does *episkopos* appear with a proper name in such a way even to suggest a title: once (3.3.4) for Polycarp of Smyrna and once (3.4.2) for Hyginus of Rome (ca. A.D. 136–ca. 140)." In neither case is the original Greek extant.

⁸Eusebius must be used with caution. Neither his paraphrasing nor his system of quoting is completely trustworthy, as T. D. Barnes points out (*Constantine and Eusebius* [Cambridge, Mass.: Harvard Univ. Press, 1981] 140–143). Eusebius's handling of the material is marked by his own interests and his own limitations, of which a principal one is the tendency to read back the situation of the Church of his own day into earlier times. Yet there is a kind of information for which Eusebius is irreplaceable. Barnes notes that "the letter of the Gallic Christians in Book Five, for example, provides important evidence for all aspects of life in Roman Lugdunum" (*Constantine* 140). While I depend here on that letter and on fragments Eusebius quotes from two letters of Irenaeus, the one to Florinus and the other to Victor, I read this material conservatively.

⁹There is broad support for a date of February 23, 167, following the analysis of Pierre Brind'Amour, "La date du martyre de saint Polycarpe [Le 23 février 167]" (*Analecta Bollendiana* 98 [1980] 456–462); the article includes review of the possible positions with bibliographical references to the works of the various advocates. See also Victor Saxer, "L'authenticité du 'Martyre de Polycarp': Bilan de 25 ans de critique" (*Mélanges de l'école française de Rome: Antiquité* 94 [1982] 979–1001).

¹⁰On the authenticity of the Eusebian report see P. Keresztes, "The Massacre at Lugdunum in 177 A.D.," *Historia* 16 (1967) 75–86. Concerning the dating of the martyrdoms, see T. D. Barnes, "Eusebius and the Date of the Martyrdoms," in Centre National de la Recherche Scientifique, eds., *Les martyrs de Lyon (177)* (Paris: Editions du Centre National de la Recherche Scientifique, 1978) 137–143. Robert Turcan, "Les religions 'orientales' à Lugudunum en 177," *Les martyrs de Lyon* 195–210, persuasively refutes the evidence for the theory that persecution began as an intra-Phrygian conflict between worshipers of Cybele and Christians. Lellia Cracco Ruggini, "Les structures de la société et de l'économie lyonnaises au IIe siècle, par rapport à la politique locale et imperiale," *Les martyrs de Lyon* 65–92, and "Nuclei immigrati e forze indigene in tre grandi centri commerciali dell' impero," *Memoirs of the American Academy in Rome* 36 (1980) 55–76 suggests that the Lyonnais trade societies of the late second century were feeling vulnerable in the light of contemporary imperial attitudes toward such societies. They were thus particularly embarrassed by the visible and offensive presence of the Christian "society" which they feared could implicate them in imperial disapproval as well. The powerful members of the trade

societies may thus have played a role in inciting the mob in order to discredit the Christians and clearly separate themselves from them. It would seem that the persecution functioned to define the boundaries of Lyonnais society as well as those of the Christian community.

[11]Debate about the authenticity of the superscription may limit its value as witness to the relation between these churches. While the bulk of opinion favors the authenticity of the superscript, Glen Bowersock, "Les Eglises de Lyon et de Vienne: relations avec l'Asie," *Les martyrs de Lyon* 249–256, has recently raised doubts on this point. Bowersock notes that Phrygia was an integral part of Asia in the second century; it would not, therefore, have made sense to address a letter to the brothers in Asia *and Phrygia*. In the fourth century, on the other hand, Asia and Phrygia were distinct provinces, and thus Eusebius and his contemporaries would have found such an address perfectly natural. Bowersock suggests that a late redactor of the document composed the superscript, possibly deriving the provinces of the addressees from the fact that the only two martyrs whose origins are specifically noted came from Asia (Attalus) and Phrygia (Alexander) respectively. He adds that Rouge has suggested that the troublesome identification of the authors as natives of Lyons *and Vienne* might likewise derive from the mention of a Sanctus "from Vienne" among the martyrs. If Bowersock is right the superscript is useless for an understanding of the origins and purpose of the document.

[12]See ch. 5 below.

[13]J. van der Straeten, "Saint Irénée fut-il martyr?" *Les Martyrs de Lyon* 145–153, notes the absolute silence about the circumstances of Irenaeus's death both on the part of his contemporaries and by Eusebius. The legend emerges at the beginning of the sixth century in Burgundy. In the east the earliest mention appears to be in Jerome, writing ca. 397 (*In Isaiam* 64 [PL 24, 623]) although this is a passing reference, conceivably interpolated; he does not refer to Irenaeus as a martyr in *De Viris Illustribus* 35 (PL 35, 650).

[14]What was recovered was a thirteenth-century manuscript of what was probably a sixth-century Armenian translation from the Greek.

[15]Adolf von Harnack, "Der Presbyter-Prediger des Irenäus (IV, 27, 1–32, 1), Bruchstücke und Nachklänge der ältesten exegetisch-polemischen Homilien," in *Philotesia zu Paul Kleinert zum LXX. Geburtstage dargebracht* (Berlin, 1907) 1–38. Wilhelm Bousset, *Jüdisch-Christlicher Schulbetrieb in Alexandria und Rom: Literarische Untersuchungen zu Philo und Clemens von Alexandria, Justin, und Irenäus*, FRLANT n.s. 6 (Göttingen: Vandenhoeck & Ruprecht, 1915). F. Loofs, *Theophilus von Antiochien Adversus Marcionem und die anderen theologischen Quellen bei Irenäus*, TU 46.2 (Leipzig: Hinrichs, 1930). M. Widmann, "Irenäus und seine theologischen Väter," *ZThK* 54 (1957) 156–173. André Benoît, *Saint Irénée: Introduction à l'étude de sa théologie*, EHPhR 52 (Paris: Presses universitaires de France, 1960).

[16]Bacq responds to the source critics in four thorough appendices to *De l'ancienne à la nouvelle alliance selon S. Irénée* in which he summarizes and evaluates the scholarship on each of the four disputed sections of *AH* IV: the Testimonia (*AH* IV. 17, 1-5); the Treatise on Prophecy (*AH* IV. 20–21; 25, 2; 33, 10-14); the section from the Presbyter (*AH* IV. 27–32); and the Treatise on Liberty (*AH* IV. 37–39).

[17]J.N.D. Kelly, *Early Christian Creeds* (3rd ed. New York: Longman, 1972) 29. On Irenaeus's use of "canon of truth" see Norbert Brox, *Offenbarung, Gnosis und gnostischer Mythos bei Irenäus von Lyon* (Salzburg and Munich: Pustet, 1966) 105–113.

[18]Rowan A. Greer, "The Christian Bible," 107–199 in James L. Kugel and Rowan A. Greer, *Early Biblical Interpretation*. LEC 3 (Philadelphia: Westminster, 1986) 157. For an excellent study of the problems treated in the following paragraphs see pp. 107–208 of that work.

[19]Ben F. Meyer, *The Early Christians: Their World Mission & Self-Discovery* (Wilmington, Del.: Michael Glazier, 1986) discusses this question, rightly rejecting both the explanation of syncretism offered by the history of religions school and the evolutionary explanation of organic process. He suggests that what occurs is a process of transposition or translation:

> It supposes that every act of meaning is embedded in a context and that the maintenance of meaning is conditioned by the more or less creative act of transposing meaning from one context to another. In contradistinction to the model of evolutionary syncretism, it affirms, as the starting point of early Christian development, not a low christology, low ecclesiology, etc., but an experience of salvation . . . the object of which was the risen Christ. . . . [The move from the Jewish to the Greek world] imposed the task of signifying in new conceptual as well as new linguistic terms the realities first encountered and thematized by the first Christians of Jerusalem. In this as in all comparable cases something of the old was (both deliberately and indeliberately) lost in the translation and significant new elements were gained. (pp. 190–191)

[20]For discussion and bibliography on tradition see W. Rordorf and A. Schneider, *L'évolution du concept de tradition dans l'église ancienne.* TC 5 (Bern and Frankfort: Peter Lang, 1982); Bruno Reynders'shorter historical review remains helpful: "Paradosis: le progrès de l'idée de tradition jusqu'à s. Irénée," RThAM 5 [1933] 155–191.

[21]Walter Bauer, *Rechtgläubigkeit und Ketzerei im ältesten Christentum* (Tübingen: Mohr/Siebeck, 1934); English translation edited by Robert A. Kraft and Gerhard Krodel, *Orthodoxy and Heresy in Earliest Christianity* (Philadelphia: Fortress, 1971).

[22]Frederik Wisse, "The Use of Early Christian Literature as Evidence for Inner Diversity and Conflict" in Charles W. Hedrick and Robert Hodgson, Jr., eds., *Nag Hammadi, Gnosticism, and Early Christianity* (Peabody, Mass.: Hendrickson, 1986) 185.

[23]Ibid.

[24]A. LeBoulluec (*La notion d'hérésie dans la littérature grecque [IIe–IIIe siècles] 1: De Justin à Irénée* [Paris: Etudes Augustiniennes, 1985]) has noted: "On reconnaît la thèse centrale: les hérétiques tirent leur doctrine de leur propre imagination; le recours á l'Ecriture n'est qu'un artifice secondaire, dont la fonction est de donner confiance, de convaincre, de séduire. En outre le grief essentiel apparaît: une exégèse aussi forcée, qui choisit dans l'ensemble des Ecritures les quelques paroles qui semblent aller dans le sens du système à soutenir, ruine la cohérence du texte sacré, et détruit par là le corps de la vérité. L'erreur doctrinale se double d'un attentat impie contre la parole de Dieu, à travers la *pithanologia* qui la met à son service" (p. 220).

[25]In K. Aland, M. Black, B. Metzger, and A. Wikgren, eds., *The Greek New Testament* (London: United Bible Society, 1966) the index of quotations is almost exclusively from the Jewish Scriptures and runs to twenty-three three-column pages (897–920).

[26]E.g., the index to Scripture texts in the ANF translation, pp. 584–586, a little less than half of which are to the Old Testament.

[27]*Apol. 1,* 67: "And on the day called Sunday, all who live in cities or in the country gather together to one place, and the memoirs of the apostles or the writings of the prophets are read, as long as time permits; then, when the reader has ceased, the president verbally instructs, and exhorts to the imitation of these good things." ANF 1, 186.

[28]For a recent review of the problem of canonicity see Raymond E. Brown, s.s., and Raymond F. Collins, "Canonicity," in Raymond E. Brown, s.s., Joseph A. Fitzmyer, s.j., and Roland E. Murphy, o.carm., eds., *The New Jerome Biblical Commentary* (Englewood Cliffs, N. J.: Prentice-Hall, 1990) 1034–1054.

[29]Since Eusebius there has been debate about whether Irenaeus understood *Shepherd of Hermas* to belong to Scripture. For discussion and a summary of the debated passages see SC 100:248–250.

[30]See Greer, *Early Biblical Interpretation* 122–154.

[31]As Greer remarks (ibid., 111): "The decision to retain the Hebrew Scriptures was a theological one. The church came to insist that the God of Israel was the God of Jesus Christ and also that the significance of the Hebrew Scriptures lay in the testimony they bore to Christ. And the decision as to which Christian writings could be considered the apostolic witness to Christ was really a decision that these books interpreted Christ correctly from a theological point of view. For Christians, the dialogue between God and his people found its fullest expression in Christ, and so Christ became the key to the whole of Scripture. The theological and even Christological convictions that determined how a Christian Bible was to be constituted then became central in shaping the interpretation of that Bible."

[32]Most scholars agree that in *AH* I. 1–9 Irenaeus depicts the position of the Ptolemaic (or Italian) branch of Valentinian Gnosticism. He, however, simply speaks of "the Valentinians."

[33]See Bacq, *De l'ancienne à la nouvelle alliance* 55, n. 2.

[34]See Bacq, ibid., "Préliminaire: Structure d'ensemble," 41–47, especially 41, where *à propos* of *AH* IV. 1–19, he writes: "Une analyse précise de ces chapitres révèle une pensée cohérente et vigoureuse. Elle ne se développe pas de façon linéaire, comme nous y sommes habitués de nos jours, mais se présente en cercles concentriques qui abordent un problème unique à partir d'angles d'approche différents."

[35]William V. Harris, *Ancient Literacy* (Cambridge, Mass.: Harvard Univ. Press, 1989) includes a review of monumental Latin inscriptions in seventeen selected western provinces. Lugdunensis, with 10.3 inscriptions per 1000 km^2 ranks twelfth. He makes a tentative assessment of literacy there during our period: "It is doubtful whether we can reach a final numerical judgement of much value about literacy in all or parts of the western provinces. But the epigraphical statistics presented above, especially when they are compared with the parallel figures from Italy, together with all the other negative considerations which have been presented, make it unlikely that the overall literacy of the western provinces even rose into the range of 10%" (p. 272).

PART TWO
The Face of the Foe

Introduction to Part Two

"Our adversaries, slippery as snakes . . ." (*AH* III. 2, 3)

Moderns, as well as Irenaeus, can find the Gnostics "slippery." Prior to 1945 the approach to Gnostic thought was primarily through citations in ancient polemical literature, sources whose reliability is questionable.[1] The recovery of the Nag Hammadi Gnostic library in 1945 with its subsequent publication, together with the publication of a one-volume English translation of all the texts[2] has inspired a renaissance in Gnostic studies.[3]

An adequate introduction to Gnosticism would require a book in itself, and many splendid ones exist.[4] For our purposes a preliminary description will be helpful. In the late second century Gnosticism was a widespread movement extending from Alexandria in the eastern Mediterranean to the Rhone valley in the west. It retained the fluidity of a movement without developing permanent, fixed structures or a tightly organized body of doctrine. There were many ways to be "Gnostic," yet common traits are discernible. The Gnostics claimed esoteric knowledge that offered saving access to the unknowable God. Gnostics tended to devalue materiality or even to equate materiality with evil. They shared what was then a popular fascination with the Genesis account of creation, and many Gnostic writers offered exegeses of that story as well as of other Jewish and Christian sacred writings. Their method of exegesis favored allegory and included personification, both common approaches to textual interpretation in that time. Finally, it is important to note that it was not unusual for Christians to be Gnostics. In fact the Gnostic Valentinus, a successful teacher in Rome, was considered for the post of bishop of Rome. Only later did he break with the community there; they in turn labeled him "heretic" (Tertullian, *Adv. Val.* 4).

In the opening lines of *Adversus haereses* Irenaeus evokes a severely condemnatory image of the Gnostics:

> Repressing the truth certain ones introduce lying words . . . . By a likeness
> fraudulently effected they win over the judgment of the inexpert and lead them
> into captivity, falsifying the words of the Lord, making themselves bad inter-
> preters of what was well said. They overthrow many, attracting them under pre-
> text of knowledge of him who founded and ordered this universe, as if they
> could show someone higher and greater than the one who made heaven and
> earth and all that is in them (*AH* I. preface 1 [SC 264:18]).

His charge is that the Gnostics use a pseudo-resemblance to the Christians to
betray the word of God, interpreting it according to an understanding of God
different from the Creator God presented by the Rule of Faith accepted by Irenaeus. According to him, not only do Gnostics view the true God and the Creator as distinct, but also as exegetes of the Scriptures they work with a principle
of interpretation peculiar to them.[5]

This text raises several questions, not the least of which is that of Irenaeus'
reliability as a witness to the Valentinian positions. Can a prosecution witness
speak for the defense? Over the last century many historians have doubted the
possibility, at least in a case where Irenaeus uses secondary sources. Discussion of the Nag Hammadi material has precipitated a reassessment. The matter remains controverted, but it seems possible to draw a fair appreciation of
the Valentinians from Irenaeus's work if one attends to his goals and methodology.[6] Study of the Valentinian documents in the Nag Hammadi corpus offers a valuable control, as will appear, for example, in the analysis of the
Valentinian threefold division of humanity in Chapter Two.

Another question suggested by the opening lines of *AH* concerns the relationship between the Gnostics and Irenaeus's own Christian community. It is
almost certain that he encountered Gnostic Christians within that community.
To observe someone who, like Irenaeus vis à vis the Gnostics, is "in opposition" to members of his own community focuses issues in a way that is illu-
minating. In *AH* I Irenaeus reviews Gnostic teaching in an attempt to unveil
the face of the adversary, a face initially masked and hidden. "Error does not
show itself as it is," Irenaeus says (*AH* I. preface 2 [SC 264:20]). He compares
it to green glass posing as an emerald, to gold adulterated with brass, and to
wolves among the lambs. (Ibid.) His comparisons suggest that the Gnostics
possess a falsely sparkling allure beneath which they debase the gold of truth.
Under these false pretenses they lurk among Christians with the same fatal results as come when wolves fall among lambs. Furthermore the Valentinians'
own doctrines are "hidden" or secret. Irenaeus writes: "We are impelled by
our love for you and all who are with you to manifest those [Valentinian]
teachings that until now were hidden" (*AH* I. preface 2 [SC 264:24]). It is his
expressed conviction that the Gnostics are among the flock where they pre-
tend to be what they are not, and that they have a secret teaching. Impelled by
concern for his readers (and, as became apparent in Chapter One, by concern
for the Gnostics themselves) he intends in *AH* I to unmask the Valentinians

and make clear to all what these Gnostics are about before proceeding to refute their teaching in *AH* II. To watch for every glimpse of the "face of the foe" will be an ongoing concern in Chapters Two, Three, and Four.

The opening lines of *Adversus haereses* quoted above also raise the issue of Gnostic exegesis. One wonders how they "falsify the words of the Lord" and in what sense they are "bad interpreters of what was well said." Throughout the study of *AH* it will remain important to question the nature of Gnostic exegesis, but particularly in these chapters devoted to the Irenaean exposition and refutation of Gnostic teaching.

NOTES

[1]Apart from the extracts in the Fathers, Kurt Rudolf, *Gnosis,* translated by R. M. Wilson (Edinburgh: Clark, 1983) identifies the Gnostic writings known to be extant before the mid-twentieth century discoveries: some tractates of the *Corpus Hermeticum,* especially the *Poimandres;* the *Pistis Sophia;* the two *Books of Jeu;* the *Gospel of Mary;* the *Apocryphon of John;* the *Sophia Jesu Christi;* the *Odes of Solomon;* the *Hymn of the Pearl;* and sections of various apocryphal acts of Apostles. For Rudolf's discussion see pp. 25–30. Of these only the *Apocryphon of John* is useful for the study of Valentinian Gnosticism, and that usefulness is almost totally in function of the question of dating: that is, how early a form of it was in circulation, since Irenaeus uses a version (*AH* I. 29) in his discussion of the immediate antecedents of Valentinianism.

[2]James M. Robinson, ed., *The Nag Hammadi Library in English* (3rd rev. ed. San Francisco: Harper and Row, 1988); for the publication history see pp. ix–xii.

[3]R. Van Den Broek, "The Present State of Gnostic Studies," *VC* 37 (1983) 41–71 offers a still useful summary. For a preliminary assessment of the scope of the revival of Gnostic studies one need only scan the contents of D. M. Scholer, ed., *Nag Hammadi Bibliography, 1948–1969* (Leiden: Brill, 1971); this has since been continued on an irregular basis as a supplement to *Novum Testamentum.*

[4]Selected studies of Gnosticism: Giovanni Filoramo, *A History of Gnosticism* (Cambridge, Mass.: Blackwell, 1990), ET of *L'attesa della fine: Storia della gnosi* (Rome: Laterza, 1983); Kurt Rudolph, *Gnosis* (Edinburgh: T & T Clark, 1983), ET of *Die Gnosis: Wesen und Geschichte einer spätantiken Religion* (German Democratic Republic: Köhler & Amelang, 1977); Pheme Perkins, *The Gnostic Dialogue: The Early Church and the Crisis of Gnosticism* (New York: Paulist, 1980); Elaine Pagels, *The Gnostic Gospels* (New York: Random House, 1979); Hans Jonas, *The Gnostic Religion* (2nd ed. Boston: Beacon, 1963); Gilles Quispel, *Gnosis als Welt-Religion* (Zurich: Origo, 1951). Selected collections: Charles W. Hedrick and Robert Hodgson, Jr., eds., *Nag Hammadi, Gnosticism, and Early Christianity* (Peabody, Mass: Hendrickson, 1986); R. Van de Broek and M. J. Vermaseren, eds., *Studies in Gnosticism and Hellenistic Religions Presented to Gilles Quispel on the Occasion of his 65th Birthday* (Leiden: E. J. Brill, 1981); J. Ries et al, eds., *Gnosticisme et monde hellénistique, Actes du Colloque de Louvain-la-Neuve (11–13 Mars 1980)* (Louvain: Université Catholique de Louvain, 1982); *The Rediscovery of Gnosticism. Proceedings of the International Conference on Gnosticism at Yale, March 28-31, 1978. I: The School of Valentinus,* ed. B. Layton (Leiden: Brill, 1980); *II: Sethian Gnosticism,* ed. B. Layton (Leiden: Brill, 1981); Henri-Charles Puech, *En quête de la Gnose* I and II (Paris: Gallimard, 1978); Barbara Aland et al., eds, *Gnosis. Festschrift für Hans Jonas* (Göttingen, 1978); U. Bianchi, ed., *Le origini dello gnosticismo, coloquio de Messina, April, 1966* (Leiden, 1967).

[5]Birger Pearson, "Use, Authority and Exegesis of Mikra in Gnostic Literature," ch. 17 in Martin Jan Mulder and Harry Sysling, eds., *Mikra: Text, Translation, Reading and Interpretation of the Hebrew Bible in Ancient Judaism and Early Christianity* (Philadelphia: Fortress, 1988) 35–52, summarizes the present state of scholarship and offers some conclusions of his own. He notes about Ptolemy's *Letter to Flora* that it: "can be seen to express the typical Valentinian Gnostic positions vis-à-vis the OT as a whole: Even though it is inspired by an inferior deity, the OT contains valuable truth which 'the Savior' fulfills, or which, when subjected to allegorical interpretation, reveals gnosis. The Valentinian use of the OT thus derives not only from Gnostic religious presuppositions (the inferior Creator, etc.) but also from general, non-heretical Christian tradition" (p. 645). In addition, the *Apocryphon of John* and the system described by Irenaeus in *AH* I. 30 fit the category of "rewritten Scripture" in which a scriptural story "is retold with the use of other biblical and extra-biblical materials in such a way as to emphasize [in this case, Gnostic doctrine]" (p. 649).

[6]See Appendix for a review of the scholarship.

CHAPTER TWO

The Valentinian Reading

Adversus haereses I. 1–9

"Why do I suffer? How did I get here? Where did I come from? Where— if anywhere!—am I going?" Sooner or later these questions trouble every human heart. The key to the meaning of human existence ever tantalizes the seeker. In this respect the second century was no different from any other. Many suspected that the longed-for key was hidden in the Scriptures; right interpretation would yield the desired knowledge, if only to the elect. Enter the Gnostic exegetes and teachers. Ptolemy was a disciple of Valentinus, and it was his version of Valentinian Gnosticism that penetrated the Rhone valley, home to Irenaeus and his co-religionists. Irenaeus describes Ptolemy's system in *AH* I. 1–8 and critiques it in *AH* I. 9.

LIFE WITHIN THE PLEROMA (*AH* I. 1–3)

Irenaeus opens with a description of the inner life of the Pleroma or heavenly world of the thirty Aeons who are the divine emanations. The first great Aeon (whose names include Pro-Father and Abyss) and his female partner (Thought, or Grace, or Silence) emit one whose names include Only-Begotten, Father, and Beginning. With the Only-Begotten (male) comes his partner, Truth (female). This pair emits Logos (male) and Life (female), who in turn emit Man (male) and Church (female) to complete the first eight, the Ogdoad (*AH* I. 1, 1). To glorify the Father these eight emit ten more Aeons, who in their turn emit an additional twelve to complete the thirty Aeons of the Pleroma (*AH* I. 1, 2).

In the second phase of the story Irenaeus tells of the fall of the youngest Aeon, Sophia, and of her restoration effected by the Aeon Limit (an emission of the Only-Begotten). Here follow as well the accounts of the emission of the first Christ, of the Holy Spirit, and of the second Christ who is the Savior (*AH* I. 2, 1–5). In its entirety this story is intended to give the hidden meaning of the gospel texts, a meaning hidden for the sake of those who cannot understand and revealed only to those who are capable of grasping it. Irenaeus describes the Gnostic position: "All of this has indeed not been said plainly, because all cannot comprehend it, but rather the Savior has shown it mysteriously through parables to those who are able to understand" (*AH* I. 3, 1 [SC 264:50]).

For example, according to these Valentinians the thirty years of Jesus' hidden life (Luke 3:23) and also the sum of the hours at which workers were sent into the vineyard (Matt 20:1-7: $1 + 3 + 6 + 9 + 11 = 30$) alike reflect the fact that there are thirty Aeons (*AH* I. 1, 3). Likewise the emission of the thirty in groups of twelve and eighteen is symbolized by occurrences of the numbers twelve, and eight plus ten. So it is significant that the Lord lived *twelve* years before disputing with the teachers in the Temple (Luke 2:42-46) and that he chose twelve apostles (Matt 10:2; Luke 6:13). As to the eighteen, Irenaeus remarks: "they say that after the Resurrection from the dead the Lord conversed with the disciples for *eighteen* months" (*AH* I. 3, 2 [SC 264:52]). The phrase "they say" probably reflects that the number eighteen is here not directly connected with a gospel text.

In addition Irenaeus explains that these Gnostics find the total number of thirty Aeons by using the numerical value of letters. The first two letters of the name of Jesus, *iota* (10) and *eta* (8) total 18 and stand for eighteen of the Aeons, and the remaining ten Aeons are symbolized by the first letter of his name, *iota*, taken alone (*AH* I. 3, 2 [SC 264:52]).

Gnostic exegetes here employ three forms of interpretation to account for the thirty Aeons in the Valentinian Pleroma. The first finds a hidden meaning in numbers present in the gospel accounts. The second assigns a numerical value (eighteen months) to the period of time the risen Lord conversed with the disciples, a period that is not quantified in the scriptural narratives. The third applies numerical interpretation to the name of Jesus. All these numerical forms of interpretation work in varying ways with the gospels to form a connection between them and the Valentinian myth of the formation of the Pleroma.

Similarly the passion of Sophia, the youngest Aeon who comes last in the group of twelve, is symbolized by the apostasy of Judas, the twelfth apostle; by the Savior's passion during the twelfth month, after he had preached for one year from the day of his baptism; and by the story of the healing of the woman who had suffered a hemorrhage for twelve years. This gospel story is interpreted to show that the woman's healing reveals many aspects of the healing of Sophia (*AH* I. 3, 3 [SC 264:54]). These forms of exegesis include finding a hidden meaning in a number occurring in the gospel account, the assigning of a meaning to a time period, and application of the story of the healing of a woman to the healing of Sophia, the connection being made between the woman's twelve years of suffering and the twelfth Aeon.

Returning to the Valentinian myth, Irenaeus continues. The Aeon Savior, he notes, emanates from all thirty of the Aeons, so he must be "the Whole" or "the All" *(omne)*. "Every male opening the womb *(omne masculinum aperiens vulvam)"* (Luke 2:23; Exod 13:2) refers to the story of the Aeon Savior opening the womb of Achamoth (the personified thought *[Enthymesis]* of the fallen Aeon, Sophia) when she had been banished from the Pleroma. The Valentinians ascribe an entire series of Pauline texts to the Aeon, Savior: "He is *all* things" (Col 3:11); *"All* things are made by him, and from him come *all* things" (Rom 11:36); "In him lives *all* the fullness of the divinity" (Col 2:9); "to [recapitulate] *all* things in Christ through God" (Eph 1:10). "Other such" passages are interpreted in the same way according to Irenaeus (*AH* I. 3, 4 [SC 264:56]). In every instance the Valentinian exegetical connection is by word association used to relate the Christ of the Pauline writings, who is "All," to the Aeon Savior, who is "All."

Irenaeus notes that the Aeon Limit has both a consolidating function and a separating function and is named differently depending on which function it is fulfilling. As Cross it consolidates and confirms, and as Limit it separates and divides. The consolidating role is indicated when the Savior in the gospel says "Who does not take up his cross and follow me is not able to be my disciple" (Luke 14:27; Matt 10:38) and "taking up your cross, follow me" (Mark 10:21). The limiting function appears when he says "I have not come to bring peace, but the sword" (Matt 10:34). So too it appears in the passage: "The winnowing fan is in his hand to clean his threshing floor; he will collect the wheat into his barn, but the chaff he will burn in unquenchable fire" (Matt 3:12; Luke 3:17). Irenaeus writes that in this text the Valentinians see the operation of Limit, for "the winnowing fan is understood to be the Cross, which consumes everything hylic as the fire consumes the chaff, but which cleans those who are saved as the winnowing fan cleans the wheat" (*AH* I. 3, 5 [SC 264:58–60]). (In this application the "consolidating" function of the cross becomes a purifying one.) The Valentinians refer the following two Pauline passages to their understanding of the cross: "The word of the cross is foolishness to those who perish, but to those who are saved, the power of God" (1 Cor 1:18) and "It does not occur to me to glory in anything except in the cross of Christ, through whom the world is crucified to me and I to the world" (Gal 6:14).

In this section, according to Irenaeus, the Valentinian exegetes seek parallels in function between the mythological Aeons and the words of the Scriptures. The cross is understood metaphorically to have functions of consolidating and of purifying and dividing. Is it, then, that a metaphor is used to interpret a metaphor, so that the metaphoric Aeon, Cross, is understood through the scriptural metaphors "cross" and "winnowing fan"? This seems to be the case. A difference between this section and the earlier ones is that the application is being made not simply to the world of the Pleroma but also to the world here below where materiality exists.

As he looks back to summarize this section of exegetical material Irenaeus writes:

> Such things do they say about their Pleroma and the formation of the universe, forcing those things which were well said to adapt to these which are badly thought by them. Moreover, they not only try to make their proofs from the gospels and the apostles, changing interpretations and adulterating explanations, but also from the Law and the Prophets: since many parables and allegories are written there and they can be taken in many ways; adapting the ambiguity to their own fiction through skillful exegesis, they lead captive from the truth those who do not guard a firm faith in one God the Father omnipotent and in one Jesus Christ the Son of God (*AH* I. 3, 6 [SC 264:60, 62]).

Not only do the Valentinians draw from a broader base of texts than might appear from the quoted sections, but they use those that are susceptible to multiple interpretations. Irenaeus suggests that this strategy is tragically important because it can separate from the truth those with weak faith in one God and one Christ. He might also have mentioned that it is extremely difficult—for him or for them!—to give a coherent exegesis of all these texts.

Thus far it is evident that the Valentinians assume that the Scriptures have a hidden meaning that, on interpretation, supports their account of the heavenly world. This is hardly surprising. Allegorical interpretation of revered writings was an accepted practice well before the dawn of the second century of the present era. When Paul used it in Galatians 4, where he remarks that Sarah and Hagar are to be read as an allegory of the two covenants, he was following established custom, and late second-century people—pagan, Jewish, and Christian—would continue to use allegory freely.

In addition, religion was a given in that world and a mythology postulating a well-populated heavenly world was standard. Again the Pauline corpus offers an example: "in him all things in heaven and on earth were created, things visible and invisible, whether thrones or dominions or rulers or powers" (Col 1:16). This text reflects a usual way of imagining reality in its time. In the case of the Pleroma, its high population density is clearly related to the necessity to separate the Supreme God as far as possible from materiality, something that will be more evident in the soteriological section of the myth. It also gives both system and place to the complexities of titles and attributes that both the Scriptures and Hellenic philosophy use in the pursuit of truth.

Furthermore, the mythological material gives indications that the Valentinians exist within the Christian community. Their familiarity with the Scriptures, the claim that they present themselves under false colors, the claim that they operate as wolves among the lambs, and the Irenaean concern for the impact of Valentinian interpretation on "the weak" of the community suggest this. Their presence, as it were "in the family," would be of immense concern to a man like Irenaeus. Finally, their alternate teaching challenges his author-ity as leader.

LIFE OUTSIDE THE PLEROMA (*AH* I. 4–5)

Irenaeus next reports the Valentinian explanation of the formation of all that is outside the Pleroma, a formation quite literally dependent upon the results of the passion and healing of Achamoth. After Sophia had fallen her "thought" (literally *enthymesis*) was expelled from the Pleroma; her very "idea" of look-ing on the Father and comprehending him was cast outside where it lived per-sonified as Achamoth (sometimes called Enthymesis). Achamoth existed there, trembling outside the Pleroma, "unformed and without figure, like an abortion" because "she knew nothing" (*AH* I. 4, 1 [SC 264:62]).

In pity, he tells us, the Christ of the Pleroma came to her and formed her ac-cording to substance (but not according to gnosis). The hope was that, be-coming aware of the passion that was in her as a result of her separation from the Pleroma, she would aspire to better things. Because she was abandoned she wept; when she remembered the light that had abandoned her she smiled; sometimes she was fearful and in anguish (*AH* I. 4, 2).

When Mother Achamoth had endured all this passion she pleaded for Christ the Light who had abandoned her. "Too lazy to come down again" *(pigritatus est secundo descendere),* according to Irenaeus, he sent the Paraclete who came to her with the angels (*AH* I. 4, 5 [SC 264:72]). Out of respect for his presence Achamoth at first drew a veil over herself; then, looking on him, she received power from him. He formed her according to gnosis and healed her passions. From her passions the Paraclete formed the evil substance, that is, the material or hylic one (*AH* I. 4, 5; see also I. 4, 2, and I. 5, 1 and 4). From her conversion he formed the substance mixed with passion, that is, the psy-chic substance (*AH* I. 4, 5; see also I. 5, 1 and 4). Achamoth herself brought forth the spiritual or pneumatic substance when she had been disengaged from passion (*AH* I. 4, 5 and I. 5, 1). She had no formative power over this pneu-matic substance that was consubstantial with her because it was born from her. Her formative power was limited to the psychic and hylic substances. In every use of that power she shaped the things she made as an image of the Pleroma in order to honor the Aeons (*AH* I. 5, 1).

Out of the psychic substance she formed the Demiurge (*AH* I. 5, 1) who him-self formed all celestial and terrestrial beings, becoming the Demiurge of the psychics and the hylics. The Demiurge created humankind. Irenaeus writes:

> He made an "earthly" human being, not taking the human being from this dry earth but from the invisible substance and from unrestrained and fluid matter. This is the human being made according to the image and likeness. The hylic human is according to the image, close to God [i.e., the Demiurge], but not of the same substance as God. The psychic human is, in truth, according to the likeness.

. . . After this, last of all they say the human being was enveloped in a tunic of skins: they suppose this to be the sensible flesh (*AH* I. 5, 5 [SC 264:86–88}).

Thus two substances, the hylic and the psychic, were accounted for. The pneumatic substance was of another order entirely. Consubstantial with Mother Achamoth, it completely escaped the purview of the Demiurge. Irenaeus remarks that the Valentinians say: "It was deposited secretly in the Demiurge so it might be sown by him in the soul that comes from him and in the material body; gestating in these elements as in a womb it would grow and be prepared for the reception of the perfect Logos" (*AH* I. 5, 6 [SC 264:88]).

Irenaeus summarizes the Valentinian anthropology to this point: "This is the human being whom they would like to see in themselves, namely that they have a soul *[anima]* from the Demiurge, a body *[corpus]* from mud, the carnal part *[caro]* from matter, and the pneumatic man from Mother Achamoth" (*AH* I. 5, 6 [SC 264:88–90]). With this summary Irenaeus completes his account of the cosmological section of the myth and turns to the soteriological section.

RETURN TO THE PLEROMA (*AH* I. 6-8)

According to Irenaeus, Valentinian cosmology accounts for three classes, kinds, or groups within humankind. With respect to salvation each has a different destiny. The hylic, whom the Valentinians also call "those of the left," will perish of necessity because they are unable to receive the breath of incorruptibility. The psychic, whom they also name "those of the right," mediate between spirit and matter; each of them will go to the side to which each one leans. The pneumatic, whom they designate as "the salt and light of the earth," are on earth to be instructed with the psychic. The Savior comes for the sake of the psychics who have free will. The final consummation will come when all the pneumatics, also identified as the "true Gnostics," have been formed and rendered perfect by gnosis (*AH* I. 6, 1). The psychics are incapable of perfect gnosis but are affirmed by bare faith. "These," Irenaeus remarks, "are we who are of the Church" (*AH* I. 6, 2 [SC 264:92]). For this group good works are essential for salvation, unlike those Gnostics whose salvation is assured by their pneumatic nature. In fact, the pneumatics may engage in acts forbidden to the others since it is not works that will introduce them into the Pleroma but the seed they possess from on high.

Thus although the Valentinians are within the community, they nevertheless consider themselves an elite. Irenaeus strongly suggests that while the Valentinians are "in" the community they are not "of" it. Reading between the lines it is possible to envision a group who consider that the rules apply only to lesser beings. Irenaeus's remark about "we who are of the Church" being identified with the "middling good" psychics hints of such a situation.

According to him the distinctions among the three groups will last into the final consummation. When the end comes Achamoth will leave the Intermediary Place and enter the Pleroma, receiving for spouse the Savior issuing from all the Aeons. The pneumatics, having become pure intellectual spirits, will also enter the Pleroma. The Demiurge will pass into the Intermediary Place where his mother Achamoth had been, accompanied by the souls of the "just," that is, the psychics who had a capacity for the heavenly seed. Then the fire hidden in the world will erupt, destroying matter (including the hylics) and reducing it to nothing. The Demiurge will know nothing of all this until the Savior comes (*AH* I. 7, 1 and 5).

For some of the Gnostics, Irenaeus notes, even the understanding of Christ and the Savior is touched by the distinctions between substances. Some of them say that the Demiurge has emitted a Christ as his son, a Christ who is psychic as he himself is. This is the Christ who spoke through the prophets, who passed through Mary like water through a tube, and on whom (during his baptism) the Savior belonging to the Pleroma descended in the form of a dove. In him is found the spiritual seed from Achamoth. Thus our Lord is composed of four elements, paralleling the primitive Tetrad: the pneumatic element from Achamoth, the psychic element from the Demiurge, the element from the economy, and the Savior from the Pleroma. It is only the psychic element and the element from the economy that suffered, doing so in figure of the actions of the Christ from the Pleroma (*AH* I. 7, 2).

When Irenaeus has completed his account of one section of the myth, he comments: "Such is their theory, which neither the prophets taught, nor the apostles transmitted, which they boast to have known better than others" (*AH* I. 8, 1 [SC 264:112]). He does not find the relation of the Gnostic myth to the Scriptures immediately apparent, nor would it help his polemic to do so. Yet the Valentinians presented this myth as scriptural exegesis. In Irenaeus's opinion their reading "exceeds the order and the text of the Scriptures and since [the truth] depends on [the Scriptures] dislocates the members of the body of truth (*AH* I. 8, 1 [SC 264:112]). He compares what the Valentinians do with the Scriptures to the arbitrary disfigurement of a lovely mosaic of the king. Their interpretation is like what would happen if someone rearranged the stones in the likeness of a dog and then insisted that this likeness is the original portrait. Because the stones sparkle attractively, and because the simple do not know what the king looks like, they are deceived. By implication this exegesis is defective because it does not reflect the truth of the Rule of Faith.

With this negative introduction Irenaeus opens his report of the Valentinian exegesis that supports the last section of the myth. According to him they "apply" the Scriptures to four major topics: (1) the events occurring outside the Pleroma,[1] (2) the three races or classes of humans,[2] (3) the situation of Achamoth outside the Pleroma in the void (the "kenoma"),[3] (4) the constitution of the first eight Aeons.[4] Three orders or levels of reality are referred to: that of the heavenly world (the "Pleroma"), that of the void outside the Pleroma (the "kenoma"), and that of this world (the "kosmos"). The form of the exegesis

reported by Irenaeus here as well as earlier in *AH* 1 is midrash. The interpretation amplifies on the Scriptures to explain God's work as understood by the
interpreter. It relates passages joined only by common words or allusions and
does not hesitate to interpret texts apart from their obvious meaning in their
context.[5] This methodology has much in common with the approach Irenaeus
himself uses. It is in the area of theological presuppositions that he and they
part company.

The Valentinian interpreter works within a framework of assumed theological presuppositions, as Elaine Pagels has shown.[6] In essence the presuppositions she identified are these: the exegete must situate an interpretation
with respect to the level of mythic history at which the passage is being interpreted; the three possible levels (pleroma, kenoma, cosmos) reflect a theology
of God that the myth expresses; this theology is a form of hierarchical monism.

The question at issue is finally a question of theology; that is, it is a question
of whether a reading that works from theological assumptions contradictory
to the Rule of Faith is acceptable. Irenaeus is certain it is not. He concludes
his presentation of the mythology with the words: "You see then, beloved, the
inventions by which they seduce themselves, calumniating the Scriptures,
forcing their own fiction to agree with them *(finctionem suam ex eis constare
adnitentes)"* *(AH* I. 9, 1 [SC 264:136]). The whole of *AH* I. 9 is a critique of
this Gnostic exegesis and a defense of a reading conformable to the Irenaean
theology.

IRENAEAN CRITIQUE OF VALENTINIAN MYTHOLOGY (*AH* I. 9)

The Johannine prologue with its emphasis on the preexistent Word and the
entry of that Word into this world was important to the Valentinians. In *AH* I.
8, 5 Irenaeus reported their exegesis of that passage. In *AH* I. 9, 1-5 he critiques
that exegesis. First he points to the lack of correspondence between the prologue and the Gnostic myth. John does not preserve the order of the emissions
in the Valentinian Ogdoad, nor does he include the name "Church" (*AH* I. 9,
1). What John does, Irenaeus notes, is to proclaim the one all-powerful God
and that God's unique Son, Christ Jesus, the very Word of God through whom
all things were made. All those titles belong to one being in John, whereas the
Valentinians take them as denoting separate beings. For them, contrary to
John, it is not the Word but the Savior who was made flesh (*AH* I. 9, 2).

Irenaeus then develops what is for him a central point. It concerns the nature of the Savior's flesh. He begins by reiterating that the Jesus who suffered
for humankind, who lived among them, *is* the Word of God. For the Gnostics,
he repeats, it was not the Word who became flesh, but the Savior. They say the
Savior's flesh was a living body *(corpus animale/sōma psychikē)* from the
economy, and made visible and palpable by an ineffable providence. By contrast, Irenaeus writes, the flesh is that very same "model" made in the begin-

ning from mud by God for Adam. It is this flesh, he says, that according to John the Word of God truly was made (*AH* I. 9, 3).

Irenaeus then introduces an example to illustrate how he sees Gnostic exegesis working. He points out that they select texts and names from different places and give them new meanings, somewhat like those who compose poems on subjects foreign to Homer, using texts and names taken from actual writings of Homer on other subjects. He offers an example, remarking that the naïve may conclude that Homer wrote this poem. In fact, he did not. Anyone who recognizes the pieces taken from Homer's work will realize that in Homer each piece refers to a different subject than the subject of the poem in question. Irenaeus then draws a moral: how important it is for the baptized to be familiar with the Rule of Faith. One who is will recognize the names, phrases, and parables found in the Scriptures and will not be deceived by those who take them out of context (*AH* I. 9, 4).

He concludes this critique with the announcement that to end the errors in question he will show how the Gnostics disagree among themselves. It is self-evident to him that the truth of the Scriptures does not allow for multiple meanings. There is but one "right reading," the reading that harmonizes with the Rule of Faith. In his view, when he contrasts Gnostic diversity with the "solid truth" proclaimed by the Church it will be apparent that the Gnostics lie (*AH* I. 9, 5).

TWO CONTEMPORARY QUESTIONS

It is often difficult for today's readers to comprehend the attraction of Valentinian mythology. Those whose world view is shaped by the theory of nuclear physics (itself more than a little abstract) may find that this ancient mythology reads like fantasy, yet in its own day it was taken seriously, even regarded as a grave threat by Christian leaders. Why was this the case? The Valentinian myth is founded on a theology that accounts for the existence of the world and the presence of evil within it, as well as the differing natures and various final destinies of humans. It reflects the common preoccupation of the age with the kinds of questions addressed by the text of Genesis 1–3. (Recent renewal of popular interest in the same text betrays similar preoccupations.) The myth also gives evidence of the ordinary second-century conviction that invisible, higher beings share the world with humans and interact with them. Thus Valentinian mythology appealed to concerns of the age and was compatible with contemporary convictions.

Furthermore, it had a particular appeal for the Christian community. It is articulated as an exegesis of texts Christians were in process of claiming as their own. It seems likely that these Valentinians were themselves Christians, offering another interpretation of the group's sacred writings. Christian elements in the myth include names like Christ and Savior and storylines treating the themes of creation, fall, passion, and salvation.

Another question of concern to contemporary scholars is whether Valentinian belief included the division of humanity into three groups with corresponding destinies. Such a division has been widely accepted, but Michel
Desjardins strongly challenges that opinion. He has analyzed the relevant
pericopes pertaining to sin among the Valentinians in both the patristic sources
and the Valentinian writings in the Nag Hammadi material.[7] He finds that only
The Tripartite Tractate clearly reflects the division of humanity into pneumatics, psychics, and hylics (104, 4–140).[8] With respect to sin (and so to the
issue of salvation), he writes:

> Sin for [the Valentinians] is an action not in keeping with the heavenly Father's
> will. They are worried about their salvation (cf. especially the moving prayer in
> *The Second Apocalypse of James*) and struggle to remain sinless in the hope that
> this will make the difference when they die. If anything, these Christians would
> have been more concerned than others about acting correctly and avoiding
> lapses. The frequent allusions to the ethical directives in the Sermon on the
> Mount are remarkable. Three works in particular show significant awareness of
> these chapters in Matthew: *The Gospel of Truth, The Gospel of Philip,* and *The
> Interpretation of Knowledge.* This buries the traditional claim that gnostics were
> not interested in ethics.[9]

While the Valentinian works agree that sin is caused "by an outside power hos-
tile to God" and that one must seek to do God's will (a significant agreement),[10]
they differ from one another on the divisions within humanity. The diversity
in the writings suggests diversity among the Valentinians themselves. All of
the midsection of *AH* I indicates that Irenaeus found such diversity. But what
of the Irenaean presentation on the three groups and their destinies?

That presentation cannot be accepted uncritically. It appears that the Valentinians with whom Irenaeus was familiar used the threefold division. Even
granted that this is the case, still an unqualified ethical interpretation of the
threefold distinction paralleling each group with a moral capacity and salvific
destiny is unacceptable. In fact, it will soon become apparent that Irenaeus
himself had doubts about the alleged immoral practices of the Valentinians.

The unqualified ethical interpretation of the triple distinction needs qualifi-
cation by an approach like that of Roger Berthouzoz.[11] In the latter's reading
of the literature (including the Valentinian documents) the Gnostic understanding of grace has to do with the constitutive presence in certain humans
of a divine element; concomitantly, liberty is rejected as an appendage of an
intermediate and imperfect form of humanity. Among the Valentinians there
are three "natures" or "races" of humanity: hylic, psychic, and pneumatic. The
hylic has no superadded gift. The psychic has the gift of soul from the Demiurge, an inferior gift but of transcendent origin. The pneumatic has the perfect
gift of Spirit from Achamoth. Thus there are three modalities of human nature
and two oppositions. The hylics are opposed to the other two, and the psychic
to the pneumatic. While the dependence of this approach on Sagnard[12] is evi-

dent and acknowledged, Berthouzoz offers entrée into a helpful understanding of nature as well as clarification of two passages of Irenaeus that some have interpreted as equivalent: first, the Valentinian picture of the three dimensions of "man" found in the individual (*AH* I. 6, 1) and second, the picture of the three races into which humanity is divided (*AH* I. 7, 5).

Prior to reaching his position Berthouzoz examined Luise Schottroff's existential interpretation.[13] On her reading, the Valentinians hold that for each individual one of the three origins of humans determines the quality of existence, but not the individual's destiny. Whatever the origin of the individual, each one's destiny is determined by a positive or negative relation to salvation, that is, to gnosis. Each thus equally stands faced with choice. What then is the meaning of claiming the pneumatic is "saved by nature"? Berthouzoz rejects her interpretation as not adequately accounting for the texts. In his view Elaine Pagels' presentation is also problematic.[14] She approaches Valentinian anthropology from the perspective of Pauline theology of election. Berthouzoz finds this to be not an interpretation of the position but simply a reiteration of it. However, Pagels' application of the Valentinian allegorical code to the reading of New Testament texts and her determination of the expressions in Romans 1–5, which for Valentinians characterize psychics and pneumatics, are helpful. Berthouzoz notes that both Schottroff and Pagels seem to read the accounts in *AH* I. 6, 1 and I. 7, 5 as if they were equivalent. As we have seen, his own reading applies the first passage to the three dimensions of "man" found in the individual, while the latter passage depicts the three races into which humanity is divided. His reading of the second passage is the same as that which Rousseau later followed.

CONCLUSION

In the first major section of *AH* I Irenaeus reviews Ptolemy's version of Valentinian Gnosticism and the exegesis supporting it. That mythology responds to religious issues of concern in the second century. People wondered then, as they do today, about the source and nature of evil and about the relation of human life to the heavenly world whose existence they accepted. They wondered about the relationship between personal morality and ultimate destiny, about whether humans are ultimately free or fated. Through the use of storytelling and ritual (to be addressed shortly) they sought to explain their world and to control it. The Valentinian myths address these questions and give as warrant for their truthfulness the emerging Scriptures of the Christian Church. This accounts in part for the passion of Irenaeus's response. The Valentinians are fellow Christians. Their teaching offers an alternative reading of the emerging Scriptures of the Christian Church. Their method of exegesis is the same as that of Irenaeus. He and they part company around the theological presuppositions governing the interpretation of the Scriptures. For Irenaeus

there is but one right reading, and that one consistent with the Rule of Faith.
No alternative reading departing from that Rule is acceptable.

Despite his own problems with the Valentinian approach, the Irenaean presentation is a helpful introduction to their mythology. One caution: what he
writes about the three classes of people and the ultimate destiny of each must
be placed within the context of a diverse Valentinianism with varying positions on these matters. Not all the Nag Hammadi Valentinian material uses the
threefold distinction, and all the Nag Hammadi Valentinian material indicates
concern about sin.

NOTES

[1]Irenaeus reviews the texts applied to events outside the Pleroma in *AH* I. 8, 2. The Lord
came "in the last age" (1 Pet 1:20) to reveal the passion of "the last of the Aeons." Christ
awakened the daughter of Jairus from death (Luke 8:41-42) as Christ formed Achamoth and
led her to awareness of the Light. That the Savior appeared to Achamoth when she was outside the Pleroma in a state of "abortion" is shown by Paul in the words "In the last place, he
showed himself to me also, as to an abortion" (1 Cor 15:8). Achamoth covered her face with
a veil as did Moses (Exod 34:33-35). Her experience of abandonment was manifested by
the Lord's word from the cross: "My God, my God, why have you abandoned me?" (Matt
27:46; NRSV Ps 22:1 [LXX Ps 21:2]). Her sadness is made known by the Lord's word:
"How sad is my soul!" (Matt 26:38), her fear by "My Father, if it is possible, let this cup pass
far from me!" (Matt 26:39), her anguish by "I do not know what I should say" (John 12:27).

[2]Irenaeus presents the Valentinian interpretation of Scripture applied to the three races of
human beings in *AH* I. 8, 3. The hylic race is revealed when someone said to the Lord, "I
will follow you," and he answered, "The Son of man has nowhere to lay his head" (Matt
8:19-20; Luke 9:57-58). The psychics are revealed when, to someone who said to the Lord,
"I will follow you, but first let me go and say farewell to my family at home," he responded:
"Anyone who, having put his hand to the plow, looks back, is not fit for the kingdom of
heaven" (Luke 9:61-62). The story of the rich young man (Matt 19:16-22) is also applied to
the psychics. The pneumatics are revealed both by the words "Let the dead bury their dead;
as to you, go and announce the kingdom of God" (Matt 8:22; Luke 9:60) and the words to
Zaccheus, "Make haste to come down because today I must stay at your house" (Luke 19:5).

The parable of the woman who hid the yeast in three measures of wheat is applied to all
three classes, the woman being Wisdom, the three measures the three classes, and the yeast
being the Savior (Matt 13:33; Luke 13:20-21). Paul says about the hylics, "As was the
earthly one, so also are the earthly" (1 Cor 15:48), and about the psychics, "The natural person does not receive the things of the Spirit" (1 Cor 2:14). He also says, "The pneumatic
judges all" (1 Cor 2:15). Then, referring back to 1 Cor 2:14, Irenaeus notes that the "natural person" in this text refers to the Demiurge.

Finally, in Paul's line, "If the first-fruits are holy, so is the whole batch of dough," (Rom
11:16) the first-fruits are the pneumatics, and the whole batch of dough refers to the psychic church, which the Savior assumed and raised with him, for he was the yeast.

[3]Irenaeus presents the texts applied to Achamoth outside the Pleroma in *AH* I. 8, 4. These
include the Savior seeking the lost sheep (Matt 18:12-13; Luke 15:4-7), she being the sheep;
she is also identified with the woman cleaning her house to find her lost drachma (Luke
15:8-10). Simeon, receiving Christ into his arms and giving thanks to God, is a figure of the
Demiurge (Luke 2:29), whereas Anna signifies Achamoth (Luke 2:36-38). Achamoth's

other name, Wisdom, is suggested by "wisdom has been justified by her children" (Luke 7:35) and "we speak of wisdom among the perfect" (1 Cor 2:6). Paul speaks of the unions within the Pleroma when he says "This mystery is great: I speak in reference to Christ and the Church" (Eph 5:32).

[4]Irenaeus reviews texts applied to the first group of eight Aeons (the "Ogdoad") in *AH* I. 8, 5, noting that he does so in the Valentinians' (i.e., Ptolemy's) own words. With one exception (Eph 5:13: "All that which is manifested is Light") all the texts used here come from the Johannine prologue, so that the whole section reads like an abbreviated Valentinian commentary on that passage. From the Father is emitted the Beginning (called Son and Only-Begotten God), from whom is generated the Logos from whom all else came. There is thus postulated what Elaine Pagels (*The Johannine Gospel in Gnostic Exegesis: Heracleon's Commentary on John,* SBL Monograph 17 [New York: Abingdon, 1973] 26) has termed "a triadic monism of the Godhead in hierarchical form." Then comes Life, partner to Logos; from them will come Humankind and the Church, the latter being indicated in the Johannine passage only by implication.

[5]The literature is extensive. For a brief discussion see the section "Derash" in Rimon Kasher, "The Interpretation of Scripture in Rabbinic Literature" in *Mikra,* 560–577; "Appendix VIII: Midrash as a Literary Genre" in Raymond Brown, *The Birth of the Messiah* (New York: Doubleday, 1977) 557–563. Brown makes the point that it is helpful to distinguish between midrash as a literary genre and as a technique. A characteristic of midrash as a genre, according to Addison G. Wright (*The Literary Genre Midrash* [New York: Alba House, 1967]) is that it is a literature used to explain literature. Brown notes that midrashic techniques were employed in texts like the infancy narratives, not to make the OT more understandable, but to make Jesus more understandable (p. 561). Wright's complete definition, which, because it is quite limited, has not won general acceptance, remains useful. It is: "Rabbinic midrash is a literature concerned with the Bible; it is a literature about a literature. A midrash is a work that attempts to make a text of Scripture understandable, useful, and relevant for a later generation. It is the text of Scripture which is the point of departure, and it is for the sake of the text that the midrash exists. The treatment of any given text may be creative or non-creative, but the literature as a whole is predominantly creative in its handling of biblical material. The interpretation is accomplished sometimes by rewriting the biblical material" (p. 74). Among recent longer treatments are Jacob Neusner, *Midrash in Context: Exegesis in Formative Judaism* (Philadelphia: Fortress, 1983) and Shmuel Safrai, ed., *The Literature of the Sages. Part 2: Midrash, Aggada, Midrash Collections, Targum, Prayer* (Philadelphia: Fortress, 1987).

[6]Pagels, *Johannine Gospel,* commenting on *AH* I. 8, 5, writes:

> The basic methodological principle of Valentinian exegesis is that the exegete must define precisely in terms of which context—pleromic, kenomic, or cosmic—he intends to interpret any given verse. So when Ptolemy sets forth the pleromic interpretation of the [Johannine] prologue, he selects for exegesis only those verses from which he can trace the members of the first ogdoad. In this context, the references he makes to the christological and soteriological interpretation of these verses remain only peripheral to his primary exegetical aim. Such exegetical decisions are grounded theologically on the ontological trinitarianism which is expressed mythically in terms of the pleroma, the kenoma, and the cosmos. *Knowledge of the myth and its theological basis forms the essential prerequisite for understanding Valentinian exegesis* (p. 34, emphasis added).

All of Pagels' first chapter develops this position.

[7]He accepts as "a defensible Valentinian corpus from Nag Hammadi" *The Prayer of the Apostle Paul* (I, 1), *The Gospel of Truth* (I, 3 / XII, 2), *The Treatise on the Resurrection* (I, 4), *The Tripartite Tractate* (I, 5), *The Gospel of Philip* (II, 3), *The Interpretation of Knowledge* (XI, 1), and *A Valentinian Exposition* (XI, 2). See *Sin in Valentinianism* (Atlanta: Scholars Press, 1990) 6, and the review of scholarly opinion, 7 n.18.

[8]Concerning the division of humanity, Michel R. Desjardins writes:

> Valentinianism according to Irenaeus distinguishes between pneumatics, psychics and sarkics [hylics]. Yet only *The Tripartite Tractate* clearly reflects this "classical" division. Indeed, in both *The Gospel of Philip* and *A Valentinian Exposition* all people seem to be treated the same. Actually, a bipartite rather than a tripartite division does more justice to these works on the whole. The distinction between "the children of the Father" and the "others" is clearly drawn in *The Gospel of Truth, The Second Apocalypse of James,* and *The Interpretation of Knowledge,* and the struggle between "those on the left" and "those on the right" is a feature of *A Valentinian Exposition.* Even in *The Tripartite Tractate* the psychics and the pneumatics are treated virtually as one group and set off from the hylics. (Ibid. 115.)

[9]Desjardins, *Sin in Valentinianism* 116.

[10]See Desjardins, *Sin in Valentinianism* 67–116, with summary of the relevant material on p. 116.

[11]Desjardins, *Sin in Valentinianism,* although otherwise quite thorough, does not cite the earlier work of Berthouzoz: *Liberté et grace suivant la théologie d'Irénée de Lyon: le débat avec la gnose aux origines de la théologie chrétienne,* Etudes d'ethique chrétienne 8 (Paris: Cerf, 1980).

[12]François Sagnard, *La gnose valentinienne et le témoignage de Saint Irénée* (Paris: Vrin, 1947).

[13]R. Berthouzoz, *Liberté et grâce* 95–99, analyzes Luise Schottroff, *"Animae naturaliter salvandae:* zum Problem der himmlischen Herkunft des Gnostikers," in W. Eltester, ed., *Christentum und Gnosis* (Berlin: Topelmann, 1969) 65–97.

[14]R. Berthouzoz, *Liberté et grâce* 99–101 on Elaine Pagels, "The Valentinian Claim to Esoteric Exegesis of Romans as Basis for Anthropological Theory," *VigChr* 26 (1972) 241–258.

CHAPTER THREE

Issues of Unity and Diversity

Adversus haereses I. 10–31

In the second and central section of *AH* I Irenaeus frames his presentation of Gnostic diversity of doctrines, practices, rites, and exegeses between two chapters that focus on the unity of the Church's faith and on the Rule of Faith that grounds this unity. He begins with attention to the implications of his understanding of unity for the role of the learned person in the Church.

UNITY OF THE CHURCH'S FAITH (*AH* I. 10)

Rule of Truth and Task of the Theologian

The kind of unity of faith the Church possesses is, for Irenaeus, such that it is as if the Church really were only one person, living in just one house, having just one soul, one heart, and one mouth. He notes:

> The Church, having received this proclamation and this faith, as we have said, being spread through the whole world, *guards* it carefully as inhabiting *one house,* and likewise *believes* in the same way, *as* having *one soul and one heart,* and it *preaches* and *teaches* and *hands this on as* if possessing *one mouth* (*AH* I. 10, 2 [SC 264:158]).

Whether or not the picture painted here is touched with hyperbole the intent is clear: unity of faith does not admit diversity. (It is perhaps too easy for contemporary readers to forget that it is only comparatively recently—and in some places—that diversity in everything from opinions to lifestyles has come to be valued in itself.)

Greater or lesser degrees of knowledge, Irenaeus holds, have nothing to do with changing doctrine. The degree of learning of the Church's teachers is not a positive correlate of the changes in doctrine or the abundance of the images of God they produce. (So much for creative theology!) Rather the sign of a person's learning is the ability of that person (1) to untangle the exact significance of parables and to make them accord with the doctrine of truth, (2) to clarify how the saving designs of God are realized for humanity,[1] and (3) to show, in an action of thanksgiving, why the Word of God was made flesh and suffered his passion (*AH* I. 10, 3). By its allusion to the eucharistic action *(eucharistein; gratias agere)*[2] this formulation suggests a context within the life of the Church. Thus one can maintain without over-reading of *AH* I. 10, 1-3 that Irenaeus sees as functions of the learned person within the Church the study of the Scriptures and theology and the work of liturgy, all performed under the Rule of Faith.[3] If the Valentinians themselves began as learned Christians (as Valentinus apparently did and as may well be suggested by the number of times Irenaeus warns of the effect of their teaching on "the simple"), this outline of the function of the learned person within the Church offers a further negative critique of the Valentinians.

GNOSTIC DIVERSITY (*AH* I. 11–21)

Different Stories

In contrast to the unity of the Church's doctrine Irenaeus proceeds to show the diversity of Gnostic doctrines, practices, rites, exegeses, and even Scriptures. First he outlines three different Gnostic presentations of the Pleroma, including a system that names the first four powers who emit the rest as Singleness, Unity, Monad, and One. He satirizes this doctrine, suggesting that one might as well speak of the royal Proarche, pro-empty of intelligibility, pro-empty of substance, and pro-pro power of rotundity that he calls "Gourd." With Gourd is a power called "Supervacuity." These two, being one, emit without emitting a visible fruit, edible and sweet, which he calls "Cucumber." Cucumber's partner is "Melon." These four have emitted all the rest of the numerous, dizzy-making Melons of Valentinus. As Irenaeus remarks: "for if it is necessary to transform the common language into the first Tetrad, and if anyone is able to place names as he or she wishes, who is to prevent these names, very worthy of credibility, being put into use and being known by all?" (*AH* I. 11, 4 [SC 264:176]). The implication is that in his eyes the normative Rule of Faith also governs language used to describe the Deity. The Valentinians evidently use language far more freely in an effort to speak intelligibly of the incomprehensible God and of the coming to be of the Savior (See *AH* I. 11 and 12).

Different Eucharistic Practices

Irenaeus then turns to various practices and rites common to the disciples of Mark the Magician, who "is thought to accomplish miracles among those who have never had any sense, or who have lost it" (*AH* I. 13, 1 [SC 264:190]). The magical practices described center around the eucharist. Among the Marcosians the eucharistic rite involves a quasi-miraculous change in the color of the wine and an equally "miraculous" filling of a large cup from a smaller one. By his prodigies Mark "removed many and dragged them after him." The practices described do not impress Irenaeus, who speaks disparagingly of those who were moved by them. The use of verbs like "removed" (*abstraxis/apageochen* [SC 264:193]) suggests that Marcosians were among the Christian community, an inference Irenaeus will confirm shortly when he mentions the number of women who followed Mark in the Rhone valley. In the circumstances one might imagine how difficult it would be for him to give a sympathetic presentation of Mark's practices.

Role of Women

All the more remarkable, then, is the way Irenaeus responds to the role of women in Mark's community. Women play significant roles as assistants to the magician and as prophets in his group. Irenaeus does not criticize the involvement of women as women; he makes no remarks about "wanton women."[4] In fact he notes that other women, more faithful, who "have the fear of God" are not seducible. He does not object to women prophesying but to anyone prophesying on human command. In his opinion "those having the God-given gift of prophecy speak where and when God wishes, not when Mark orders" (*AH* I. 13, 4 [SC 264:198]). He also objects to Mark's preference for elegant and rich women whom he flatters and seduces in a "nuptial rite." From Irenaeus's remarks it is evident that in his opinion neither women's involvement in the Church, nor their beauty, nor their riches should be used as an excuse to take advantage of them physically, psychologically, or spiritually. He mentions that there are women who resist Mark's invitations, that some who followed Mark's teachings repented of it and did penance, but that a great many women "in our Rhone region" were taken in (*AH* I. 13, 3-7). Apparently, at least among the followers of Mark known to Irenaeus, prophecy is important, women have a central role, and a form of Eucharist is celebrated as well as a "nuptial rite."

Rites of Redemption

After a discussion of their doctrines and the supporting exegesis Irenaeus will return to the Marcosian rites of redemption, portraying a variety of rituals. These include use of a nuptial chamber and the carrying out of a mystagogy to effect a pneumatic marriage in imitation of the partnerships in the Pleroma, baptism in water with varying invocations, and ending the rite with an anointing with balsam (*AH* I. 21, 3). In still another form the water is replaced with an anointing of the head with a mixture of oil and water, and balsam is used. Another group rejects all physical ritual since true gnosis is incorporeal. Others employ the ritual at the moment of death and include with the anointing some invocations to be used by the soul in its journey after death.[5]

Understanding of Scripture

Mark's preoccupation with women continues to set the tone as Irenaeus reviews Mark's understanding of revelation, leading into an examination of the latter's use of word, letter, and number symbolism. The first Tetrad "descended on [Mark] under the form of a woman because the world is not able to bear her [its?] masculine element" (*AH* I. 14, 1 [SC 264:206]). She then revealed to him (and only to him) the genesis of all things. The Word itself took form through the enunciation of his Name by the Father. From this follows an analysis of word, syllable, letter, and number symbolism (*AH* I. 14, 1-15, 3; 16, 1-2).

In the remainder of the middle section of the first book of *Adversus haereses* Irenaeus reviews a variety of doctrines and supporting exegesis concerning the Pleroma and the unknown Father. The multiple forms of exegesis are not attacked in themselves; rather the difficulty remains the same as in the opening section of *AH:* these people interpret the Scriptures to refer to another than the Creator who *is* the invisible God (*AH* I. 19, 2). In addition, not satisfied with offering such false interpretations of the true Scriptures, these people invent scriptures of their own: "Beyond this they also bring forward a vast multitude of apocryphal and bastard scriptures, composed by themselves, for the amazement of the simple and those who are not knowledgeable of the literature of truth" (*AH* I. 20, 1 [SC 264:288]). As an example Irenaeus tells the story of the child Jesus learning his letters, a story found in most of the apocryphal infancy gospels.[6] The teacher said, "Say *a.*" Jesus said, *"a."* The teacher then said, "Say *b.*" Jesus replied, "First you tell me what *a* is and then I will tell you what *b* is." According to Irenaeus the Gnostics say this means that Jesus alone knew the Unknowable, symbolized by *a.*

In this mid-section of *AH* I, Irenaeus contrasts the unity of the faith of the Church with Gnostic pluriformity in doctrines, practices, and rites, as well as in the number of writings recognized as scriptures. He condemns the Marcosians both for misinterpreting the Scriptures and for unduly expanding them. While he also attacks this group for their actions and attitude toward women, he himself never criticizes the involvement of women as women. The face of the adversary begins to emerge as the face of a fellow Christian who is far more at ease with plurality of interpretation in many areas of life than is Irenaeus. The Gnostic is intellectually adventuresome in terms of both doctrine and interpretation, and given to the development of new liturgical forms.

THE RULE OF TRUTH AND THE ONE GOD (*AH* I. 22)

Irenaeus drives home the contrast between Gnostic pluriformity and the unity of truth in a summary of the Rule of Truth (another name, as we have seen, for the Rule of Faith), recalling that the Father by himself made all things: visible, invisible, sensible, intelligible, temporal in view of the economy, or eternal. By the Word and the Spirit the Father made all, disposes all, governs all, and gives all to be, and that "all" includes humankind. In fact, as Irenaeus remarked earlier, "holding on to this Rule we are easily able to show them to have deviated from the truth, although they may say many different and numerous things" (AH I. 21, 1 [SC 264:310]). Such an assertion that rebuttal will be "easy" reveals either a bit of bravado on Irenaeus's part or else an immense confidence in the truth and power of his own position. After all, Ptolemy's Valentinians and the followers of Mark the Magician must have been numerous—or at least extremely effective in winning adherents—in the Rhone valley. If not, would even so ardent a conviction have matured into so thorough a work of rebuttal? Yet Irenaeus remained confident of the force of his position.

THE VALENTINIAN FAMILY TREE (AH I. 23–31)

In the third and final part of Book One Irenaeus undertakes to complete his unmasking of the Valentinian teaching by outlining their "family tree," sketching both their remote (AH I. 23–28) and more immediate ancestors (AH I. 29, 1–31, 2), for whom he describes systems of doctrine,[7] practices as opposite as encratism and libertinism,[8] rituals,[9] and, at least to some extent, use of the Scriptures.[10]

Doctrine and practice are assumed to have mutual implications. Among Irenaeus's remarks on Carpocratian practices is a passage particularly worth attention. He writes: "They have entered such a degree of insanity that they say they have the power to do whatever things are irreligious and impious. Good and evil, they say, are only human opinions" (AH I. 25, 4 [SC 264:338]). In fact, until they use their liberty to experience everything humans will suffer the penalty of continuous reincarnation. What is desired is the practice of absolute liberty. But whether actual Gnostics live out the implications of this position is another question. Irenaeus remarks: "Do they do among themselves these things which are irreligious and unjust and forbidden? I simply do not believe it" (AH I. 25, 5 [SC 264:340]). In his view they have not "lived down" to their teaching, a most important observation in light of the bent of his polemic. This passage is one in which he betrays discomfort with the absence of connection between Gnostic lived experience as known to him and the theory of relativity he had expounded earlier, a theory he viewed as supporting moral depravity. He apparently does not know Valentinians who live according to this notion of "absolute liberty."

The real problem, he thinks, is that teaching that destroys any real difference between good and evil also breaks the link between faith and love. Irenaeus continues: "Through faith and love we are saved; all the rest is indifferent. According to the opinion of these men a thing is sometimes able to be called good, sometimes evil, since nothing is of its nature evil (*AH* I. 25, 5 [SC 264:340–342]). His judgment of this group is that, first, it is unlikely that their actions will correspond with their teaching. This is noteworthy since an accusation of libertinism is more likely to be used polemically to tar an opponent than to be weighed by the polemicist and found wanting. Second, the problem he finds with the teaching is that by denying the possibility of genuinely evil actions it destroys the connection between belief and life. In his reports of most of the groups portrayed as ancestors of the Valentinians Irenaeus consistently mentions the consequences of their doctrines for one's way of life without, however, illustrating those consequences in Valentinian living by any but the most general examples.

ADVERSUS HAERESES I: SUMMARY

The "face of the adversary" peers through a threefold presentation that includes a summary of the Valentinian myth, a contrast between the Church's unity and Valentinian diversity in doctrine, practices, rites, and exegeses, and a review of Valentinian ancestry attentive to the link between belief and life. On Irenaeus's presentation the mythology is complex and internally consistent; it betrays an intelligent understanding of the religious questions of the day. It is supported by an interpretation of the Scriptures that works from a different theological principle than that used by the community led by Irenaeus. The rich diversity in expressions of the myth and in forms of ritual contrasts with the emerging common Christian experience. Some Marcosians, Irenaeus notes, seduce women; at the same time, among them women have a prominent place in prophecy and worship. In addition, not only do these thinkers use a different principle to support their exegesis but they also make use of a wider variety of scriptural texts than those in use in the Church. Furthermore, the many shadings of Gnostic mythology support quite diverse life choices, including encratism. When Irenaeus considers the family tree of the Valentinians he finds a doctrine that eliminates the possibility that certain actions are genuinely evil (or genuinely good). In his view such a position subverts the connection between faith and love, and so between belief and life. Interestingly, in this area he finds it difficult to illustrate the doctrine with examples of lived Gnostic practice.

Has the Gnostic face become any clearer? It presents itself as intelligent, probably educated, creative, and unafraid of the challenges of diversity, whether in the Scriptures or in rite, in myth or in life choices. It is the face of one at home with women's leadership (which Irenaeus does not attack). The arguments Irenaeus uses against the Valentinians may further sharpen this picture.

NOTES

[1]Irenaeus specifies further ways in which the duty to make clear God's saving designs for humanity is to be carried out: the Christian teacher is to show how God has been patient

with both apostate angels and disobedient men and women; to show how the one God has created all things; to show how the invisible God has appeared to the prophets in different ways; to show why several testaments were given to the human race, and the unique character of each; and to show why "God has consigned all to disobedience, that he may have mercy upon all" (Rom 11:32).

[2]On this interpretation see SC 263:227, the note marked 165, n. 1.

[3]The Greek reading in two manuscripts is *tēs pisteōs* rather than the Latin *veritas;* the editors argue for the Latin reading on a parallel with the text of II. 25, 1. However, what is of greater importance to my argument here, they also note the closeness between the two readings. See SC 263:226, n. 1 on SC 264:163.

[4]By contrast his near contemporary, Tertullian, writes: "And the women of these heretics, how wanton they are! For they are bold enough to teach, to dispute, to enact exorcisms, to undertake cures—maybe even to baptize" (*Praesc.* 41.5).

[5]Elaine Pagels, "A Valentinian Interpretation of Baptism and Eucharist—and Its Critique of 'Orthodox' Sacramental Theology and Practice" (*HThR* 65 [1972] 153–169 studies these rituals in the fragments of Heracleon.

[6]See, e.g., *GThom* 6; 14; *Gospel of Pseudo-Matthew* 31; 38; *Arabian Infancy Gospel* 48–49 (SC 263:263, n. 1 from p. 289).

[7]Sections dealing with doctrine are *AH* I. 23, 2 and 5; 24, 1-7; 25, 1-2; 26, 1-2; 27, 1-3; 29, 1-4; 30, 1–31, 2.

[8]Sections dealing with practices are extensive; they include references to the practice of magic (e.g., *AH* I. 23, 1 and 4), references both to refraining from intercourse (e.g., I. 28, 1) and to practicing indiscriminate intercourse (e.g., I. 28, 2), mention of the notion that all impieties and sacrileges can be committed because good and evil are only human opinions (I. 25, 4), and mention of groups in which Jewish practices are followed (I. 26, 2-3.)

[9]Only two occur: *AH* I. 23, 5 and I. 26, 2.

[10]Examples of interpretation of the Scriptures include *AH* I. 24, 1 and 4; 25, 4; 26, 2; 27, 2; 29, 2.

CHAPTER FOUR

Toward a Right Reading

Adversus haereses II

Face to face with such an adversary, Irenaeus carefully plans *Adversus haereses* II as a five-part refutation of the Valentinian teaching. As he treats their claims his own face appears: the content, order, and force of his writing show him to be an intelligent, organized, and formidable thinker. He takes his organizing principle from the Rule of Faith and orders the theses he intends to refute from most important to least.[1] In that order these are: (1) Valentinian theses on a Pleroma superior to the Creator God (*AH* II. 1–11), (2) Valentinian theses concerning the emission of the Aeons, the passion of Sophia, and the seed (*AH* II. 12–19), (3) Valentinian number speculation (*AH* II. 20–28), (4) Valentinian theses on the final consummation and the Demiurge (*AH* II. 29–30), and (5) some non-Valentinian theses (*AH* II. 31–35). In addition his organizing principle governs the selection and use of arguments; thus theological in both principle and method, Book Two becomes an exercise in the practice of theology. Bearing in mind his readers, Irenaeus remarks that those fearing too long an argument may be comforted to know that he does not plan to use all possible materials, but only those that are *"apta"* and that time permits. What he is after are the key pieces. Once these are destroyed he is confident the rest of the structure will collapse for lack of support.

PART ONE: PLEROMA SUPERIOR TO CREATOR (*AH* II. 1–11)

Granted Irenaeus's plan, his opening can hardly be unexpected. He writes:

> It is well, therefore, for us to begin with the first and greatest point, with God the Demiurge, who made heaven and earth and all that is in them, which these

50

blasphemers call the fruit of a fall,[2] and to show that there is not anything above him or after him, and he made all things not by motion from some other but by his own purpose and freely, since he is sole God and sole Lord and sole Creator and sole Father and solely contains all things and is himself responsible for the being of all things (*AH* II. 1, 1 [SC 294:26]).

He begins with an assertion of the supremacy of the Creator God, the Demiurge, who is himself the Father of all. "Sole God, sole Lord, sole Creator, sole Father, sole container of all things" echoes as a leitmotif throughout his work, picking up as it does fundamental insights of the Rule of Faith.

As was the case in Book One, the Rule of Faith will function as touchstone to supply Irenaeus with the understanding of God against which he measures the Gnostic understanding of the Deity. Here as there that same Rule will also play a determinative part in his assessment of Gnostic exegesis. The basic thrust of his argument is that to hold a Pleroma superior to the Creator God contradicts both principles of sound thought (Irenaeus accepts that one cannot argue for an infinite regress: *AH* II. 1, 3) and the common understanding of God as one who is neither ignorant, negligent, nor bound by necessity.

PART TWO: EMISSION OF AEONS, SOPHIA, THE SEED (*AH* II. 12–19)

Irenaeus goes on to refute theses concerning the emissions, the passion of Sophia, and the seed. One of his first steps is to criticize the literal application of the analogy of human thought to the emission of the Aeons. Having said God is unknowable, the Valentinians still use the human thought process to describe processes within the Pleroma so that God emits Thought, Thought emits Intellect, and Intellect emits Word. Irenaeus remarks: "If they had known the Scriptures and have been taught by truth they would have known that God is not like human beings, and that God's thoughts are not like human thoughts" (*AH* II. 13, 3 [SC 294:114]).

This position separates Irenaeus from the theology of someone like Justin, who used the analogy between human thought and speech to distinguish between the Word within God and the uttered Word of God. At the same time it serves as a reminder that the Valentinian teaching has a place in early theological speculation on the procession of the Word.[3]

The heart of the Irenaean argument against the emissions lies in *AH* II. 17 and again rests on the innate contradictions within the position, presuming one accepts his understanding of God. He postulates three possible modes of emission. First, generation can be on the human model, where from two beings having the same substance *(eiusdem substantiae)*[4] comes a third having that same substance. But if God is impassible, how could a passible Aeon be generated in this way? He notes, too, that the Aeons are assumed to exist as discrete beings with magnitude. But magnitude is a property of matter, not of spirit (*AH* II. 17, 3-5). Second, generation can be on the model of branches from a tree, but the same problem arises: tree and branch are of one substance. Either that substance is impassible or passible. Either Sophia is incapable of suffering or God is capable of suffering. Neither option fits the situation (*AH* II. 17, 6). Third, generation can be on the model of rays from the sun. Exactly the same objection applies: identity in substance issues in identity in qualities. An impassible God cannot generate a passible Aeon (*AH* II. 17, 7-8).

PART THREE: VALENTINIAN NUMBER SPECULATION (*AH* II. 20–28)

In addition, while attacking the Valentinian exegesis of Ptolemy, Irenaeus presents what he views as conditions for the right use of the Scriptures. Here he explores the role of theology, a highly debatable role if, as Irenaeus argues, all interpretations of the Scriptures incompatible with the Rule of Faith are to be rejected.

The development occurs in the context of an attack on Valentinian speculations involving the interpretation of numbers. Irenaeus does not attack the possibility of doing such interpretation, but rather the validity of their particular interpretations. To take one example, he writes:

> All agree that Judas, the traitor, was the twelfth, twelve being named apostles in the Gospel. However this Aeon [Sophia] was not the twelfth but the thirtieth, for according to them there were not only a dozen Aeons emitted by the will of the Father nor was it emitted the twelfth in order, they reckoning it as emitted in the thirtieth place (*AH* II. 20, 4 [SC 294:206]).

It is not the Valentinians' number speculation as such but their poor use of it that is attacked here. This is also the case in their interpretation of the Passion of the Lord in the so-called "twelfth month" (*AH* II. 22, 1-6) and their interpretation of the woman who hemorrhaged for twelve years (*AH* II. 23, 1-2). Equally, the Marcosian number and letter interpretation is off base (*AH* II. 24).

Speculations of this type are common in second-century exegesis, but in Irenaeus's view they need to be handled correctly. It is not that numbers and letters do not signify anything; rather, symbols and the things symbolized must be kept in proper relation to one another: "For measure *(regula)* does not come from numbers, but numbers from measure, nor does God come from the things that are made, but the things that are made come from God" (*AH* II. 25, 1 [SC 294:252]). The movement is not from created things to God, but from God to created things. The point is not that created things can tell nothing about God but that, quite literally, created things like numbers *have their origin* in God. Irenaeus uses the example of music, where one hearing the separate tones issuing from an instrument does not assume separate artists or authors. So, to paraphrase him, those who listen to the melody of creation should praise the Artist who made it, without ever transforming the measure, or distancing themselves from the Artist, or rejecting faith in one sole God, Author of all things (*AH* II. 25, 2).

The question of how to interpret the Scriptures correctly is a central one. As part of this response to the Gnostic exegetes Irenaeus reflects on the conditions of the correct use of the Scriptures (*AH* II. 25, 3-28). "Sane" and "religious" or pious study is not only governed by the true understanding of God but also respects the fact that there are some things humankind cannot know.

> Insofar as the human person who was made, and only today received the beginning of existence, is less than the one who made that person and who is always the same, to that extent the human person is less than the one who made that person in learning and in the investigation of the causes of all things (*AH* II. 25, 3 [SC 294:254]).

It is true that there are some things that surpass the capacity of human knowledge; however, it is also true that an invaluable help has been given to humankind: "Having therefore the very Rule of Truth and a testimony about God placed in the open, we ought not reject the solid and true knowledge of God by seeking the answer to questions in all sorts of directions" (*AH* II. 28, 1 [SC 294:268]). Thus it is important to distinguish between the things human beings can know and those that they cannot know, and in doing so to let oneself be guided by the Rule of Faith. As Schoedel has shown, the distinction Irenaeus makes is not simply between difficult and easy problems either in the study of nature or in Scriptural exegesis.[5] Rather in the study of nature humans know that natural things are; knowledge of how such things come to exist is left to God. With respect to things in the Scriptures the contrast is between the assertions (as "there is one God who created matter") and speculation about such assertions (as when or how God created matter). Schoedel remarks: "The important point, then, is that when Irenaeus worries about the gnostic interpretation of parables, it is because such exegesis reflects dissatisfaction with knowing 'that' and an unhealthy desire to know 'why.'"[6] The parables must be read in harmony with the rest of the Scriptures. The Irenaean approach explains unclear passages in the Scriptures via the clear passages and in conformity with the Rule of Faith, always bearing in mind that speculation into the why of God's actions is not for humankind.

PART FOUR: VALENTINIANS ON FINAL CONSUMMATION AND THE DEMIURGE (*AH* II. 29-30)

After this instruction on the right reading of Scriptures, Irenaeus continues his rebuttal of the Gnostic teachings. He returns here to the final destiny of the three natures or substances. According to the Valentinians whom Irenaeus knows, the destiny of each of the three natures is attained by the joining of like to like. The pneumatics, having been separated even from their souls and being rendered pure intelligences, will become the spouses of the pneumatic angels in the Pleroma. The Demiurge (being psychic and so inferior to human pneumatics) will go to the place of the Mother, and the souls of the "just" will go to the intermediary place, below the Pleroma (*AH* II. 29, 1). The hylics will remain in the lower regions and will be destroyed by fire.

Irenaeus finds a fundamental inconsistency in the claim that it is the psychics who are just who will enter the repose of the intermediary place. His argument is that if they are saved by nature there is no need for a Savior. If they are saved by justice it is not because they are souls but because they are just that they are saved. But if justice can save souls otherwise destined to be lost, why can it not save bodies also? After all, the body also had a part in doing justice. He notes: "Justice appears either impotent or unjust if indeed it saves some things because of their participation in justice, but not others" (*AH* II. 29, 1 [SC 294:296]). This approach is fundamental to the almost naively literal Irenaean argument for resurrection of the body, an argument he will develop in *AH* IV and V. The force of his objection in this place, however, is directed to the conflict he finds in the Valentinians he knows between salvation by nature and salvation by justice.

PART FIVE: SOME NON-VALENTINIAN THESES (*AH* II. 31–35)

In the final part of his refutation Irenaeus turns to the non-Valentinian Gnostics, including Simon and Carpocrates. In his critique of magical practices (*AH* II. 31, 2-3) he notes that the magicians have not healed the sick, expelled demons, or raised the dead, all deeds accomplished by both the Lord and the apostles. He even recalls one instance when, by prayer and fasting, the local church had raised a dead man (*AH* II. 31, 2). By contrast he complains that if one were to observe the day-to-day life of the Gnostics "one would find their daily activity to be one and the same as that of the demons" (*AH* II. 31, 3 [SC 294:332]). Yet the only instances he gives are general accusations of "fraudulence, an apostasizing spirit, demonic activity, and idolatrous trumpery," omitting any specifics (*AH* II. 31, 3 [SC 294:330]). Even in dealing with other than the Valentinian Gnostics with whom he is acquainted Irenaeus uses only generic accusations of wrong conduct. He moves promptly from accusation to speculation.

Turning to what he terms the "pretended necessity" of giving oneself to all possible practices, he takes an ingenuous approach. First he compares this doctrine to the Lord's teaching that even evil thoughts are to be rejected (*AH* II. 32, 1). Then he points out that "all possible actions" would include practicing all virtue, performing every difficult deed, and every glorious exploit. In fact, mastery of all the theoretical and practical arts would also be required (*AH* II. 32, 2). Plainly no one person could accomplish this in one lifetime. If one then raises the possibility of transmigration of souls, so that what is impossible in one lifetime may be accomplished in several, he points to the absence of memory of previous lifetimes, a memory that would be necessary if in each successive life one is to add to the roster of things accomplished previously (*AH* II. 33, 1). On every one of these points the Gnostics contradict the teaching of the Scriptures (*AH* II. 32, 1; 34, 1-2).

ADVERSUS HAERESES II: SUMMARY

In the organization of his refutation Irenaeus reveals himself as deeply committed to the Rule of Faith as he understands it. It supplies the understanding of God with which he works: there is one God who is alone Lord, Creator, Father, and container of all. He employs this notion to undermine the Valentinian theories of the Pleroma and of the emissions. This understanding of God also undergirds his critique of the Valentinian use of number speculation in the interpretation of the Scriptures. Right use of a method of interpretation for him means a use guided by the true understanding of God. Where Scripture study brings one up against matters unknowable by humans one should accept the guidance of the Rule of Faith.

In addition Irenaeus rejects the Valentinian teaching on the destiny of the psychics because of the conflict he finds between salvation by nature and salvation by justice. He ends by refuting several positions concerned with implications for action in which he holds that the Gnostics contradict the Scriptures. He is relentless in his attack, moved by concern for those whom wrong teaching is leading astray in understanding and consequently in action, as well as by care for their erring teachers. He clearly understands his own work as including right teaching. In each area—in the order, the content, and the force of *AH* II—Irenaeus shows himself as a man passionately committed to the one God. His service is wholehearted, and brooks no halfway measures. One of his particular concerns focuses on the misinterpretation of the Scriptures by the Valentinians.

NOTES

[1]Pheme Perkins, "Ordering the Cosmos: Irenaeus and the Gnostics," in Charles W. Hedrick and Robert Hodgson, Jr., eds., *Nag Hammadi, Gnosticism, and Early Christianity* (Peabody, Mass.: Hendrickson, 1986) 221–238, has studied the philosophical substructure behind Irenaeus's refutation of the Valentinian system in *AH* II. 1–19. She notes: "Irenaeus' stock arguments against the Valentinians have a parallel in Philo's arguments against the Platonists. Philo's reconciliation of Genesis with Platonic speculation providing for the divine creation of the intelligible world concludes with a list of five points that characterize the truth taught in Moses' story" (p. 223). These five points are the eternity of the deity, the oneness of God, the temporality of the world, the oneness of the world, and the providence of God. She comments that "Philo's five points provide a 'handbook defense' by which one can evaluate competing claims about the origin of the cosmos and its relationship to God" (p. 224). Her thesis is that "such a pattern of stock argumentation also underlies Irenaeus' arguments. The anti-Platonic character of these arguments forms part of a persistent theme in Haer. II" (p. 224).

[2]The Latin is *extremitatis;* "fall" describes what is suggested.

[3]See Antonio Orbe, *Hacia la primera téologia de la procesion del verbo.* Estudios Valentinianos 1 and 2 (Rome: Gregorian University, 1958).

[4]It would be anachronistic to read into Irenaeus's language the fourth- and fifth-century debates about substance.

[5]See William R. Schoedel's valuable study of this section, "Theological Method in Irenaeus (*Adversus haereses* 2. 25–28)," *JThS* n.s. 35 (1984) 31–49. He seeks to reconcile the opinions of Robert Grant, who concludes that Irenaeus here "inclines toward Scepticism" ("Irenaeus and Hellenistic Culture" [*HThR* 43 (1949) 41–51]; also in *After the New Testament* [Philadelphia: Fortress, 1967, 158–164]) and W. C. van Unnik, who argues that "the experiment with doxographical knowledge did not lead to scepticism, but to differentiation in our human knowledge of physical phenomena: some things are known, other things are not" ("Theological Speculation and its Limits" in W. R. Schoedel and R. L. Wilken, eds., *Early Christian Literature and the Classical Tradition, In Honorem Robert M. Grant,* Théologie historique 53 [Paris: Beauchesne, 1979] 33–43).

[6]Ibid. 35.

CONCLUSION TO PART TWO

Valentinians and the Christian Church

As one comes closer to Irenaeus it is increasingly apparent that the "demonic" daily activity of the Valentinians that upsets him has to do with their use of the Scriptures. Irenaeus repeatedly identifies his opponents as "evil interpreters of the good word of revelation" (*AH* I. preface, 1), calling them such things as "perverters" and "abusers" of the Scriptures (*AH* I, 3, 6; I, 8, 1; I, 9, 1). He accuses them of evildoing like "making wrong use of the prophets" (*AH* I, 19, 1-2), and "garbling the Scriptures" (*AH* II. preface, 1). In addition he urges that the Church expel the Valentinians, something the latter themselves find puzzling:

> [The Valentinians] ask why—when they think as we do—without cause *we absent ourselves from communion with them*—and when they say the same and have the same doctrine—*we call them heretics!* (*AH* III. 15, 2 [SC 211:280], emphasis added).

To "think as we do," to "say the same," even "to have the same doctrine" is, in the Valentinians' thinking, a satisfactory basis for communion in one people. Equally clearly Irenaeus does not see it as such. He is aware that people using the same verbal formulas can differ in their interpretation. While the Valentinians accept the same Scriptures as the rest of the Christian community he finds that they propose an interpretation of the Scriptures not in accord with the Rule of Faith. Therefore "we" (the Christian Church) separate ourselves from them and name them "heretics," that is, those who teach "another doctrine."

What is at issue fundamentally is the unity proper to the New Testament experience of faith in Jesus Christ, a unity in baptism and Eucharist, a unity proper to members of the Church. That unity found its expression in practice and in proclamation, in sacrament and in word. Valentinian exegesis challenged both dimensions. In addition, as we shall see, Valentinians refused or preferred to ignore the authority of Church leadership. Irenaeus will respond not by contributing a theory of development (something the mentality of his times precluded), but by contributing both a theory of authority that correlated the right of teaching (and so of interpretation) with succession in office, and an authoritative interpretation of the Christian faith.

PART THREE

One God, One Christ

Introduction to Part Three

"The glory of humankind is God." (AH III. 20, 2)

Problems centered on interpretation, both the right interpretation and the right to interpret, have moved Irenaeus to attack the Valentinians. Because the underlying issue is a matter of the content and transmission of Christian faith he sees that an adequate response to his opponents requires him to present an authoritative interpretation of the Christian faith. Since, in his opinion, the Scriptures belong to the Christian community in such a way that any valid interpretation must be consistent with the faith of the community, an authoritative interpretation of the faith for him includes authoritative interpretation of the Scriptures. In this sense there is but one right reading.

Following conventions of ancient rhetoric, he organizes his presentation in a style that involves repetition, and this in several ways. His predominant method of exegesis, as Philippe Bacq has demonstrated, has three steps: announce the word of the Lord, cite the word, and comment on it, using linking words or phrases to unite various units of thought of varying lengths. (By the time he begins to comment he has thus already repeated the word two times.) In addition he regularly employs chiasm, a structure marked by repetition and having characteristics of inversion, balance, and climactic centrality.[1] Finally, he repeatedly contrasts his "authentic" interpretation with that of the Gnostics here and throughout *Adversus haereses*. His exegetical procedures are evident in *AH* III where Irenaeus teaches the doctrine of the one God and his Son, Jesus Christ, supported by an exegesis opposed to that of the Valentinians. The purpose of chapters five and six is to present the thought of Irenaeus in *AH* III with attention to his method of exegesis[2] (especially his use of chiasm), bearing in mind that he develops his "true" exegesis in response to the Valentinians' "false" exegesis.

The body of *AH* III consists of two parts, framed by an extended introduction and a shorter conclusion. Irenaeus uses *AH* III. 1–5 (found here in the prologue to chapter five) to outline his theory of authority. He does this in such a way as to establish a correlation between the right to teach (and so to interpret) and succession in office. The first major part, *AH* III. 6–15 (presented in the body of chapter five) treats the scriptural witness to one God, the Creator of all, and the second, *AH* III. 16–23 (discussed in the body of chapter six) examines the scriptural witness to one sole Christ, Son of God become Son of Man. There follows a short concluding section on the Church, *AH* III. 24–25 (found in the epilogue to chapter six) that balances the notion of Church as vehicle of tradition, a concept explored in the extended introduction to *AH* III, with the image of Church grasped as "place" of the Holy Spirit.[3]

NOTES

[1]Centrality requires that the principal argument be located in the center of the exposition. Balance requires that the same number of arguments precede and follow the principal one, each of the preceding arguments being paired with a succeeding one, whether as completion or amplification. Inversion requires that the succeeding arguments follow in reverse order from the preceding ones. Thus the pattern of a seven-membered chiasm would take the form: A, B, C, D, C', B', A'. See Augustine Stock, o.s.b., "Chiastic Awareness and Education in Antiquity," *BTB* 14 (1984) 23. Also helpful are John Breck, "Biblical Chiasmus: Exploring Structure for Meaning," *BTB* 17 (1987) 70–74; David J. Clark, "Criteria for Identifying Chiasm," *LingBibl* 35 (1975) 63–72; and John W. Welch, ed., *Chiasmus in Antiquity: Structures, Analyses, Exegesis* (Hildesheim: Gerstenberg, 1981).

[2]By applying Bacq's method of analysis to *AH* III, I both extend and confirm his work, which was limited to *AH* IV. It is not the intent here to repeat Bacq's study on *AH* III. Rather, profiting from his work, this study builds on it, directing attention to the unfolding of Irenaeus's thought.

[3]For discussion of the plan of *AH* III see SC 210:171–205.

PROLOGUE

The Church,
Place of Authoritative Teaching

Adversus haereses III. 1–5

Correlative to the notion of one right reading is that of one true teacher. For Irenaeus there is but one teacher, Jesus Christ; access to his teaching will be through his designated successors and in the Holy Spirit. It is for this reason that Irenaeus employs his theory of succession to link *AH* I and II with *AH* III–V, and that he balances his presentation of the Church as locus of authoritative teaching with that of the Church as place of the Spirit. Irenaeus begins by recounting the process of transmission: after the resurrection of the Lord and the coming of the Spirit the apostles were filled with certitude and possessed "perfect knowledge." Then they traveled throughout the world proclaiming the good news; indeed, "all together and each separately they had the Gospel of God" (*AH* III. 1, 1 [SC 211:22]). Irenaeus then affirms that this teaching of the apostles is handed on ("traditioned"—so "the tradition") through the bishops, whom they established as their successors in the churches (*AH* III. 3, 1 [SC 211:30]). He buttresses his argument by referring to the "succession lists" maintained by the churches and enumerating that of the church of Rome (*AH* III. 3, 2-3 [SC 211:32–38]).[1]

An assumption basic to Irenaeus's argument is that there is one God, one Church, and—effectively—one bishop speaking for God in that Church. Such a position has immense implications for Church organization since, as Elaine Pagels has noted, theology and polity exert reciprocal influence. Referring to the Valentinian puzzlement over being called heretics when "they confess the same things, and hold the same doctrines," she writes:

I suggest that here again we cannot fully answer this question as long as we consider this debate exclusively in terms of religious and philosophical arguments. But when we investigate how the doctrine of God actually functions in gnostic and orthodox writings, we can see how this religious question also involves social and political issues. Specifically, by the latter part of the second century, when the orthodox insisted upon "one God," they simultaneously validated the system of governance in which the church is ruled by "one bishop." Gnostic modification of monotheism was taken—and perhaps intended—as an attack upon that system. For when gnostic and orthodox Christians discussed the nature of God, they were at the same time debating the issue of *spiritual authority*.[2]

Orthodoxy implied accepting the authority of the bishop in teaching as well as in sacramental practice. By contrast, Valentinians understood their sacrament of redemption as initiating them into a higher way of life, beyond the authority of the bishop who represented the Demiurge. In their own meetings they chose officers by lot each time they gathered.[3] This resulted in a quite different structure of authority. The problem was compounded because among the Valentinians were some leaders of the Christian community.[4] When in a later section of his work Irenaeus addresses the problem of assisting the faithful to distinguish true priests from false he will invoke the principle of apostolic succession:

> One must obey the priests who are in the Church—that is . . . those who possess the succession from the apostles. For they receive simultaneously with the episcopal succession the sure gift of truth. One must hold in suspicion others who depart from the primitive succession, and assemble themselves in any place at all. These one must recognize as heretics . . . or as schismatics . . . or as hypocrites. All of these have fallen from the truth (*AH* IV. 26, 2 [SC 100:718]).[5]

Valentinian Gnostics offered a threat not only by advancing an exegesis of the Scriptures incompatible with that structured by the Rule of Faith, but also by separating themselves from the assemblies led by those "in succession." Irenaeus stood for faith in one God revealed by the one Son, Jesus Christ, whose teaching was preserved in the one Church through the one authoritative episcopal succession.

As a consequence of this theory the right and duty of interpreting the Rule of Faith, that is, the doctrine of Christianity, becomes the responsibility of the bishops. So Irenaeus affirms:

> It is not necessary to search among others for the truth which it is easy to obtain from the Church, for the apostles most fully deposited in her, as in a rich bank, all things which are true, so that everyone who wishes might take from her the water of life. This is the gate of life; all others are thieves and brigands. On account of this it is necessary to avoid them, but to love with great attentiveness those things which are of the Church and to know the tradition of truth (*AH* III. 4, 1 [SC 211:44]).

This graceful allusion to John 10:1-10 ("Who does not enter the sheepfold by the gate . . .") encapsulates the conviction underpinning all the Irenaean teaching. The apostles gave all truth to the Church in the persons of its leaders, their successors. The truth is life, and anyone who wants genuine life must reject alternate points of view, love what comes from the Church, and know the tradition. In sum: reject the false, love the true, know the tradition.

Yet the role of the Spirit must never be underestimated. In the Irenaean perspective the bishops succeed to the apostles through the gift of the Spirit. Thus for him the faith is ordinarily validated by the Church's authoritative teachers, the bishops; however, even his strongest passages on this concept also refer to those whose belief seems to have been more immediately under the action of the Spirit of God. There are those who have come to "the old tradition" without the direct influence of written teaching: "To this order [of the Tradition] the many peoples of the barbarians who believe in Christ give their assent, having salvation written in their hearts without paper or ink by the Spirit, and guarding diligently the old tradition" (*AH* III. 4, 2 [SC 211:46]).

Ultimately faith rests on the Jesus of the Church, and the movement of the Spirit will always have to be allowed for. The situation undoubtedly was somewhat more ambiguous than Irenaeus's analysis of the doctrine of succession would suggest.

NOTES

[1]Recent interest in the interpretation of this passage is a consequence of the appearance of the Sources chrétiennes edition. Decisions made not only in establishing the Latin text but also in the French translation and the Greek retroversion favor the "Roman" interpretation, i.e., that every church must necessarily agree with the church at Rome for reasons connected with its origin. For the editors' explanation of their choices see SC 210:223–236, note marked p. 33, n. 1.

Norbert Brox ("Rom und 'jede Kirche' im 2. Jahrhundert: Zu Irenäus, adv. haer. III 3, 2," *AHC* 7 [1975] 42–78) views the controversy as turning on the meaning of *propter potentiorem principalitem,* which itself turns on the disputed meaning of *principalitas.* He rejects *archē* in the sense of "early source." The superiority in question is linked with foundation by Peter and Paul as eminent, not as chronologically prior. *Potentior* does not mean that Rome has priority over the whole Church or a central function. Rather Rome has an exemplary role, which it fulfills particularly for the Western Church. (Brox makes use here of Tertullian, *Praescr.* 36.1-3 to illustrate similar regional roles played by other churches.) Rome's importance lies in possessing in a clear and decisive way the public teaching received through the bishops in succession to the apostles. Rome is thus a regional exemplar of sound doctrine.

Luise Abramowski ("Irenaeus, Adv. haer. III. 3, 2: Ecclesia Romana and omnis Ecclesia; and ibid., 3.3: Anacletus of Rome," *JThS* n.s. 28 [1977] 101–104) suggests a reading that eliminates the need to postulate an error in the Latin (the path taken by the SC edition). Her reading supports the non-Roman interpretation, in her judgment the only correct Irenaean reading of the passage.

The crux of the question is whether the primacy of the Roman church was, in the mind of Irenaeus, an "exemplary" primacy or something more. If it was exemplary, as seems likely, then confirmation or rejection of Brox's regional exemplary model will come through further study of the relation of the churches to one another.

For a review of the abundant literature on *AH* III. 3, 2 see my "Irenaeus in Recent Scholarship," *SecCen* 4 (1984) 238–240.

[2]Elaine Pagels, *The Gnostic Gospels* (New York: Random House, 1979) 33. The entire chapter develops the thesis.

[3]For texts from the Gnostic documents, Clement of Rome, Tertullian, and Irenaeus, see Pagels, loc. cit. Klaus Koschorke, "Gnostic Instructions on the Organization of the Congregation: The Tractate Interpretation of Knowledge from CG XI" in Bentley Layton, ed., *Rediscovery of Gnosticism* 2, discusses the attitude of the Gnostics to ecclesiastical offices on pp. 764–768, making three points: (1) Gnostics were indifferent toward the offices of that time, granting them an auxiliary but not exclusive function in the appropriation of salvation; (2) they understood outside mediation of salvation (as through the sacraments or the teaching of the bishop) to be a lesser participation in salvation; (3) they leveled a polemic against the exclusive claims of the Church, which they regard as baseless and leading to a confusion between earthly assemblies and the heavenly *ecclesia.*

[4]Some were apparently presbyters: "For they constitute a stumbling-block to many, who simply and unreservedly receive, as coming from a presbyter, the blasphemy which they utter against God" (Irenaeus, Frag. 51 ANF 1.576]). As noted earlier, Tertullian (*Adv. Val.* c. 4) claims that Valentinus himself was a candidate for bishop of Rome.

[5]Elaine Pagels' translation, see eadem, *The Gnostic Gospels* 45.

CHAPTER FIVE

The One God

Adversus haereses III. 6–15

Irenaeus presents the witness of the Scriptures to the One God, Creator of all, in three sections, and devotes a fourth section to a special problem raised by some Gnostics. In the first section (*AH* III. 6, 1–III. 9, 1, line 11) he considers the "global witness" of the Scriptures to the one Creator God. A detailed examination of his exposition will accomplish three things: (1) it will make clear what Irenaeus means by the "global witness" of the Scriptures to one God, the Creator, (2) it will deepen understanding of how his method of exegesis functions and in so doing (3) it will verify that Irenaeus employs in *AH* III the same method Bacq observed in *AH* IV. In the second section (*AH* III. 9, 1–III. 11, 9) Irenaeus considers the evangelists' witness to the one God. He does so by analyzing the opening verses of each of the four gospels. Here one can see how his exegetical method utilizes chiastic structure. After a brief third section (*AH* III. 12) Irenaeus devotes a fourth section (*AH* III. 13, 1–III. 15, 3) to a response to questions about the authority of Paul and Luke.

"Global Witness" of the Scriptures to the One Creator God (*AH* III. 6, 1–III. 9, 1 lines 1–11)

In this section Irenaeus chooses texts from three strata of scriptural sources: prophetic books, a name he uses for the Old Testament taken as a whole (meaning unit 1, including *AH* III. 6, 1–III. 6, 4);[1] apostolic books, represented by Paul (unit 2, including *AH* III. 6, 5–III. 7, 2); and "the words of the Lord," understanding as such the words attributed to Christ in the gospels (unit 3, including *AH* III. 8, 1–III. 9, 1). The works he chooses he treats as belonging to the

Scriptures.² Since he believes that the Scriptures are consistent within themselves
evidence from selected texts in each stratum serves to illustrate the position of
that entire stratum. Thus he achieves his "global witness" of the Scriptures.

Irenaeus affirms that according to the Lord, the Holy Spirit, and the apostles
the strict use of the term "God" is reserved to the true God, and "Lord" in the
absolute sense is applied to the Father and his Son. This affirmation serves as
a general introduction to the entire section; it reappears in the conclusion of
the section, where the only significant difference is that "the Holy Spirit" of
III. 6, 1 becomes in III. 9, 1 "the prophets." Irenaeus typically associates the
Spirit with the work of prophecy,³ so the shift in wording serves as a reminder
of the fullness of the concept stressed throughout the section.

Close examination of Irenaeus's methodology in this section reveals the pattern Bacq found in *AH* IV: announce the word, cite the word, and comment on
it, using linking words and phrases to connect various units. After the intro-
ductory phrase, the first unit of the section opens with the announcement and
citation of a word of the prophetic Spirit: "The Lord said to my Lord, 'Sit at
my right hand, while I make your enemies the footstool of your feet" (Ps 110:1
[LXX 109:1]).⁴ Irenaean commentary on the text takes the form of associat-
ing with it other Old Testament texts in which the twofold use of "Lord" enables him to see the presence of both Father and Son (e. g., "the LORD rained
fire on Sodom and Gomorrah and sulfur came from the LORD of heaven," Gen
19:24). Thus he asserts the first of his three principal themes in the unit: both
Father and Son are truly Lord.

His second principal theme is that Son and Father are both truly God. He
takes up this theme with the text: "Your throne, O God, is forever; the scepter
of righteousness is the scepter of your realm. You have loved justice, and hated
iniquity; therefore, O God, your God has anointed you" (Ps 45:6-7 [LXX
44:7-8], quoted at *AH* III. 6, 1 [SC 211:66]). In typical fashion Irenaeus sees
the Father as God the anointer, and the Son as God the anointed. He finds roles
for Father, Son, and Church in the text: "God stands in the assembly of God;
in their midst he judges the gods" (Ps 82:1 [LXX 81:1]).⁵ Here he introduces
the notion of the Church as God's adopted ones gathered by the Son. These
adopted ones are gods only derivatively and in a secondary sense. Irenaeus explains that the true God is the one who comes and is not silent (Ps 50:1-3
[LXX 49:1-3]), who appears to those who do not seek him (Isa 65:1). According to Irenaeus the "gods" are those to whom it was said: "I have said,
'You are gods and you are all children of the Most High" (Ps 82:6 [LXX
81:6]).⁶ Thus it is these, Irenaeus writes, who have received the grace of adoption (cf. Rom 8:15; Gal 4:5-6). In *AH* III. 6, 2 he reiterates that the only God
and Lord is the God who spoke to Moses and his Son, Jesus Christ our Lord,
who makes children of God those who believe in his name. Explicit citations
include "I AM WHO I AM" and "Thus you shall say to the Israelites: 'He who is
sent me to you'" (Exod 3:14).

The third theme of the unit, presented in *AH* III. 6, 3, is to recognize the status of those the Scriptures name "gods" who nevertheless are not truly God. Beginning from "the gods of the nations, idols of demons" (Ps 95:5), Irenaeus points to the presence of phrases that show that the gods in question are not God in the absolute sense.[7]

With one exception, the text that locates the place of Christians in the overall scheme (Rom 8:15), all of the texts cited throughout *AH* III. 6 are drawn from the Old Testament: Psalms, Genesis, Isaiah, Exodus, Jeremiah, 1 Kings, and 1 Chronicles. This procedure is consistent with Irenaeus's intention to show that "the prophets" know only one who is truly God and that same God's one Son. Echoing up and down the pages of the unit are the words "Dominus Deus," linking words that open the prayer that ends the unit on the note of a fiery plea:

> Therefore I invoke you, Lord God of Abraham and God of Isaac and God of Jacob and Israel, you who are the Father of our Lord Jesus Christ, you who in the multitude of your mercies have delighted in us insofar as we know you, you who have made heaven and earth and rule all things, you who are sole and true God above whom there is no other God, you who through the gift of our Lord Jesus Christ also are giving the Spirit of holiness: give to all who read this book to know that you are the one God, to be confirmed in you and to separate themselves from all heretical doctrine which is without God and impious (*AH* III. 6, 4 [SC 211:74]).

Irenaeus then begins unit two with a Pauline reference to the ones who serve "those who are not gods"; in this way he joins unit two to unit one. Analysis of this section makes it evident that he follows the same methodology that Bacq noticed in *AH* IV.

A constant concern to establish the true exegesis in opposition to the Valentinians' false exegesis is apparent in the remaining two units of this section. In unit two (*AH* III. 6, 5–III. 7, 2) Irenaeus lets Paul's teaching represent that of the apostles. Recognizing that "an idol is nothing" Paul avows one God, the Father, and one Lord Jesus Christ in the face of those who call others gods, whether these others be in heaven or on earth (1 Cor 8:4-6). Irenaeus notes that the phrase "whether in heaven or on earth" is incorrectly applied to the "makers of this world"; he finds support not only from Paul but also from Moses (Deut 5:8; 4:19). The same ones who read "whether in heaven or on earth" wrongly also misinterpret "the god of this world" of 2 Cor 4:4. Irenaeus prefers to render the verse: "God has blinded the spirit of the unbelievers of this age."[8] Irenaeus claims that the inverted structure of the Pauline verse is an example of *hyperbaton,* the transposition of normal word order for the sake of emphasis. (He devotes *AH* III. 7, 2 to examples of this figure in Paul.) He remarks sarcastically, "We are not to blame if those who claim to know mysteries that are above God don't know how to read Paul!" (*AH* III. 7, 1 [SC 211:80]).

A similar concern to rectify false readings governs Irenaeus's presentation of the words of the Lord on the one God. Thus he holds that in the verse that speaks of "giving to Caesar what is Caesar's and to God what is God's" one should recognize "God" for the true God, while in the reference to "not serving two lords" one should be reminded that there is but one Lord who alone is God (*AH* III. 8, 1). Not only must wrong interpretations be rejected but the very language referring to God should take into account the difference in nature between Creator and creature, as did Christ, who called Caesar "Caesar" and recognized "God" for God (*AH* III. 8, 2). Only the Creator, who made all things with his Word, can be called God and Lord (*AH* III. 8, 3). An obvious implication: this line of argument leads to the claim that it is false to postulate a Creator-Demiurge who is an inferior sort of deity in relation to the supreme God, the Father.

In summoning the global witness of the Scriptures to the truth that there is but one God the Lord, Irenaeus has used his typical method of interpretation to show the incompatibility between his readings and those proposed by his opponents.

Evangelists' Witness to One True God (*AH* III. 9, 1, line 12–III. 11, 9)

Irenaeus's treatment of the synoptic gospels, drawing on passages from the beginning of each, offers a somewhat loose example of chiastic organization. The pattern is:

A.   The Baptist, Matthew (*AH* III. 9, 1)
B.   The Infancy Narrative, Matthew (*AH* III. 9, 2)
C.   Jesus' Baptism, Matthew (*AH* III. 9, 3)
B'.   The Infancy Narrative, Luke (*AH* III. 10, 1-5)
A'. The Baptist, Mark (*AH* III. 10, 6)

Irenaeus quotes the great Isaian text (Isa 40:3-5) about the voice crying in the wilderness, "prepare the way of the Lord" that the gospels apply to John the Baptist in both the opening and the closing sections on the Baptist. He interprets it in Matthew's gospel thus:

> There is one and the same God who is Father of our Lord, who through the prophets promised to send the precursor and who made his Salvation, that is, his Word, visible to all flesh, making him flesh himself so that he might make himself manifest to all things as their King. For it is necessary that those who will be judged see their Judge and know him by whom they are judged, and it is also necessary that those who will attain glory know him who gives them the reward of glory (*AH* III. 9, 1 [SC 211]).

This comment is paired with the one with which he ends the section, writing about Mark's use of the same passage:

He says plainly that the beginning of the gospel is the voices of the holy prophets, and he shows that he whom they confess Lord and God is the Father of our
Lord Jesus Christ, who promised he would send his messenger before his face;
this was John, "in the Spirit and power of Elijah," crying in the desert: "Prepare
the way of the Lord, make straight the ways before our God." For the prophets
did not announce now one and now another God, but one and the same under
various significations and many names. . . . It is this same God whom we
Christians honor and love with our whole heart, the Maker of heaven and earth
and of all that is in them (*AH* III. 10, 6 [SC 211:136–138]).

What is important to Irenaeus here is, first, to claim as one and not several beings both the Father, who is the Creator, and the Lord, his Word and Son, who
is our Salvation; second, to indicate that the Word is visible in the flesh where
he can be known by all; and third, to affirm that the God of the prophets is one
with the God of Christians.

The theme of knowledge recurs in both passages on the infancy narratives.
In the earlier passage, commenting on Matthew, there is simply a single-word
allusion. Among the texts Irenaeus calls to witness is: "In Judah God is *known*
. . . his abode has been established in Salem, his dwelling place in Zion"
(NRSV Ps 76:1-2 [LXX 75:2]). Later he comments on the words: "you, child,
will be called the prophet of the Most High, for you will go before the Lord
. . . to give *knowledge* of salvation to his people by the forgiveness of their
sins" (NRSV Luke 1:76-77). Responding to Gnostic claims, he expands on
the meaning of this "knowledge of salvation":

This therefore was the knowledge of Salvation, not another God, nor another
Father, nor Abyss, nor the Pleroma of thirty Aeons, nor the Mother Ogdoad; but
the knowledge of Salvation was the knowledge of the Son of God, who is called
and is Salvation, Savior, and the Power Who Saves. Salvation, thus: "In your
salvation I have endured, O Lord." Savior, thus: "Behold my God, my Savior, I
trust in you." The Power Who Saves, thus: "God has made known his Saving
Power in the sight of the nations." He is Savior because he is Son and Word of
God. He is Saving Power because he is Spirit: for it is said, "The Spirit of our
face is Christ the Lord." He is salvation, because flesh: for "the Word was made
flesh and dwelt among us." This therefore was the knowledge of salvation which
John offered to those doing penance and believing in the Lamb of God who
takes away the sin of the world" (*AH* III. 10, 3 [SC 211:124]).

What Irenaeus is concerned to do is to unite in the one figure, Christ, attributes that the Gnostic myth splits among several figures. God's word in the
Scriptures provides the warrant for recognizing the diverse qualities in the one
Christ. It does not worry Irenaeus that the connection among the cited passages is merely verbal, without any contextual relationship. Though he never
put it this way, his argument would move like this: "all the Scriptures speak
of the one God and his Christ. These passages use the vocabulary of salvation;
therefore they are applicable, (or even they *best* apply) to the Savior and his

saving work." In addition he notes that Christ, Son and Word of God, is voluntarily in flesh, in the very materiality so despised by the Gnostics. He will develop this point in more detail later. The passage just quoted comes immediately after the presentation of the idea central to the chiasm, the Baptism of the Lord, which thus is preceded by a reference to the knowledge of the Lord and is succeeded by an explanation of the nature of such knowledge.

Irenaeus presents the central theme of the baptism of Jesus through a commentary on a tissue of scriptural texts. He begins with the Matthean narrative: "the heavens were opened and he saw the Spirit of God descending as a dove upon him. And behold a voice came from heaven saying, 'This is my beloved Son in whom I am well pleased'" (Matt 3:16-17). Keeping the Gnostics in mind, he writes:

> For Christ did not then descend on Jesus, nor was there one Christ and another Jesus; but the Word of God, who is Savior of all and ruler of heaven and earth, who is Jesus, as we have shown before, and who took flesh and was anointed by the Father in the Spirit, was made Jesus Christ (*AH* III. 9, 3 [SC 211:108]).

That is, "the Word was made Jesus Christ." The clauses "who is Savior" and "who is Jesus" are paralleled by "who took flesh" and "was anointed by the Father in the Spirit." The one who is Savior, who is Jesus, took flesh; in that flesh the one who is Jesus the Savior was anointed. Thus, the Word from the heavenly realm was made flesh in Jesus in the earthly realm, and that same Word who is Jesus was anointed Christ in the flesh. Heaven and earth, Word and flesh are held together. So, too, do Father and Spirit meet the Word who is in the flesh. The difference is that these Three are shown to meet, while the Word, Savior, Jesus, Christ are identified as one.

Irenaeus introduces two additional Isaian texts to develop his thought. First he recalls verses associated with the Spirit of God:

> A shoot shall come out from the stump of Jesse, and a branch shall grow out of his roots. The spirit of the LORD shall rest on him, the spirit of wisdom and understanding, the spirit of counsel and might, the spirit of knowledge and the fear of the LORD. His delight shall be in the fear of the LORD. He shall not judge by what his eyes see, or decide by what his ears hear; but with righteousness he shall judge the poor, and decide with equity for the meek of the earth; he shall strike the earth with the rod of his mouth, and with the breath of his lips he shall kill the wicked (NRSV Isa 11:1-4).

Then, thinking of the "anointed" Christ, he recalls another Isaian text:

> The spirit of the LORD God is upon me, because the LORD has *anointed* me; he has sent me to bring good news to the oppressed, to bind up the brokenhearted, to proclaim liberty to the captives, and release to the prisoners; to proclaim the year of the LORD's favor, and the day of vengeance of our God; to comfort all who mourn . . . (NRSV Isa 61:1-2).

Led by these texts, Irenaeus continues his thought:

> For, insofar as the Word of God was a human being from the root of Jesse and son of Abraham, the Spirit of God rested on him and he was anointed for evangelizing the lowly; but, insofar as he was God, he did not judge according to appearances nor blame according to hearsay. . . . In giving forgiveness to those led captive by their sins, he dissolved their bonds, of which Solomon said: "Each is constrained by the ropes of his own sins" (*AH* III. 9, 3 [SC 211:110]).

The one Word, a human, was anointed by the Spirit to bring good news to the least of humans; that same one Word, God, rendered just judgment to humans. Again Irenaeus reiterates that the same one, the Word of God, is both God and human. His coming as human was not for an elite but for the sake of even the least among humankind. While he brought judgment, far from being harsh, the judgment was a word of forgiveness and release. This very fact confirms that it was indeed the Spirit *of God* who was at work. Irenaeus completes the passage: "The Spirit, therefore, of God descended on him, the Spirit of the one who through the prophets had promised that he would anoint him, that we might receive from the abundance of his anointing and be saved" (*AH* III. 9, 3 [SC 211:112]).

It was God's Spirit anointing Jesus as Christ who made possible human salvation. Here Irenaeus reiterates a central motif in his account of the Baptism of Jesus. He has framed it with two references to "knowledge" and he will develop the second of these by way of reflection on the infancy narrative in order to clarify the meaning of the knowledge of salvation brought by the Son of God. The whole section then concludes with a return to the opening figure, the Baptist, recalling that John, sent in the Spirit and the power of Elijah, prepared the way of the one and only God, the very one whom Christians love and serve.

Assessment of This Instance of Chiasm

As he presents the opening of the three synoptic gospels Irenaeus has followed a loose chiastic pattern. Returning to our diagram we see that inversion and balance occur when section A' repeats and balances the theme of section A, while section B' (to some extent) repeats and balances section B. The central section, C, is where the weight of the whole and Irenaeus's emphasis falls. The pattern is "loose" in that only in the broad outline of the section can one discern the typical structure of inversion, balance, and climactic centrality; grammatical units are not balanced although citations are. In addition, section B' is somewhat longer than good balance would call for.

Both in the section on "global witness" of the Scriptures and in the one devoted to opening verses of Matthew, Mark, and Luke, Irenaeus uses a carefully crafted structure to make plain his own thought, always kept in contrast to that of the Gnostics. The structure gives coherence and emphasis to his thought; it enables him both to show the relationship among the three synoptic accounts and, by centrally locating the passage on the baptism, to stress the person of the Savior and the nature of the salvation brought by him. In addition the structure allows various stages of the argument to be weighted (for example, closer to the center = more important), and is supple enough to permit ongoing reference to rejected positions.

Throughout the remainder of the section Irenaeus keeps a sharp eye on "the opposition"; he even goes so far as to attribute his own motives to a biblical author. When he turns to the opening verses of John's gospel Irenaeus holds that John wrote his gospel to counteract the "false knowledge" of Cerinthus and the Gnostic Nicolaitans by presenting the "rule of truth" of the Church. Surely he here contributes what must be one of the earliest opinions about the authorial intent of any gospel! (AH III. 11, 1).

The method is simple. He cites the verses he will comment on (John 1:1-5); his exegetical development employs other verses of John that echo key words, regularly pointing to the contrary Gnostic interpretation.[9] The major theme is the one Creator God. The verse "all things came into being through him, and without him not one thing came into being" (NRSV John 1:3) refers to this created world, and not to the "all things" of the Pleroma (AH III. 11, 1). The Word who makes "all things" was in the world he made, contrary to both Marcion and the Valentinians (AH III. 11, 2). Despite the Valentinians that same Word, who is at once Jesus, the Christ, Son of God, and Savior, became flesh, that is, was born, was baptized, and suffered (AH III. 11, 3). John the Baptist was sent by the one creator God to testify to the Light whom he saw and pointed out, and in whom he persuaded many to believe. For this reason John was "more than a prophet"; Irenaeus considers him an apostle, both gifts coming from the one God (AH III. 11, 4).

The immediacy of the Creator God is even more apparent in the story of the wedding feast at Cana (John 2:1-11). Irenaeus recalls that the first wine served at the marriage, fruit of the normal divine creative process, was good wine. The wine made from water by the Word was better. And the Word made it, using water, to show that the one who made heaven and earth has now given the human race, through his Son, the food and drink by which the Incomprehensible becomes comprehensible and the Invisible visible, "for the Son is not outside of him but exists in the bosom of the Father" (AH III. 11, 5). After all, "only the Son knows the Father, the Son who is in the bosom of the Father" (John 1:18, in AH III. 11, 6). The pattern in AH III. 11, 1-6 is as elsewhere: announce the word, cite the word, and explain it, using linking words to join units of explanation.

In the last three paragraphs of AH III. 11 Irenaeus summarizes the section on the four evangelists. His point is that there can be neither more nor less than four gospels. Here Irenaeus embarks on number symbolism, not different in kind from that indulged in by the Marcosians (AH II. 24).[10] He finds arguments for four gospels in the four winds, the four columns supporting the world, the four living figures (Rev 4:7), the four revelatory activities of the

Word, and the four covenants (Adam, Noah, Moses, and the gospel) (*AH* III. 11, 8). Criticism of Gnostic variations on the number of the gospels precedes and follows his arguments for the number four. What the evangelists give is the complete gospel, from which each heretic extracts a scrap. Thus the Ebionites use Matthew, while Marcion favors Luke, and those who separate Jesus from Christ, saying that only Jesus suffered, choose Mark; the Valentinians prefer John (*AH* III. 11, 7). By contrast Marcion edits the gospel, keeping only parts; others, rejecting the prophetic Spirit, reject John (thereby, according to Irenaeus, losing both the Spirit and the gospel). These last evidently also reject at least some of Paul. Finally, others add gospels, like the Valentinians with their "Gospel of Truth" (*AH* III. 11, 8).[11]

Other Apostles' Witness to One True God (*AH* III. 12, 1-15)

Now Irenaeus turns to the witness of other apostles and disciples to the one God, offering an interpretation of the passages of Acts dealing with Peter, Philip, Paul, and Stephen. Peter preached[12] the God known already to the Jews, calling them to acknowledge Christ as God's Son. Not only Peter, but Philip (*AH* III. 12, 8: Acts 8), Paul (*AH* III. 12, 9: Acts 9 and 17), and Stephen (*AH* III. 12, 10: Acts 7) affirm that the God of the Jews and the God of the Christians are one and the same God (*AH* III. 12, 11). According to Irenaeus the Gnostics, especially the disciples of Marcion and Valentinus, err because of their ignorance of the Scriptures and of the economy[13] of God (*AH* III. 12, 12). Irenaeus insists that what the apostles preach is what the Church teaches, and it is that for which the martyrs die:

> to the Jews they proclaimed that Jesus, whom they crucified, was the Son of God, judge of the living and the dead, who received from the Father eternal rule in Israel, as we have shown. To the Greeks they announced one God who made all things and his Son Jesus Christ (*AH* III. 12, 13 [SC 211:238]).

As a leader in the church of Lyons, whose martyrs were still fresh in memory, Irenaeus does not hesitate to offer the witness of the martyrs as a warrant for the truth of the gospel. He will turn to the martyrs again in Part Two of *AH* III, when he will situate their sufferings in relation to the suffering of Christ. Here he summons the blood of the martyrs to witness to the truth of apostolic preaching.

The evidence from the apostles is completed by their teaching at the Council of Jerusalem. Even to raise the possibility of requiring circumcision of new Christians is an indication to Irenaeus that the God of the Old Testament is the God of the Apostles. After all, no other God had required circumcision. The apostles resolved their difficulty, as Irenaeus points out, not by teaching another Father but by giving the new testament of liberty to those who believed in God in a new way, through the Holy Spirit (*AH* III. 12, 14 [SC 211:244]).

Irenaeus's primary concern thus far in the first part of *AH* III has been to show that the Scriptures witness to one God who is the Creator who made all things by his own Word. Using his characteristic method of exegesis, he has given a reading of texts from every stratum of the biblical books. He then follows with a more detailed analysis of the opening verses of each of the four gospels, to which he has appended the teaching of four apostles and disciples found in Acts. He has mentioned the problem caused by those Gnostics who either abbreviate the gospels or add to them. Now he interrupts the development of his argument to respond to those who raise questions about the authority of Paul and his associate, Luke.

Authority of Paul and Luke (*AH* III. 13, 1–III. 15, 3)

Some maintain, according to Irenaeus, that Paul alone of all the apostles knew the truth because he was taught "the mystery" by a revelation. But Irenaeus adduces three texts showing that Paul recognized the apostleship of Peter (Eph 3:3), and referred to others who announce the good news (Rom 10:15 and 1 Cor 15:11). This dispute is a good example of what may have happened often during the Gnostic controversy: both sides claimed Paul for themselves (*AH* III. 13, 1).[14]

The Lord himself, according to Irenaeus, told Philip that those who knew him knew the Father (John 14:7, 9-10); how then, Irenaeus inquires, could the Twelve who knew the Father not have known the truth? (*AH* III. 13, 2). The truth Paul knew, he taught plainly to all (Acts 20:25-28 in *AH* III. 14, 2). Irenaeus betrays himself as a careful student of the gospels who realizes that the gospel of Luke contains information not in other gospels. Nonetheless he engages in circular argument, holding that one who rejects Luke rejects the gospel since so much is only found there (*AH* III. 14, 3) and applying the same argument to Paul. Some do not accept Paul, but that is to reject Luke's veracity, and so Luke's unique gospel (*AH* III. 15, 1). Irenaeus concludes: "Therefore [Luke's] witness is true and the doctrine of the apostles manifest and firm and omitting nothing, not teaching one thing in secret but another in the open" (*AH* III. 15, 1 [SC 211:278]).

The procedure of the Valentinians is quite different. They talk to the crowds, counterfeiting the accepted word of Christian teachers as it was usually heard. Some of those who hear their teaching ask for explanations or contradict them, but the Valentinians say these people do not really know the truth; they are "psychics." Only the ones initiated into their private mysteries, the "spiritual," are perfect. However, because their public teaching is the same as that of other Christian teachers the Valentinians object to being called heretics (*AH* III. 15, 2). It is again evident that the argument is not only about the interpretation of Paul or Luke but about the validity of any "secret" interpretation, and hence about authority.

Irenaeus ends this discussion somewhat abruptly, writing: "But let us return to the original topic" (*AH* III. 15, 3 [SC 211:284]). He then summarizes what he has accomplished thus far in *AH* III. He is satisfied that he has shown that the one Creator God of Christian belief is, together with his Word, the sole Lord God acknowledged in the Scriptures produced by the apostles and their disciples. With that task behind him, Irenaeus turns to the figure of Jesus Christ.

NOTES

[1]Following Bacq's practice, I subdivide the section into meaning units.

[2]The evolution of the biblical canon moves from recognition of works as sacred works to accepting them as Scripture to designating them as canonical. Irenaeus is involved in steps 1 and 2, but not yet in step 3. For him the "canon" refers to the "canon" or rule of faith, not to the "canon" or rule of Scripture.

[3]This is evident in the extended discourse on prophecy in *AH* IV. 20 examined below, ch. 8. The Spirit works through the prophets to effect their vision: for example, of the coming of the Son. However, there are also places where the words of the prophet are presented as the words of Christ; e.g., *AH* IV. 2, 3-4. Such words are understood as Christ's because both prophets and Christ speak of the one Lord God who made heaven and earth (Bacq, *De l'ancienne à la nouvelle alliance* 52, n. 1, a position contradicting Antonio Orbe, *Parabolas evangelicas in San Ireneo.* 2 vols. [Madrid: Biblioteca de Autores cristianos, 1972] 2.424–426). Bacq devotes Annexe II, 315–342, to a study of the scholarship on the questions surrounding Irenaeus's treatment of prophecy and the place of that treatment as an integral part of *AH* IV.

[4]The text here cited and commented on is noteworthy from several perspectives. It is the text from the Old Testament most often cited in the New. (See D. M. Hay, *Glory at the Right Hand: Psalm 110 in Early Christianity.* SBL MS 18 [Nashville: 1973].) It also figures in the "two powers" heresy condemned by the early rabbis who viewed "two powers" in heaven as "two authorities" and so objected to the "two powers" theology. It is worth noting that from the rabbis' perspective both Christians and Gnostics were suspect in this area. (See Alan F. Segal, *Two Powers in Heaven: Early Rabbinic Reports About Christianity and Gnosticism.* Studies in Late Antiquity 27 [Leiden: E. J. Brill, 1977].) Justin, a source used by Irenaeus, cites the text three times, once in *Apol.* 1.45 and twice in *Dial.*, at 56 and 127, where he makes the typical Christian application of the second use of "lord" to Christ. While we do not know why Irenaeus selected this verse, he did have available both the New Testament writings and Justin. The text was a prominent one in Christian affirmation of the role of Christ; moreover, it was recognized as messianic by the rabbis.

[5]I follow Rousseau who argues that the context justifies the translation "God stands in the assembly of God." He suggests that the Greek text before Irenaeus was *"en synagogei theou."* The received Latin reads: *Deus stetit in synagoga deorum, in medio autem deos discernit. De Patre et Filio et de his qui adoptionem perceperunt dicit; hi autem sunt Ecclesia: haec enim est synagoga Dei, quam Deus, hoc est Filius, ipse per semetipsum collegit.* On Rousseau's reading *de patre* refers to *Deus; Filio* refers to *deorum* for which he would read *dei.* For his arguments, see SC 210:252–253.

[6]Irenaeus's words here, as given by Rufinus, are: *qui filios Dei facit credentes in nomen suum,* that is, "who makes sons of God those believing in his name." The thought is a clear allusion to John 1:12: *tekna theou genesthai, tois pisteuousin eis to onoma autou,* that is, "who makes children of God those believing in his name." Rufinus used the appropriate

Latin convention, but a literal English translation of the Latin communicates to the modern reader an androcentrism missing from the NT Greek and—in my opinion—from Irenaeus.

[7]Texts include "you shall not follow strange gods" (RSV Ps 81:9 [LXX 80:10]); "They are all confounded who model God and sculpt useless works" (Isa 44:9-10); "The gods who did not make the heavens and the earth will perish from the earth which is under heaven" (Jer 10:11); "How long will you straddle the fence?* One is the Lord your God; come after him" (RSV 1 Kings 18:21 [LXX 3 Kings 18:21]); "You will call on the name of your gods, and I will call on the name of the LORD my God; and the God who hears today, he is God" (RSV 1 Kings 18:24 [LXX 3 Kings 18:24]); "LORD God of Abraham, God of Isaac, God of Jacob, hear me today; and let all people here know that you are the God of Israel" (RSV 1 Kings 18:36 [LXX 3 Kings 18:36]).

*A literal rendition of the Latin gives "How long will you limp/hobble along on two hams?" *[Quousque claudicabitis vos in ambobus suffraginibus?]* The intent seems to be to ask how long one will remain unable to go cleanly ahead neither on one side nor the other; thus the choice of the English idiom.

[8]In this instance the NRSV agrees with Irenaeus's opponents, giving the reading: "In their case the god of this world has blinded the minds of the unbelievers . . . ." The Greek reads: *"en hois ho theos tou aiōnos toutou etuphlōsen ta noēmata . . . ."*

[9]He has already reviewed Gnostic exegesis of the opening verses of John in *AH* I; see ch. 2, n. 4.

[10]In so doing he illustrates again that it is not the method to which he objects so much as its results.

[11]While this last gospel may be a version of the "Gospel of Truth" found at Nag Hammadi, Irenaeus mentions only that its content differs from the evangelists' gospels. See James M. Robinson, general editor, *The Nag Hammadi Library in English* (3rd rev. ed. San Francisco: Harper & Row, 1988) 38–51 for introduction and text.

[12]Irenaeus reviews Peter's leadership in replacing Judas (*AH* III. 12, 1: Acts 1:15-26), his Pentecost sermon (*AH* III. 12, 1 and 2: Acts 2:14-39), Peter and John's healing of the man born lame (*AH* III. 12, 3: Acts 3), Peter's discourse to the chief priests (*AH* III. 12, 4 and 5: Acts 4:1-31), and Peter's role in the conversion of Cornelius (*AH* III. 12, 7: Acts 10).

[13]By "economy" in this context Irenaeus means the divine plan for salvation, spanning all of time from creation to the end, and turning on Christ as its hinge. Notable studies of Irenaeus's concept of the divine economy are those of A. d'Alès, "Le mot oikonomia dans la langue théologique de Saint Irénée," *REG* 32 (1919) 1–9, and M. Widmann, *Der Begriff oikonomia im Werke des Irenäus und seine Vorgeschichte,* Theol. Diss. Tübingen, 1956.

[14]Elaine Pagels, *The Gnostic Paul: Gnostic Exegesis of the Pauline Letters* (Philadelphia: Fortress, 1975) gives evidence "of the process whereby Paul became known in the second century as the 'apostle of the heretics'" (p. 157), making clear the appeal as well as the forcefulness of the Gnostic interpretation. To the contrary, Andreas Lindemann's later analysis of a broader body of literature, *Paulus im ältesten Christentum: Das Bild des Apostels und die Rezeption der paulinischen Theologie in der frühchristlichen Literatur bis Marcion* (Tübingen: Mohr, 1979) suggests that there is not an overtly clear Gnostic preference for Pauline texts. The same themes are exemplified through Old Testament and synoptic texts as much as through Pauline and Johannine ones. See especially pp. 305–306.

CHAPTER SIX

Jesus Christ, the Son of God Incarnate

Adversus haereses III. 16–23

From Irenaeus's perspective the genuine humanity of Christ is of key soteri-ological significance. He begins by stressing the reality of the incarnation; his intent is to show from the Scriptures that the Son of God was truly made a man (*AH* III. 16, 1–III. 18, 7). Then he employs all his techniques of scriptural exegesis to emphasize that Jesus is not simply a man, but the Son of God in-carnate in the womb of the Virgin. The real divinity of Jesus Christ also car-ries soteriological significance. Both these sections offer good instances of chiastic organization (*AH* III. 19, 1–III. 21, 9). Then, specifically working against the Ebionites and the Valentinians, he presents his interpretation of the Pauline doctrine of the recapitulation, in which he examines Christ, the Sav-ior, as the antitype of Adam (*AH* III. 21, 10–III. 23, 8). In the epilogue (*AH* III. 24, 1–III. 25, 7) Irenaeus balances the notion of Church as vehicle of tradition, explored in the introduction to *AH* III, with the image of Church as "place" of the Holy Spirit.

God's Only-Begotten Word, Truly Incarnate (*AH* III. 16–18)

Three themes occupy Irenaeus in this section: (1) the place of the incarna-tion in the economy; (2) the role of the Holy Spirit in the economy; (3) the ne-cessity of the incarnation for human redemption. Throughout he is preoccupied with the contradiction he finds between Valentinian speech and thought; it is in the first part of this section that he calls the Gnostics those "sent by Satan" and "Antichrists" who are "outside the economy." As always, he opposes their interpretation of the Scriptures to his own.

The first theme is introduced by a reprise of the doctrines of three Gnostic groups, with attention centered on the Valentinians. They "confess one Jesus Christ with their tongues but divide him in their thought" (*AH* III. 16, 1 [SC 211:288]). Here he reduces the complexities of Valentinian christology to these elements: there are Aeons called Christ, Only-Begotten, and Savior; these are all distinct from the Jesus of the economy who only "passed through" Mary; it was this Jesus of the economy on whom the Savior from on high (called "Christ") descended, and who suffered while Christ returned to the Pleroma. This schematization sharpens the two aspects of Gnostic christology which Irenaeus criticizes most severely. First, they distinguish between the Christ from on high and the earthly Jesus, who are linked in merely a transitory way; and second, they put in question the real humanity of the earthly Jesus.[1] The gravity with which Irenaeus regards this teaching is marked by the censure he levels against it: he regards its teachers as those whom the Holy Spirit warned would be "sent secretly by Satan to corrupt the faith of many and to drag them away from life."

Against this position he aligns the Scriptures. Because he is focusing on the incarnation, the synoptic material with which he is primarily concerned is contained in the infancy narratives. The basic assumption governing his interpretation in this section is the continuity of the action of the one God, from creation through prophecy to the coming of Jesus Christ. He announces that Matthew intends to recount the human generation of Jesus Christ from the Virgin, as God had promised David and Abraham before him. The text he then cites is Matt 1:1: "The book of the generation of Jesus Christ, the son of David, the son of Abraham," which locates Jesus' birth as fulfillment of prophecy. He continues with Matthew's description of the dream in which Joseph learns that Mary has conceived by the Holy Spirit, linking the conception (following Matthew) to Isaiah's prophecy about the virgin who will conceive and bear a son to be called Emmanuel. He points out that Matthew could have written "the genealogy of Jesus," which would have supported Gnostic teaching of a separation between Jesus and Christ, but instead Matthew wrote "Christ," and specified that Jesus Christ is called Emmanuel (*AH* III. 16, 2).

To similar effect Irenaeus cites Rom 1:1-4, a text that Ignatius of Antioch had already used to account for the one Jesus Christ, Son of David according to the flesh, and predestined Son of God in power.[2] Commenting on this and other Pauline texts (Rom 9:5 and Gal 4:4-5), Irenaeus writes:

> [these texts] clearly signify one same God, who through the prophets made a promise about his Son, and one Jesus Christ our Lord, of the seed of David according to his generation of Mary, this same Jesus Christ appointed Son of God in power according to the Spirit of holiness after the resurrection from the dead, that he might be first-born from the dead as he was first-born of all creatures,

the Son of God made Son of humankind,[3] that through him we might receive the adoption, humankind bearing and taking hold of and embracing the Son of God (*AH* III. 16, 3 [SC 211:296]).

In and through the humanity of the risen incarnate Son the humanity of the entire race is affected. The last three participles—bearing, taking hold of, embracing—are typical Irenaean expressions meant to stress the immediacy of God to humanity, an immediacy brought about through the incarnation and resurrection of the Son and quite different from the usual remoteness of the Valentinian Pleroma, and especially of the Father within that Pleroma.[4]

After reviewing passages from Mark and Luke touching the generation of Jesus Christ, Irenaeus remarks that near the end of his gospel John wrote: "These things have been written so that you might believe that Jesus is the Christ, the Son of God, and that believing you may have eternal life in his name" (John 20:31). Carrying the idea farther, he notes that John also writes: "Who is the liar if not the one who denies that Jesus is the Christ? This is the antichrist" (1 John 2:22, in *AH* III. 16, 5).

Such are those who, he repeats, confess with the lips one sole Jesus Christ but think one thing and say another. This group, the Valentinians, separate the Jesus of the economy, born of Joseph and able to suffer, from the Christ who is invisible, incomprehensible, and impassible. Irenaeus comments that they wander from the truth because they deny the true God when they deny that God's only-begotten Word was made flesh and suffered for us. He then summarizes the connection between the incarnation and the divine economy or plan, which he extends to include creation and the end time, with the incarnation in the center.[5] Thus he affirms:

> Therefore as we have shown there is one God the Father, and one Christ Jesus our Lord, coming through the universal economy and recapitulating all things in himself. In all things, moreover, is humankind molded by God; therefore he also recapitulated humankind in himself, the invisible being made visible, and the incomprehensible being made comprehensible, and the impassible being made passible, and the Word being made a human being, recapitulating all things in himself, so that, as the Word of God is first in things supercelestial and spiritual and invisible, so he would also have the primacy among visible and corporeal things and, in assuming to himself this primacy and placing himself as head of the Church, he will draw all things to himself at the right time (*AH* III. 16, 6 [SC 211:312, 314]).

The qualities of invisibility, incomprehensibility, and impassability that the Gnostics assign to the Christ Irenaeus identifies as qualities of the Word reversed by the incarnation. Jesus Christ is visible, comprehensible, and passible. The incarnation is a stage in the divine plan that encompasses all of creation. In becoming a human being the Son of God "recapitulates" or sums up the entire creation in himself.[6] Those who deny the incarnation cut themselves off from the divine economy. Such an excision is the equivalent of being cut off from true life, so Irenaeus describes their position as "homicidal" (*AH* III. 16, 8).

Turning to his second theme in this section, the role of the Spirit in the economy, he insists again that the apostles could have written that "Christ" descended on "Jesus," or that the "higher Savior" came down on the "Jesus of the economy," but "since they knew no such thing, neither did they say it; if they had known it they would surely have said it" (*AH* III. 17, 1 [SC 211:328]). Instead what they did say is that the Spirit of God rested on him in the form of a dove. This happened for a reason:

> [The Spirit of God] descended on the Son of God made Son of Man so that with him he might accustom himself to dwell in the human race and to rest among humans and to dwell in the work molded by God, working the will of the Father in them and renewing them from old age into the newness of Christ (*AH* III. 17, 1 [SC 211:330]).

What the Spirit accomplishes in Jesus Christ is the beginning of what the Spirit will do in the human race. Irenaeus introduces several metaphors to explain the meaning of such an assertion. Thus:

> as dry wheat cannot be made into one lump and one loaf without moisture, so we are not able to be made one from many in Christ Jesus without the water from heaven. And as arid land, if it does not lay hold of moisture, does not bear fruit, so we, being at first dry wood, will never bear the fruit of life without the willing heavenly rain. For, through that washing [that is, baptism], our bodies received the union which is for incorruptibility as did our souls through the Spirit (*AH* III. 17, 2 [SC 211:332]).

The point is that the Spirit is the heavenly moisture that alone enables human beings, in all that makes them human, to experience heavenly life. The Spirit, then, has a role in the economy both with respect to the incarnation, and with respect to the destiny of the human race. Such being the case, those who teach otherwise are liars. Worse, Irenaeus remarks that some who speak "as we do" think the opposite, and in doing so kill those who, deceived by the verbal similarity, take in the poison of the inner sentiment (*AH* III. 17, 4).

The third theme in this section is the necessity of the incarnation for redemption. Irenaeus introduces it in this way: "When [the Son of God] was made incarnate and made a human being, he recapitulated in himself the long history of humankind, procuring salvation for us in the compendium, that what we lost in Adam, that is to be according to the image and likeness of God, this we would recover in Christ Jesus" (*AH* III. 18, 1 [SC 211:342, 344]). Salvation is defined as recovering through Christ what was lost in Adam, that is, to be according to the image and likeness of God.[7] The losing was "in Adam"; the recovery is "through Christ." The Adam-Christ inversion is rooted in Romans 5, but Irenaeus does not refer directly to that text until he begins the discussion of recapitulation in *AH* III. 21–22, three chapters later. Here, in *AH* III. 18, he continues with his explanation of why it was important that the restoration be "through Christ":

> Because it was impossible that humankind, who had once been conquered and shattered by disobedience, should be remolded and obtain the prize of victory, and it was as impossible that the one should receive salvation who fell under sin, the Son accomplished both, being the Word of God, descending from the Father and being incarnate, and going down even to death, and completing the economy of our salvation (*AH* III. 18, 2 [SC 211:344]).

Christ did what human beings could not do for themselves, having been wounded by sin.

This passage opens a carefully structured section on the necessity of the incarnation for salvation:

A.   Necessity of incarnation (*AH* III. 18, 2)
B.   Paul on the reality of Christ's redemptive suffering, death, and resurrection (*AH* III. 18, 2-3)
C.   Christ's teaching on his suffering and that of his disciples (*AH* III. 18, 4)
D.   If Christ did not suffer but flew away from Jesus, by what right did he exhort disciples to follow him? (*AH* III. 18, 5)
E.   Suffering of martyrs: differing views (*AH* III. 18, 5)
D'.   If Christ's suffering was not real, by what right did he exhort disciples to follow him? (*AH* III. 18, 6)
C'.   Paul teaches that Christ was a man who by his obedience redeemed human disobedience (*AH* III. 18, 6)
B'.   Christ teaches that he chained the strong man, freed the weak and gave salvation to the work of his hands in destroying sin (*AH* III. 18, 6)
A'.   Necessity of incarnation (*AH* III. 18, 7)

The witness of the martyrs is given the emphatic central place in a passage about the flesh of Christ. The understanding of who Christ is stands inseparably united to what he means for human belief, so for human life and death. With the persecution at Lyons so fresh in memory, the question of the validity of martyrdom could hardly be an insignificant one to Irenaeus and his community. Irenaeus writes:

> Some have advanced to such temerity that they even spurn the martyrs and vituperate those who are killed on account of confessing the Lord and who accept everything preached by the Lord and who, according to this, strive to follow the traces of the passion of the Lord, witnesses of him made passible. We give them up to the martyrs themselves: for when their blood is inquired into and they attain to glory, then all who dishonor their martyrdom will be confounded by Christ (*AH* III. 18, 5 [SC 211:358]).

Clearly there is comfort in the faith that God will vindicate those who suffer for the sake of Christ. The reality of Christ's flesh and so of his suffering gives meaning to the suffering the martyrs endure in their flesh. As one who suffered himself, Christ taught his followers by word and example to love and pray for their persecutors. Such a one is far better, in Irenaeus's opinion, than a Christ who flew away, suffering neither injury nor opprobrium!

In the conclusion of this section Irenaeus outlines his christology and soteriology. On the one hand, he maintains that it was necessary for a human being to defeat humanity's enemy, or the victory would not be just. On the other hand, he claims that if God did not give salvation humanity would not hold salvation firmly, and if a human being were not united to God, human beings would not be able to participate in incorruptibility. Accordingly "it was necessary for the Mediator between God and humanity, through his own being at home in both, to lead both back to friendship and concord, and to effect not only that God would take humanity to Godself but also that a human being would give himself to God" (*AH* III. 18, 7 [SC 211:364]).[8] Christ had to be both; God needed to come close to humanity and humanity to God for the saving work to be accomplished. The language clearly indicates a closeness proportionate to consequences. Irenaeus here gives an early enunciation of the soteriological principle[9] so central to later developments in Greek christology.

The section concludes with a powerful description of the redeeming work accomplished by the incarnate Son of God, which once again emphasizes a major point of the entire development, the reality of the flesh of Jesus Christ:

> For it was necessary that he who would undertake to kill sin and to redeem humanity, who were condemned to death, should himself become what humanity was, that is, a human being, who was indeed dragged into slavery by sin and held fast by death, so that sin should be destroyed by a human being and humanity should go forth from death. . . . However if he was not made flesh and yet appeared as flesh, his work was not true. But what he appeared [to be], this he was, God recapitulating in himself the primitive fashioning of humanity, that he might kill sin, destroy death, and vivify humanity: and for this reason his works are true (*AH* III. 18, 7 [SC 211:70]).

To accomplish the saving work God became truly human in Jesus. Some, however, can see only the humanity of Jesus. It is this difficulty that Irenaeus addresses in the following section of *AH* III.

Incarnate One, God's Only-Begotten Word (*AH* III. 19, 1–III. 21, 9)

This section, somewhat shorter than the previous one, is equally tightly organized, an organization best seen when the units are laid out in the chiastic structure:

   A.   To consider Jesus human only misinterprets Emmanuel (III. 19, 1)
   B.   Jesus God and human (III. 19, 2)

C.   Because humans could not imagine it, the sign of Emmanuel
         was given (III. 19, 3)

D.   Sign of Jonah: God's plan (III. 20, 1)

E.   Glory of human: God. Receptacle of God's action: the
                 human (III. 20, 2)

D'.   God became Savior, carrying out the plan (III. 20, 3-4)

C'.   Sign of Emmanuel badly translated (III. 21, 1-3)

B'.   Emmanuel sign means Jesus God and human (III. 21, 3-4)

A'. Extended interpretation of Emmanuel, with other texts supporting
     this interpretation (III. 21, 5-9)

Read as a chiasm, with the characteristics of inversion, balance, and climactic centrality, this section offers profound and even surprising insight into the Irenaean view of God, humanity, and Jesus Christ. In a passage that, as a whole, is concerned with the divinity of Jesus Christ the core is a statement about humanity and its relation to God: "The glory of the human being is God; in truth, the receptacle of the operation of God and of all God's wisdom and power is the human being" (*AH* III. 20, 2 [SC 211:388]). "Glory" carries the sense of splendor; the true splendor of the human being is what God accomplishes in that one. God's action, described as God's "magnanimity," has been to permit humans to pass through all sorts of situations, including death, in order to arrive at resurrection, and so to learn by experience the evil from which they have been delivered. Having experienced their own mortality and weakness, humans are better able to admire the eternity and power of God, so to thank and love God, who gives them immortality (*AH* III. 20, 2). What, then, of Christ? When this paragraph is placed in the context of the development of Irenaeus's thought in the section it will become clear what this understanding of humanity contributes to the Irenaean presentation of the divinity of Christ.

To understand Jesus as solely human is, in Irenaeus's view, to misunderstand the meaning of Emmanuel born of a virgin. Anyone in this position cannot receive the Word's gift of incorruptibility, but remains in mortal flesh. The word "incorruptibility" will recur with increasing frequency from this point. Irenaeus uses it to refer to human participation in the Divine Spirit, a participation that is the gift of God.[10] The Son of God became a human so that humans might become sons and daughters of God, and thus receive the characteristic of such filiation, incorruptibility. In other words, his incorruptibility joined to our mortality empowers our mortality to become incorruptible (*AH* III. 19, 1).[11]

Surely one might think that such reasoning compromises the absolute oneness of God that Irenaeus has struggled to defend. He sees the problem: "That no one of all the children of Adam may be called God other than [the one God] or named Lord, we have demonstrated from the Scriptures" (*AH* III. 19, 2 [SC 211:376]). But in those same Scriptures that acclaim only one God, and clearly name Christ a man, Irenaeus finds evidence that "anyone touched with a modicum of truth" will recognize, evidence that all the prophets, the apostles, and the very Spirit properly call Christ, alone of all humans, God and Lord and eternal King and Only-begotten and Word incarnate (*AH* III. 19, 2).[12]

Because no one would have expected such a thing, the sign of Emmanuel was given: a virgin, remaining virgin, would conceive and bear a son who would be "God with us." The Word would come down among his lost sheep, human beings, his own work molded by him, to find them and return them to the Father. Just as he, the head, passed through death to life, so too would humankind, his members (*AH* III. 19, 3).

Lost humanity, like the prophet Jonah, had been swallowed by the great sea monster, the author of lies. As Jonah was cast up and brought glory to God by converting the Ninevites, so it will be with lost humanity. Jonah is a model of what, from the very beginning, God planned to do for humankind. Like Jonah, humans would receive an unexpected salvation; risen from the dead, they would glorify God as did Jonah. Their blind pride would no longer mask God's love for them (*AH* III. 20, 1).

For this reason, as we have seen, God permitted humans to pass through all sorts of situations, including death, in order to arrive at resurrection, and so to learn by experience the evil from which they have been delivered. Knowing their own mortality and weakness, humans are better able to admire the eternity and power of God, so to thank and love God, who gives them immortality. To illustrate his point Irenaeus introduces another metaphor: "as a doctor is proved among those who are ill, so it is with God among humankind." He links this metaphor with Rom 11:32: "God delivered all to disobedience that he might have mercy upon all" (*AH* III. 20, 1 [SC 211:388]). As he remarks, it is not a question of the pneumatics but of disobedient humanity, who rejected immortality, obtaining mercy and divine filiation through the Son of God. He expresses himself with typical grace when he writes: "The Word of God dwelt among humankind and was made the Son of Man, that humankind might become accustomed to know God and God might become accustomed to dwell among humankind according to the good pleasure of the Father" (*AH* III. 20, 2 [SC 211:392]). To accustom humans to God, and God to them: to accomplish this purpose, indeed, it was necessary that the God-Word become a human. In fact, the Word of God become a human being is the God-desired link between God and humanity. So the divinity of the Word incarnate in Jesus says something about him, something about human beings, and something about God. The salvation Christ brings is described in the language of the prophets in *AH* III. 20, 3-4.

Irenaeus returns to the sign of Emmanuel with the words: "God therefore was made a human being and the Lord himself saved us, he himself giving the sign of the virgin" (*AH* III. 21, 1 [SC 211:398]). He notes that some would translate the word he renders as "virgin" as "young woman." The difficulty he recognized in the text of Isa 7:14 is a real one.[13] The Greek translation, circulating before Jesus' birth, uses *parthenos,* which normally means virgin. The translator may have meant that a woman who is now a virgin will conceive, so the child will be a firstborn.[14] Be that as it may, when Matthew quoted the verse he quoted it in Greek with *parthenos* (Matt 1:23).

Irenaeus was aware of the conflict, one that Justin before him had addressed (*Dial.* 43.8, 67.1, 70.3, 84.3); he names the Ebionites, influenced by the translation "young woman," who "say Jesus was generated by Joseph" (*AH* III. 21, 1 [SC 211:398]). Against them first he offers the translation of the Septuagint which he regards as inspired (*AH* III. 21, 2-3). Then he interprets Isa 7:10-16 to refer to the generation of Christ from the virgin, and to his substance, which is God (from the name Emmanuel) and human (because he would eat butter and honey, and would know good and evil) (*AH* III. 21, 3-4). As Irenaeus proceeds, giving a word by word, phrase by phrase explanation he employs the technique of midrash, explaining a text through other texts to make it understandable. He is, of course, governed in this interpretation by the conviction he owes to the Rule of Faith that indeed Jesus Christ is God and human (*AH* III. 21, 5-6). Finally he turns to other scriptural evidence for the virgin birth of the one who will recapitulate all things in himself (*AH* III. 21, 7-9).

Jesus Christ, Recapitulation of Adam (*AH* III. 21, 10-23, 8)

The theme of recapitulation is a Pauline one, notably developed by the apostle in the fifth chapter of Romans,[15] invoked at the opening of this section: "just as through the disobedience of one man sin had entry and through sin death prevailed, so through the obedience of one man justice, having been introduced, produced the fruits of life for those persons who formerly were dead" (Rom 5:19; *AH* III. 21, 10 [SC 211:426, 428]). The parallel between Adam and Christ is such that Christ's obedience undoes the consequence of Adam's disobedience. Christ is presented as a "second" or "new" Adam. Through his reading of the Genesis and Pauline texts Irenaeus develops the parallelism so as to address the christological concerns of both the Ebionites and the Valentinians.

The first Adam was formed by the Hand of God, that is, by the Word of God, using intact or virgin earth; so the second Adam was formed by that same Word, using an intact woman, the virgin Mary: "If [the first Adam] was taken from the earth and formed by the Word of God, it was necessary that the same Word, making a recapitulation of Adam in himself, should have the similitude of the same generation" (*AH* III. 21, 10 [SC 211:428, 430]. See also *AH* III. 22, 1-2; *Proof* 32). The recapitulation is so important that the possibility of God modeling Christ anew from fresh mud, as it were, is excluded. The likeness or similitude between the two Adams is at two levels: both are formed by the Word of God, and both are from the original virgin earth. In the case of the first Adam it is the mud of that virgin earth that is utilized; in the case of the second Adam it is the flesh of a descendant of the first Adam that is utilized (so there is continuity), but that flesh is virginal (so there is parallelism): "Therefore why did not God take up mud anew but work from Mary to make the modeled thing? That there would not be one modeled work made and another saved, but the same thing which is itself recapitulated [is protected by] retaining the similitude [in the stuff from which it is modeled]" (*AH* III. 21, 10 [SC 211:430]. See also *AH* III. 18, 7; *Proof* 33). If Christ is the recapitulation of the first Adam, then he is born of a virgin through the action of the Word of God.[16] This interpretation is an argument against the Ebionites, those who say he was the son of Joseph, born of human seed.[17]

In addition there are the Valentinians; Irenaeus writes that they hold that Christ received nothing from the virgin. If he did not receive flesh from a human being then he was not what we are, and so his sufferings did not affect us. Irenaeus continues: "We are flesh drawn from earth and soul receiving spirit from God. . . . It is this same thing that the Word of God was made, recapitulating in himself his own work made by him" (*AH* III. 22, 1 [SC 211:432]; also *AH* V. 21, 1-2; *Proof* 37). If Christ did not receive flesh from Mary one would not read in the Scriptures that he ate, was hungry after fasting, grew tired, wept, sorrowed, sweated blood, and that from his pierced side there flowed blood and water. Irenaeus comments: "These are all signs of flesh which has been drawn from earth, which he has recapitulated in himself, saving the work he modeled" (*AH* III. 22, 2 [SC 211:436]). The fullness of the recapitulation includes all nations, tongues, and generations beginning with Adam (*AH* III. 22, 3).

In this there is a role for Mary, who inverts Eve's role as Christ inverted Adam's.[18] The twinned typology is related to the Irenaean desire to join the Old and New Testaments in a single pattern of salvation history. Eve and Mary, both virgins and betrothed, differ in that Eve disobeyed while Mary obeyed, and Eve brought death while Mary brought life. Absent here is any suggestion of the impact of sexuality on either Eve's sin or Mary's obedience.[19] What is striking is the strength of the parallel between Adam and Eve on the one hand, and between Christ and Mary on the other. Adam and Eve both disobey and equally become the cause of death; Christ and Mary both obey and become the cause of salvation.[20] In fact, Irenaeus writes: "the obedient virgin is made the cause of salvation for herself and the whole human race" (*AH* III. 22, 4 [SC 211:440]; also *AH* V. 19, 1; *Proof* 33). He is quite clear that her action undoes the bonds in which humanity was tied by Eve's action, just as Christ's action reverses the destructive work of Adam. This approach, as Lyman remarks, does not detract

> from the significance of Christ whose incarnation accomplished salvation, but it affirms powerfully the humanity of Christ as the place where all Christians, male and female, are one with Christ in renewed human nature. . . . Irenaeus' high view of Adam and Eve together with his emphasis on Christ as recapitulating

the original fall of humanity allows the image of both sexes as part of the paradisical recovery. This does not seem to be the androgyny of the Gnostics nor the masculinization of the Encratite tradition, but as in baptism, the restoration of both sexes to their full potential.[21]

The final chapter devoted to the theme of recapitulation (*AH* III. 23) concerns the salvation of Adam. Salvation must include Adam or else humanity, created in the image and likeness of God, created to live, would have lost its definitive life, and God would have been defeated by the serpent (*AH* III. 23, 1). Adam is included in recapitulation because it would be unreasonable to think that one whom the enemy had wounded gravely and who was the first to be taken captive would not have been delivered by the One who conquered the enemy. "Our God," writes Irenaeus, "is neither impotent nor unjust" (*AH* III. 23, 2 [SC 211:450]). He thinks it important to remember that God never cursed Adam or Eve, but only the serpent (Gen 3:17). He remembers the gospel teaching (Matt 25:41) that the eternal fires of hell were originally made not for humans but for unrepentant angels, that is, for those who seduce humans (*AH* III. 23, 3). He holds up Cain (Gen 4:11) as an example of an unrepentant human cursed by God (*AH* III. 23, 4). By contrast Adam was repentant, and God, who hated the serpent, pitied Adam and Eve (*AH* III. 23, 5). It was this same pity that led God to send them away from the Garden, far from the tree of life (Gen 3:23-24). It was necessary that they taste physical death lest they be immortal in their sinful state, a state that (it will become apparent)[22] is a state of final or absolute death.[23] The function of physical death is "that when human beings cease to live to sin and die, they might begin to live to God" (*AH* III. 23, 6 [SC 211:462]). There is enmity between the woman and the serpent (Gen 3:15), and ultimately he, the enemy, will be defeated, and with him death. When this defeat occurs Adam will live, according to the meaning of the saying: "the last enemy to be defeated will be death" (1 Cor 15:26). Only then can it legitimately be said: "Where, O death, is your victory? Where, O death, is your sting?" (1 Cor 15:55). Therefore, the Lord having vivified "man," that is, Adam, death has been destroyed (*AH* III. 23, 7). Irenaeus here gives full weight to Adam as an individual.

As a final point in his discussion of the death of Adam, Irenaeus points out that his contemporary Tatian, a Christian who became a Gnostic teacher,[24] was wrong to exclude Adam absolutely from life. (The reference is to a lost work of Tatian's.) Irenaeus warns that such teaching places Tatian among the abusers of the Scriptures. He cautions that while it is true that "all die in Adam" (NRSV 1 Cor 15:22), it is also true that "where sin increased, grace abounded all the more" (NRSV Rom 5:20). So Irenaeus concludes:

Just as the serpent profits nothing from seducing humans except to show himself a transgressor, having the human person as the beginning and matter of his own apostasy, so those who contradict the salvation of Adam profit nothing except to make themselves heretics and apostates from the truth and show themselves advocates of the serpent and of death (*AH* III. 23, 8 [SC 211:468]).

NOTES

[1]Antonio Orbe, *Cristologia Gnostica: Introducción a la soteriología de los siglos II y III* 1 (Madrid: Biblioteca de Autores Cristianos, 1976), reviews Gnostic formulations on the preexistent Christ (pp. 16–54), devoting pp. 44–47 to the Valentinians. Gnostic docetism is the subject of pp. 380–412, with pp. 398–403 devoted to the Valentinians.

[2]For Ignatius's text see his letter to the Ephesians 2:7, studied in Aloys Grillmeier, *Christ in Christian Tradition* 1. Translated by John Bowden (2nd ed. rev. Atlanta: John Knox, 1974) 86–89.

[3]I have chosen to render *hominis Filius* with "Son of humankind" in this text; the comparison is between God and "man" in the generic sense, a sense made even clearer by the first person plural form of the verb *percipio*. The passage in question is *Filius Dei hominis Filius factus, ut per eum adoptionem percipiamus, portante homine et capiente et complectente Filium Dei.*

[4]However, in the Gospel of Truth the Son is brought forth to speak about the Father: "For that very reason he brought him forth in order to speak about the place and his resting-place from which he had come forth, and to glorify the pleroma, the greatness of his name and the sweetness of the Father" (*Gospel of Truth* 40.30–41.3 (Robinson, *Nag Hammadi Library,* 50).

[5]While a definition of the Irenaean notion of economy was supplied above where the term first occurred (ch. 5, n. 17), it is here that Irenaeus develops his notion of the divine economy, as Grillmeier has noted *(Christ in Christian Tradition)* 1.101.

[6]Irenaeus takes over the notion of recapitulation from Paul; the term appears here, but he develops it at *AH* III. 21, 10 to III. 23, 8, where it will be considered in more detail. The pattern of introducing an idea but delaying the development occurred with the notion of "economy" and will recur with the notion of "image and likeness." It resembles the pattern of announce, cite, comment that Irenaeus applies to the Scriptures. In this case he announces an idea on which he will comment subsequently.

[7]Because he is concerned here with Christ the Savior rather than with the nature of humanity's salvation experience Irenaeus does not pause to explain what he means by the "image and likeness" that were lost. He will discuss the meaning of image and the first meaning of likeness in *AH* IV. 37–39; he will discuss the second meaning of likeness in *AH* V. 6, 1–V. 8, 3.

[8]The translation of necessity eliminates some of the word play apparent in the Latin *homo;* the Latin text reads: *Oportuerat enim Mediatorem Dei et hominum per suam ad utrosque domesticitatem in amicitiam et concordiam utrosque reducere, et facere ut et Deus adsumeret hominem et homo se dederet Deo.*

[9]In essence the principle affirms that what the preexistent one "assumed" or took to himself in becoming a human being is what was saved; thus to understand the fullness of Christ's humanity one asks whether the aspect of humanity in question is part of what was saved. The principle was used in the fourth century against Apollinarius to affirm that Christ had a human soul; for discussion, see Grillmeier, *Christ in Christian Tradition* 1.329–343.

[10]This definition of the Irenaean notion of "incorruptibility" is the work of Ysabel de Andía, *Homo Vivens. Incorruptibilité et divinisation de l'homme selon Irénée de Lyon* (Paris: Études Augustiniennes, 1986). The question is how God, through the Word and the Spirit, communicates the incorruptible divine life to humankind, become mortal and cor-

ruptible through sin. De Andía organizes her work to make apparent the correspondence between the process of divinization and the movement of the economy from creation (Part 1) through incarnation and salvation (Part 2) into the time of the Church (Part 3) and the eschatological age (Part 4). This has the advantage of emphasizing the trinitarian dynamism at work in Irenaeus's view of the economy, an emphasis that de Andia rightly stresses.

[11]Antonio Orbe devotes "¿San Ireneo Adopçionista?" (*Gr.* 65 [1984] 5–52) to *AH* III. 19, 1. First he reviews the classes of sonship attested to by the Valentinians and by Irenaeus. Then he studies the four principal second-century understandings of the baptismal generation of Jesus, which he lists as: "the Ebionite of the *Gospel of the Nazareans,* clearly adoptionist; that of the Ophites (Iren I. 30) and Valentinians; the intermediate solution of the *Gospel According to Philip;* and that of St. Justin, Irenaeus, and other churchmen. . . . Although from the Irenaean lines (III. 19, 1) one does not infer with certitude the adoption of Christ as man, just as little is this excluded. Irenaeus combats on equal terms the Ebionite adoption of Christ, mere man, and the Valentinian adoption of Christ, as Word, and of the 'spirituals,' sons *phusei* of God" (p. 51).

[12]Comparative texts cited are, as man: man without beauty and suffering (Isa 53:2-3); seated on the foal of an ass (Zech 9:9); drinking vinegar and gall (Ps 69:21 [LXX 68:22]); hated by the people (Ps 22:7 [LXX 21:7]); and gone down to death (Ps 22:16 [LXX 21:16]). As God: wonderful Counselor (Isa 9:6 [LXX 9:5]); fair in beauty (Ps 45:2 [LXX 44:3]); strong God (Isa 9:6 [LXX 9:5]); universal Judge coming on the clouds (Dan 7:13, 26) (*AH* III. 19, 2 [SC 211:376, 378]).

[13]Raymond E. Brown, *The Birth of the Messiah* (New York: Doubleday, 1977) 147, remarks that the Hebrew text uses a word that "normally describes a young girl who has reached the age of puberty and is thus marriageable. It puts no stress on her virginity, although *de facto,* in the light of Israelite ethical and social standards, most girls covered by the range of this term would be virgins."

[14]Ibid. 148–149. In neither case does the sign center on the manner of the child's conception.

[15]See also Romans 6, Col 1:15-20; Eph 1:9-10.

[16]Irenaeus delights in extending the concept of recapitulation, applying it even to his speculation on the length of Christ's earthly life. Because Jesus Christ came to save all, including infants, little children, adolescents, young adults, and mature people, it was necessary that he himself pass through every age! (*AH* III. 18, 7). Irenaeus assumes here a disarming (if not dismaying) physical literalness in his application of the concept. See also *AH* II. 22, 4 (SC 294:220).

[17]Here Irenaeus completes the anti-Ebionite discussion begun at *AH* III. 19, 1, and returns to the anti-Valentinian discussion of the earlier parts of *AH* III.

[18]Rebecca Lyman, "Irenaeus on Eve: The Christological Connection," developed these ideas in an unpublished paper presented at the Pacific Coast Theological Society, Fall 1988.

[19]I cannot agree with Antonio Orbe, who gives great weight to the contrast at *AH* V. 19, 1 between the angel who "seduced" Eve and the angel who "evangelized" Mary, seeing in this the intimation that Eve's disobedience consisted in untimely marital intercourse with Adam. In fact Irenaeus simply does not discuss the nature of the disobedience. Much as I respect Orbe's interpretation of the mind of Irenaeus, here his reading goes well beyond the text. See Orbe, *Antropologia de San Ireneo* (Madrid: Biblioteca de Autores Cristianos, 1969) 237–253, especially 249, where he writes:

> El argumento adquiere su verdaders fuerza si el acto de obediencia o de inobediencia afecta positivamente al estado matrimonial de ambas (Eva y María). Eva *concibió* perdiendo la virginidad, en virtud de su desobediencia, al conocer (indebidamente)

a Adán. El acto la interesó de manera específica en su doble condición de esposa y virgen. En lugar de mantenerse esposa virgen el tiempo señaldo por Dios, faltó al mandato y, "desobedeciendo," hízose para sí y para el género humano causa de muerte. Perdió culpablemente la virginidad y concibió de Adán hijos de muerte. Siguió siendo esposa de Adán, dejó de ser virgen y comenzó en lugar la maternidad de muerte para todos los hombres.

Orbe presents a similar argument in "La Virgen María abogada de la virgen Eva; en torna a s. Ireneo *adv. haer.* V. 19, 1)," *Gr.* 63 (1982) 453–506, as well as in *Teología de San Ireneo, Comentario al Libro V del "Adversus Haereses."* Biblioteca de Autores Cristianos, serie maier, 25 (Madrid: La Editorial Católica, 1985–1988) 2.256–283.

[20]Thus Lyman, "Irenaeus on Eve" 3.

[21]Ibid. 4.

[22]See ch. 11 below.

[23]Here, however, Irenaeus is not so much interested in the distinction between physical and final or absolute death as in the absoluteness of Christ's final victory over death, and through Christ, that of Adam.

[24]Robert M. Grant, "The Heresy of Tatian," *JThS* n.s. 5 (1954) 62–68, concludes that Tatian's Valentinianism is already evident in the extant *Oration to the Greeks,* which he dates after 176.

EPILOGUE

The Church, Place of the Spirit

Adversus haereses III. 24, 1–25, 7

In the introduction to *Adversus haereses* III Irenaeus wrote that anyone who wants the truth should go to the Church. There is the truth, free as the water of life to anyone who wants to drink it (*AH* III. 4, 1). He returns to that theme in the conclusion, contrasting the false teaching about God, Christ, and the economy with the preaching of the Church, to whom has been confided the "gift of God," the "communicating of Christ, that is, the Holy Spirit" (*AH* III. 24, 1 [SC 211:472]). False teaching and evil action cut persons off from the Church, so from the Spirit and life. Thus:

> Where there is the Church, there is the Spirit of God; and where the Spirit of God, there is the Church and all grace: for the Spirit is Truth. That is why those who do not participate in it are not nourished for life from the breasts of the Mother nor do they lay hold of the most brilliant stream flowing from the body of Christ, but they dig for themselves broken cisterns, and they drink water putrid with filth, fleeing the faith of the Church lest they be exposed, rejecting the Spirit lest they be taught (*AH* III. 24, 1 [SC 211:474]).

The notion of the Church as place of Truth, and of separation from the Church as separation from Truth, is brought forward from the introduction to *AH* III but is shifted and deepened by the selection of metaphors. The Church is defined by the Spirit: "Where there is the Church, there is the Spirit of God; and where the Spirit of God, there is the Church and all grace: for the Spirit is Truth." The use of this figure richly complements the image of the Church as a bank or repository of the apostolic tradition (*AH* III. 4, 1), while expanding on an idea present in germ when Irenaeus earlier mentioned "the barbarians who believe in Christ, possessing salvation written in their hearts by the Spirit without paper or ink" (*AH* III. 4, 2). The Church, presented earlier as guided by the teaching of the bishops, is here described as the place of the Spirit of God. Irenaeus seems to intuit the need to hold together the institutional and the charismatic.

What this approach emphasizes is the *living* nature of truth, equated with the living Spirit of God. Truth so understood is sovereignly free, and the Church as "the assembly of those gathered by the Son" (*AH* III. 6, 1) finds her place as docile to that Spirit. The actions of the Church even in teaching are presented as the activity of a nursing mother. Her milk should be like (or perhaps should *be*) the limpid stream flowing from Christ's body. It is precisely by contrast with this vision of the Church that false teaching can be seen as putrid water flowing from broken cisterns.

Irenaeus turns to that "putrid water," to the teaching written in sand. The false teachers are perpetually searching but not finding; when they do "find" they find another God, another Pleroma, even another economy. In his opinion

> they spurn God, holding God for less because, on account of God's love and immense kindness, God has come to humans in knowledge; a knowledge not according to greatness or substance, for no one has measured or felt God, but according to this: that we should know that the one who made us and formed us and breathed into us the breath of life and who nourishes us through creation, confirming us by God's Word and holding us together by God's Wisdom, this one is the sole true God (*AH* III. 24, 1 [SC 211:476]).

God has given true knowledge of God to humans, knowledge commensurate at once with God's greatness and our capacity. Such knowledge is revealed in the "making" of humans (that is, in their being created) and in their "nurturing" (that is, in their being held in life). Thus revelation comes to them through the events of the economy. Such knowledge is saving knowledge rather than the pseudo-knowledge of the Gnostics with their imagined God. The themes introduced here will be developed in *AH* IV, where Irenaeus will defend the oneness of the history of salvation recounted through the Old and New Testaments.

PART FOUR

The One Story of Salvation

Introduction to Part Four

"The glory of God is the human person, fully alive, and the life of the human person is the vision of God." (*AH* IV. 20, 7)

Irenaeus used *AH* III to interpret the teaching of the apostles so as to show the unity of God and of Christ. In opposition to the distinctions in the sphere of the divine that the Valentinian interpretation supported, his interpretation showed that the Supreme God is one with the Creator God of the Old Testament, and also that the only-begotten Son, the Word, Christ, and Jesus are one and the same figure. This reading, he has stressed, is one with the Rule of Faith found in the Scriptures, and as such is the teaching of the Church. In *AH* IV he takes the argument to another stage. Working from the words of Christ found in the Scriptures, he maintains that the one God, together with the Word and Spirit, acts continuously in history for the salvation of humanity. That is, there is only one history of salvation and it runs from the Old Testament through the New. The first purpose of Part Three is to follow Irenaeus as he interprets the Scriptures in *AH* IV, observing how he structures the work to clarify his understanding of the one story of human salvation. The second and equally important purpose is to throw into relief the interrelationships Irenaeus sees among the nature of the Creator, the nature of salvation, and the nature of the human person.

As Irenaeus interprets the Scriptures to demonstrate the unity of the story of human salvation, at the same time he begins to unfold his understanding of the human person. The nature of the Creator, the nature of salvation, and the nature of the human person are, for both Irenaeus and the Gnostics, tightly bound up with each other. He differs from them in how he understands the essential definitions, most particularly in the value he attaches to materiality and in the consequences for materiality which he assigns to human freedom. Materiality for him is the direct product of the Creator God and a component of

97

all human reality. In addition, human beings as ensouled are free. All of this affects the nature of salvation. Irenaeus remarks:

> For all of [the Gnostics], although they come from different places and teach different things, nevertheless agree in the same blasphemous proposition, wounding mortally in teaching blasphemy about God our Maker and our Nurturer and diminishing the salvation of humanity. For the human person is a mixture of soul and flesh, formed according to the likeness of God and molded by God's Hands, that is, by the Son and the Spirit, to whom God said: "Let us make humankind." This therefore is the proposition of him who envies our life: to make humankind incredulous of their salvation and blasphemous toward God the creator (*AH* IV, preface 4 [SC 100:390]).

According to Irenaeus, Gnostics of every stripe falsify the teaching about God, humankind, and salvation. It is the work of "the envious one" to undercut this teaching, distorting it and falsely separating its parts from one another. Christ's own words tell a different story, and it is to those words that Irenaeus now turns.

He divides *AH* IV into three parts. In the first (corresponding here to chapter seven) he treats the unity of the two testaments as seen from the words of Christ (*AH* IV. 1, 1–IV. 19, 3). In the second (here chapter eight) he considers the Old Testament as prophecy of the New, including examples of the ecclesial reading of Scriptures in the post-New Testament Church (*AH* IV. 20, 1–IV. 35). Finally, in the third (here chapter nine) he reflects on one sole God, the author of both covenants, proved through the parables of Christ (*AH* IV. 36–41).[1] Throughout Irenaeus follows the same method he used in Book III, the method analyzed by Philippe Bacq in his groundbreaking study of *AH* IV itself.

NOTES

[1]This is substantially the outline presented by André Benôit, *Saint Irénée. Introduction à l'étude de sa théologie*. Études d'Histoire et de Philosophie religieuses 52 (Paris: Presses universitaires de France, 1960) 182–192, followed by the Sources chrétiennes editors, SC 100:181–182, and modified by Bacq, *De l'ancienne à la nouvelle alliance selon S. Irénée. Unité du livre IV de l'Adversus haereses* (Paris: Lethielleux, 1978) 29–31.

CHAPTER SEVEN

One Creator, One Christ, One Story

Adversus haereses IV. 1–19

The overall movement of *AH* IV. 1–19 is designed to establish from the words of Christ that the one Creator God who is Lord of heaven and earth is the author of both testaments. The development is in six sections with a conclusion.[1] First Irenaeus shows the oneness of the Father of Christ with the Creator and Author of the Law (*AH* IV. 1, 1–5, 1); only then does he proceed to show the oneness of the Father of Christ with the God of the Patriarchs (*AH* IV. 5, 2–8, 1). In a third brief passage he portrays Christ as observer of the Law (*AH* IV. 8, 2-3). Then he moves to examine law and gospel as stages of a growth (*AH* IV. 9–11). In the fifth section he examines the gospel as fulfillment of the Law (*AH* IV. 12–16), and in the sixth he examines the Eucharist as fulfillment of the figurative sacrifices of the Old Testament (*AH* IV. 17–19, 1a). The conclusion of Part One reflects on the absolute transcendence of God (*AH* IV. 19, 1b-3).

Part 1, Section 1: *AH* IV. 1, 1–5, 1.
Oneness of the Father of Christ with the Creator and Author of the Law

The oneness of God across the two testaments as well as the oneness of Christ with creation is apparent from this opening section of *AH* IV. First of all, Christ's words in the gospels, according to Irenaeus, witness to the oneness of the Supreme God with the Creator. It was this God to whom Christ witnessed with the words, "I praise You, Father, Lord of heaven and earth" (Matt 11:25; Luke 10:21). His words echo Moses (Deut 32:1), David (Ps 121:2 [LXX 120:2]), and Isaiah (Isa 1:2; 42:5), and through them the whole of the Scriptures. In fact the words of Moses and of the prophets *are* his words; Irenaeus recalls what Christ says in John: "If you believed Moses, you would believe me, for he wrote about me. But if you do not believe what he wrote, how will you believe what I say?" (NRSV John 5:46-47). Thus the two testaments are one since only the one Christ speaks through both of them, praising in both testaments the One God, his Father, the Creator and the author of the Law (*AH* IV. 1, 1–2, 4). The very singleness of the message of the two testaments also suggests to Irenaeus that Moses, Abraham, and the prophets are "from one substance" *[ex una substantia]*[2] as also is the risen Christ whose coming they announce.

Irenaeus then further clarifies his understanding of the Creator God and of materiality. He does this by commenting on a text, the interpretation of which is in contention between him and his opponents. Jesus said: "Do not swear at all, either by heaven, for it is the throne of God, or by the earth, for it is his footstool, or by Jerusalem, for it is the city of the great King" (NRSV Matt 5:34-35; *AH* IV. 2, 5 [SC 100:406]). The text alludes to Isa 66:1: "Heaven is my throne and the earth is my footstool." Irenaeus reports the Gnostic reading thus: "These malicious ones say: 'If heaven is the throne of God and the earth God's footstool, but it is said that heaven and earth will pass away, and with them will also necessarily pass this God who is seated upon them, therefore this is not the God who is above all things'" (*AH* IV. 3, 1 [SC 100:412]). As Irenaeus remarks, such a statement comes from someone who does not know what God is; rather "they think God is like a human being, who sits and is contained, and not that God is the one who contains" (*AH* IV. 3, 1 [SC 100:412]). Irenaeus understands that a specific note of the Creator God as distinct from the things of creation is that the Creator is the one in whom all else is, but who is in no other. The Gnostic reading contradicts this position, and it also misunderstands the passing of heaven and earth.

Irenaeus says David resolved this latter question in Ps 102:25-28.[3] According to the psalmist heaven and earth will pass but God and the servants of God will remain forever (*AH* IV. 3, 1 [SC 100:412, 414]). While God is quite different from created things that are limited and passing, there is nevertheless a kind of commonality between God and the servants of God in that both "will remain forever."

To clarify this commonality Irenaeus moves to the final section of the Matthean passage, referring to Jerusalem. The Gnostics say the city would not have been destroyed if it were truly the city of the great King. This, says Irenaeus, is like saying:

> If the stubble were a creature of God, never would it be parted from the grain of wheat! Or again, if the vine twigs were made by God, never would they be cut down when they have been stripped of grapes. But just as these things were not made principally on account of themselves but on account of the fruit growing on them . . . so with Jerusalem (*AH* IV. 4, 1 [SC 100:416]).

Jerusalem bore its fruit, the fruit of liberty, and now is abandoned. So it is, for "all that begins in time must necessarily end in time" (*AH* IV. 4, 1 [SC 100:416]).

We saw in chapter two that the Gnostics, too, hold that materiality will end with time. How then does Irenaeus differ? Having shown from his reading of the Scriptures that the Creator God is radically different from created things, and that things created in time will end in time, he turns from the end of Jerusalem to the end of the whole world, an end that will arrive with "the day of the Lord." On that day Christ will separate the wheat from the chaff (cf. Matt 3:11-12; Luke 3:16-17). Here Irenaeus introduces a distinguishing characteristic of his theology of the human person. He writes:

> But indeed grain and chaff, beings without soul and reason, are naturally made such; *the human person, by contrast, is reasonable, and according to this like God, made free in will and with his own power, he himself being the cause for himself whether he will become sometimes grain, sometimes chaff.*[4] Wherefore he will be justly condemned, because created rational he departed from true reason, and living irrationally he turned against the justice of God, handing himself over to all earthly spirits and to all serving voluptuousness (*AH* IV. 4, 3 [SC 100:424]).

The human person is like God in rationality (closely associated in this place with free will, "reasonable" choice). Herein Irenaeus finds the seed of immortality.

In this opening segment of *AH* IV he concludes his thought in the following words: "Therefore there is one and the same God, who rolls the heavens like a book, and renews the face of the earth; who made temporal things on account of human beings, so that maturing among them they might bear fruit for immortality, and who made eternal things on account of his loving friendship for human beings" (*AH* IV. 5, 1 [SC 100:424]). God the Creator is radically distinct from materiality, yet among the Creator's material creatures is one, the human person, who is like God in possessing the power of a free and rational choice, and therefore capable of sharing immortality.

Both Irenaeus and his opponents agree that material things will necessarily end with time; both recognize that humans share in materiality. Both also hold that human freedom plays a role in human destiny. In Irenaeus's view freedom enables humans to become either chaff or wheat and therefore to share in immortality. Ultimately as Irenaeus unfolds his argument in *AH* IV and V it will become clear that this immortality concerns the human being quite specifically *as* material. It is with this last stroke that Irenaeus will most sharply position his understanding of material temporality vis-à-vis the Gnostic understanding.

PART 1, SECTION 1: SUMMARY

Here in the very first section of *AH* IV is an indication of the unity of the two testaments through the person of Christ and the oneness of his Father with the Creator God, the giver of the Law. There is also an initial presentation of the kind of relationship Irenaeus perceives between the Creator and the human person, and—in the introduction of the concept of free will—a hint of how he will develop the notion of salvation.

Part 1, Section 2: *AH* IV. 5, 2–8, 1.
Oneness of the Father of Christ with the God of the Patriarchs

A further link Irenaeus sees between the two testaments is that the Father of Jesus Christ is the God of the patriarchs. This includes the idea that Jesus Christ, as the preexistent Word, is himself the agent of revelation in the Old Testament. As such he made himself known to the patriarchs. As will become evident, the Gnostics do not accept this position.

Following the text of Irenaeus, we begin with a key passage on the resurrection. Jesus taught that "He is God not of the dead but of the living" (NRSV Luke 20:38). Irenaeus holds that when Jesus said this he both revealed the resurrection and manifested God:

> For if he is not the God of the dead but of the living, and if he himself is called the God of the fathers who are asleep, undoubtedly they are living in God and not asleep, "since they are sons of the resurrection" [Luke 20:36]. But the resurrection is our Lord himself, as he himself said: "I am the resurrection and the life" [John 11:25]. Therefore the fathers are his sons; for it is said by the prophet: "For your fathers are made your sons for you" [Ps 45:16 (LXX 44:17)].[5] Therefore Christ himself with the Father is the God of the living, who has spoken through Moses, who manifested himself to the fathers (*AH* IV. 5, 2 [SC 100:430]).

Irenaeus in typical fashion here links texts thematically and freely interprets one by another to explain what he already holds: namely that Christ, the preexistent Word, is the one author of Revelation in Old Testament as well as New. (This procedure continuously illustrates his conviction, reiterated throughout *AH,* that the Scriptures are rightly interpreted within the Church and according to its Rule of Faith.) In the whole of *AH* III Part 2 Irenaeus stressed the divinity of Jesus Christ. What is critical here is the revelatory role assigned to Christ in the Old Testament as well as in the New. So for Irenaeus it is in the light of his faithful assent to the revealing Word that Abraham can be said to have known Christ, Abraham who left his home to follow the Word just as in their day the apostles left their boats, and as we in our day, he says, take up our cross to follow the same Word (*AH* IV. 5, 3-4).

The Gnostics interpret the Old Testament stories differently; for them everything hinges on the ability to know God. In this area there is one key text that

Irenaeus claims they seriously misinterpret. "All this however, those who hold evil opinions think to overturn, on account of one saying which, indeed, is not well understood among them" (*AH* IV. 5, 5 [SC 100:436]). The scriptural text in question, Matt 11:27 (Luke 10:22), is then cited: "No one knows the Son except the Father, nor does anyone know the Father except the Son, and those to whom the Son wishes to reveal [them]"[6] (*AH* IV. 6, 1 [SC 100:436]). His opponents, he remarks, cite and explain the text differently. He writes:

> [They say] no one *knew* the Father except the Son, nor the Son except the Father, and those to whom the Son wishes to reveal [them]. They interpret this as if the true God had been known by no one before the coming of our Lord; the God who had been announced by the prophets was not the Father of Christ (*AH* IV. 6, 1 [SC 100:438]).

The problem Irenaeus finds with the Gnostic variant is a shift in tenses[7] which has the effect of asserting that the Father was not known before the coming of Christ.[8] If this were true, then, according to Irenaeus, the right project would be to ask why God had been unknown before Jesus Christ, and not to imagine another God (*AH* IV. 6, 2).

His interpretation of the text allows for more subtlety. Certainly it means that the invisible Father is known through the Word and the inexpressible is expressed by the Word; in turn the Word is known only by the Father (*AH* IV. 6, 3). But Irenaeus also insists that the Lord did not say the Father and the Son can be known in no way at all. If this were true, as he says, then the Lord would have said to us: "Do not seek God for God is unknowable and you will not find God." But what the Lord did teach is: "no one is able to know God unless God teaches that person, that is, without God there is no knowing God; but that he should be known is the will of the Father. For they know him to whom the Son will reveal him" (*AH* IV. 6, 4 [SC 100:446]). While the text protects the essential unknowability of God, at the same time it makes clear that the Father desires to be known, and becomes known through the revelatory activity of the Son.

Why the Father should reveal the Son or the Son the Father is the next question. Irenaeus finds a reason for the Father revealing the Son in the just judgments of God. The Father reveals the Son in order justly to admit those who believe in him to eternal life, while justly excluding those who refuse him (*AH* IV. 6, 5 and 7). The Son, in turn, reveals the Father to lead all to belief, and does so progressively: first through creation, then through the Law and the prophets, and finally through becoming flesh. The one same God who is the Father of Jesus Christ and the Creator is the God known to the patriarchs. This is how the Father has become seen: "for the invisible of the Son is the Father, and the visible of the Father is the Son. That is why, he being present, they say 'Christ' and name him God" (*AH* IV. 6, 6 [SC 100:450]).

Because revelation has always been through the Son who is the Word it is true that Abraham, through the Word, knew the Father and expected the coming of the Son, and through the Spirit saw the Son's day and rejoiced in it (*AH* IV. 7, 1-4). It is through the Son as the sole revelatory agent that some knowledge of Father, Son, and Spirit was given to Abraham. Thus Irenaeus allows for a certain anticipatory knowledge of the triune God, if only as appearing in the economy. He includes the Three in the one God known to Abraham, although *how* Abraham knew them as "three and one" is certainly not specified any more than it is for Irenaeus himself, working at least a century and a half before the flowering of patristic trinitarian speculation.

The closest Irenaeus comes to an explanation of the way Father, Son, and Spirit relate to one another is through the metaphor of the "Hands" of God, introduced here according to the Armenian version of *AH*.[9] Irenaeus writes:

> The Father did not need angels to make the world and form humankind for whose sake he made the world, nor was he in need of assistance for the construction of the things which were made and for the disposition of their affairs which were for humankind, but he possessed a rich and ineffable assistance; for there assisted him in all things his first born and his Hands, that is, the Son and the Spirit, the Word and the Wisdom, whom all the angels serve and to whom they are subject. Vain therefore are those who on account of the saying, "No one knows the Father but the Son," introduce another unknown Father (*AH* IV. 7, 4 [SC 100:462, 464]).

The metaphor is faithful to the New Testament insight according to which *ho theos* signifies the Father with whom are associated the Son and the Spirit,[10] and allows Irenaeus to affirm the one God within a Christian perspective. While the association of the Father with his "Hands" may suggest an internal relationship among them (and so, in the language of a later theological development, the "immanent trinity"), that association is more explicitly external and for the economy (and so, in that same later language, suggests the "economic trinity"). The notion of the "Hands" of God will serve Irenaeus well a little later in *AH* IV.

PART 1, SECTION 2: SUMMARY

Having pricked his reader's imagination with this idea and defended his interpretation of "no one knows the Father but the Son," Irenaeus rests his case for the Father of the Lord as the God of Abraham and the patriarchs.

Part 1, Section 3: *AH* IV. 8, 2-3. Christ as Observer of the Law

Christ's words and actions in the Sabbath healing of the bent-over woman, a daughter of Abraham, represent a fulfillment of the Law, as he himself indicated, for healing is permitted on that day (*AH* IV. 8, 2). So, too, his words and actions in excusing his disciples for picking grain and eating it on the Sabbath represent a fulfillment of the Law. They were following the example of David, the king. According to Irenaeus all the disciples share in the priestly privilege that belonged to David by right of kingship. That privilege includes nourishing themselves while about the service of God (*AH* IV. 8, 3). From Irenaeus's perspective the point of both the healing and the eating episodes is that Christ respected and fulfilled the Law. In his very observance of the Law Christ thus represents continuity with the Law rather than severance from it.

Part 1, Section 4: *AH* IV. 9–11. Law and Gospel as Stages of Growth

Not only did Christ observe the Law, but Irenaeus has also shown from Christ's very words that his Father is one and the same as the Creator God, author of the Law and God of the patriarchs. Now Irenaeus sets out to clarify further, still from Christ's words, the relationship between "old" and "new." He writes: "All things therefore are from the same substance, that is from one and the same God, as the Lord said to the disciples: 'Therefore every scribe who has been trained for the kingdom of heaven is like the master of a household who brings out of his treasure what is new and what is old (NRSV Matt 13:52)'" (*AH* IV. 9, 1 [SC 100:476]). Irenaeus interprets the text allegorically, explaining that the new and old things "certainly refer to the two testaments; the old are the former Law, and the new, the gospel" (*AH* IV. 9, 1 [SC 100:478]). He finds support for this reading in a set of texts referring to a *new* song (NRSV Pss 96:1; 98:1 [LXX 95:1; 97:1]: "Sing to the LORD a new song,") *new* hymn (NRSV Isa 42:10-12: the passage begins "Sing to the LORD a new hymn,") and *new* testament (NRSV Jer 31:31-32: the passage begins "I will make a new testament [covenant]").

In this interpretation the master of the household is the Word of God, Jesus Christ, who in the Old Testament conversed with Abraham and Moses, and in the New Testament restored us to liberty. Continuing in the allegorical mode, Irenaeus applies to the grace of liberty the verse "more than the temple is here" (Matt 12:6). He remarks that "more" and "less" are said of things of similar nature that differ in size and quality. According to this reasoning the grace of liberty is superior to the Law of servitude. The one Lord gives to human beings a gift greater than the Temple, more than Solomon, and more than Jonah. This gift (the grace of liberty) is the knowledge of his own presence and the resurrection from the dead. The more his disciples grow in love, the more and greater the gifts he will give them. But the one whom we know in this way is not another God or a different Christ from the one God the Father and his Son who were preached by the prophets (*AH* IV. 9, 2).

The prophets knew and predicted the New Testament. God willed the movement from one to the other so that, through the testaments, humans might mature into perfect salvation. Keeping in mind his opponents, Irenaeus notes that God and salvation are one; multiple are the precepts that form human beings and the steps that lead human beings to God. Progression or growth is not from one Father to another; it is not at the divine level but on the human level (*AH* IV. 9, 3).

All of the Scriptures speak of the one Word of God; as Irenaeus puts it, "Everywhere in the Scriptures the Son of God is sown" (*AH* IV. 10, 1 [SC 100:492]). Not only the prophets but many of the just were led by the Spirit to hunger for his coming. As the Lord himself told his disciples, "Many prophets and righteous people longed to see what you see, but did not see it, and to hear what you hear, but did not hear it" (NRSV Matt 13:17). But, Irenaeus argues, this could only have been because they had preknowledge that must have come from the Scriptures; the Scriptures, in turn, depend on the one sole God who, through the Word, revealed all, giving the Law, freeing the enslaved and raising them to the status of children, and finally giving them the inheritance of incorruptibility for the perfection of humankind. In fact "he modeled humans to increase and grow to maturity, as the Scriptures say: Increase and multiply" (*AH* IV. 11, 1 [SC 100:498]).

This capacity for growth distinguishes humanity from God, as Irenaeus writes: "God makes, the human being is made. And the one who makes is always the same, but the one who is made must receive a beginning and a middle state, and an adding to, and growth" (*AH* IV. 11, 2 [SC 100:500]). This being the case, "God is always the same, but the human person finds itself in God always moving to God: for God will not at any time cease doing good for and enriching humanity, nor will humanity cease to receive benefits from and to be enriched by God" (*AH* IV. 11, 2 [SC 100:500]).

There is a reciprocity between God the Creator and humanity, the creature. Through the very process of change the unchanging God draws changeable humanity Godward; humans who resist the attraction are justly deprived of its fulfillment. To those who are fruitful God will give even more, as the master rewarded the good servant who cared for a little by placing him over much. With the shadow of his adversaries never far away Irenaeus is careful to note that this "much" is "according to the gift of God's grace, but not according to a change of [our] knowledge" (*AH* IV. 11, 3 [SC 100:502]). The one God of both testaments, he notes, rewards with liberty those who keep the Law with their whole heart and soul, but leads into eternal perdition the hypocrites who observe only externals, cutting them off from life.

PART 1, SECTIONS 1–4: SUMMARY

Part One of *AH* IV is concerned with the unity of the two testaments based on the words of Christ. Irenaeus devoted the first three sections to showing from the gospels how the Father of Christ is the Creator and the God of the patriarchs, introducing the important metaphor of the Hands of God. He also showed Christ as himself observing the Law. Section 4, just completed, shows Law and Gospel as stages of the growth of humanity toward God. Thus in the first section of Part 1 Irenaeus has not only introduced the theme of continuity in the history of salvation but he has also suggested implications of that unity for the understanding of God and Christ, as well as for the understanding of humanity itself.

Part 1, Section 5: *AH* IV. 12–16. The Gospel as Fulfillment of the Law

Before one can speak of fulfillment of the Law it is important to identify the true Law. Irenaeus notes that "their teachers" have adulterated the Law, equating with it traditions that are, in fact, contrary to it, as Christ made clear when he asked: "Why do you break the commandment of God for the sake of your tradition?" (NRSV Matt 15:3). As Irenaeus points out, what is missing is the love of God (*AH* IV. 12, 1 and 4). This love, Irenaeus continues, is the greatest and first commandment and the second is love of neighbor; the Lord teaches this in saying that the whole Law and the prophets depend on these commandments, which he himself renewed (*AH* IV. 12, 2). If, then, both testaments agree in the two greatest commandments this must be because, in Irenaeus's view, there is but one Lawgiver at work in both (*AH* IV. 12, 3). In fact he holds that the Law taught human beings in advance to follow Christ, and Christ himself made this evident when he said: "If you wish to enter into life, keep the commandments" (Matt 19:17). This teaching admits of degrees of entry into life, Irenaeus thinks, for, speaking to all through the one young man he is addressing, Christ explains what one must do to be perfect. It is not necessary to follow any of the Gnostic figures (another Son, the Mother, the Enthymesis of Sophia) or even the whole Pleroma, but rather to keep the commandments and follow Christ (*AH* IV. 12, 5).

Irenaeus accepts the commandments (including the two "great commandments") as the precepts of the natural law. Far from abolishing them, Christ extended and fulfilled them; thus Irenaeus reads the "it was said . . . but I say" passages from the Sermon on the Mount (Matt 5:21-22, 27-28, 33-34, 38-39).[11] He interprets the Law as educator. Using exterior and bodily things it led the soul, as by a chain, to the commandments so that humans might learn to obey God. By contrast, Irenaeus says, "the Word, freeing the soul, taught that the body should be purified by it voluntarily" (*AH* IV. 13, 2 [SC 100:528]). In this way the chains of servitude will be broken and humanity will follow God without chains (*AH* IV. 13, 2).

Returning to the "it was said . . . but I say" passages Irenaeus repeats that these directions of the Lord were not for the dissolution of the Law but rather for its amplification and fulfillment by his followers. He writes:

> He did not free us that we should detach ourselves from him . . . but that having obtained more of his grace we might love him more; then, the more we have loved him, the greater glory we will receive from him when we will be always in the presence of the Father (*AH* IV. 13, 3 [SC 100:532]).

The amplifications were given for the people of the New Testament, but the natural law (in Irenaeus's view, as noted above, this includes the two great commandments) is common to the people of both the Old and the New Testaments. It is the people of the New Testament, his disciples, that Christ called not servants, but friends. Servitude belonged to the Law, but freedom follows the coming of the Lord. However, Irenaeus notes, in giving the title of "friend" to his disciples Christ showed himself one with the Word, who had called Abraham the "friend of God" (*AH* IV. 13, 4). This is another instance of his principle that consistency between the two testaments indicates a single author.

The reference to friendship with Abraham must not be taken as a sign of neediness in God, according to Irenaeus, any more than God created Adam out of neediness. As God befriended Abraham to give him life, so God made humanity to give them salvation. In this context Irenaeus introduces the metaphor of light that will be increasingly prominent in *AH* IV. He writes:

> To follow the Savior is to participate in salvation, and to follow the light is to perceive light. For those who are in the light do not themselves illumine the light, but they are illuminated and made lustrous by it, they themselves indeed giving nothing to it, but laying hold of its benefit they are illuminated by the light. So it is with service to God: it gives nothing to God, for human obedience is not necessary to God. But to those who follow and serve God, God gives life and incorruptibility and eternal glory, offering the benefit to those who serve because they serve God, and to those who follow because they follow, but receiving no benefit from them, for God is rich, perfect, and without need (*AH* IV. 14, 1 [SC 100:538, 540]).

It is as if Irenaeus were saying: to understand humanity's relationship to God one need only reflect on their relationship to the sun. People give nothing to the sun, and yet, being in the light, they receive illumination and a kind of luster from it. So humans give God nothing, but, following God, they receive life and glory. It is a matter, not of God's need, but of human need: "For to the extent that God has need of nothing, to that extent humanity has need of communion with God. For this is the glory of humanity: to persevere and to remain in the service of God" (*AH* IV. 14, 1 [SC 100:540]).

In *AH* III Irenaeus said that the glory of humanity is God; the insight here simply shows how that first theoretical statement becomes practical. God will actually be the glory of humankind in response to people's following and serving God. Irenaeus relates this to the Lord's words to the disciples: "You have not chosen me, but I have chosen you" (John 15:16) taking this to signify that they do not glorify the Son of God in following him, but having followed him they will be glorified by him.

God has molded humanity from the beginning in view of the divine gifts, preparing the race for its part in the "symphony" of salvation (*AH* IV. 14, 2).[12] The Law has served as educator, leading people (as Irenaeus notes) through types to reality, through temporal things to eternal, through carnal things to spiritual, and through earthly things to heavenly (*AH* IV. 14, 3–16, 5). Unlike the decalogue which reflects the natural law and is valid for both testaments, and the exhortations of Christ which are proper to the New Testament, the cultic prescriptions of the Old Testament were given when the people separated themselves from God and so were in servitude. All these laws served a limited educative function during the period of the old covenant and are abolished with the new covenant of liberty (*AH* IV. 15, 1-2).

In addition, the practices of circumcision and the Sabbath did not justify but signified. Physical circumcision served as a sign of the alliance between God and the people (Gen 17:9-11) and prefigured spiritual circumcision (Col 2:11). The Sabbath signified that the people knew the God who sanctified them (Ezek 20:12), taught perseverance in God's service (Rom 8:36), and also, in reminding of God's seventh-day rest, served as a reminder of the repose promised to those who persevere in God's service (*AH* IV. 16, 1-3).

Corresponding to the idea of the Law as educator are both Irenaeus's position on human freedom (for example, *AH* IV. 15, 2 and 16, 5) and the Irenaean notion of the human race as needing to grow to its maturity. The latter concept is strikingly apparent in the *Proof* where he depicts Adam and Eve as children in the moral sphere (*Proof* 12 and 14).[13]

PART 1, SECTION 5: SUMMARY

The fifth section of Part One presents Irenaeus's understanding of the gospel as the fulfillment of the Law. We saw that for him the New Testament continues the natural law represented by the decalogue and the two great commandments, and the teaching of Christ expands this aspect of the Law. Prescriptions that reflect the people's condition of servitude vis-à-vis God have no standing among those who accept the liberty offered by Christ. Prefigurative aspects of the Law, like circumcision, find their fulfillment in the New Testament. All this is colored by the Irenaean understanding of human freedom.

Part 1, Section 6: *AH* IV. 17–19, 1a.
Eucharist as Fulfillment of the Figurative Sacrifices of the Old Testament[14]

In the same way that the gospel is linked to the Law as its fulfillment, so the Eucharist is joined to the Old Testament sacrifices as their completion.[15] Irenaeus opens this development by considering why God required sacrifices, citing multiple texts on God's preference for obedience over sacrifice (*AH* IV. 17, 1-2a).[16] He points out that if the sacrifices were rejected because the offerers were unworthy, then God would not have added to the rejection advice on what they should do to be saved. He illustrates this with texts, largely from the prophets (*AH* IV. 17, 2b-3).[17] All of this is summarized by the word of the Lord,

"But if you had known what this means, 'I desire mercy and not sacrifice,' you would not have condemned the guiltless" (NRSV Matt 12:7, at *AH* IV. 17, 4).

Yet, Irenaeus notes, the Lord taught the disciples to offer bread and wine, creatures, not because God had need of it but so that the disciples would be neither sterile nor ingrates. So he taught them to declare the bread his body and the wine his blood, and named this the new sacrifice of the New Testament (Matt 26:26-28). This the Church does, as Malachi (1:10-11) had prophesied, so that God's name would be glorified (*AH* IV. 17, 5). The name being glorified is that of Jesus Christ (*AH* IV. 17, 6).

This is the sacrifice pleasing to God, Irenaeus teaches (*AH* IV. 18, 1), but it is different in the Church because it is no longer offered by the enslaved but by the freed (*AH* IV. 18, 2). As in the beginning with Cain and Abel, what God cares about is the dispositions of the giver: does the offering come from a pure heart in communion with one's neighbor? It is the lack of such dispositions that the Lord condemned in the scribes and Pharisees, calling them "whitewashed tombs" (Matt 23:27-28). Irenaeus writes: "Therefore sacrifices do not sanctify human beings, for God does not need sacrifice, but the conscience of the one who offers, being pure, sanctifies the sacrifice, and is responsible for God accepting it as from a friend" (*AH* IV. 18, 3 [SC 100:604]). One could not ask a more concise summary of his view of sacrifice. Such a sacrifice is offered only by the Church, according to Irenaeus, and not by the Jews or the heretics (*AH* IV. 18, 4,a).

Reflecting on the heretics, Irenaeus asks how they could be sure that the bread and wine are the body and blood of the Lord "if they do not recognize him as Son of the Maker of the world, that is, his Word, by which the wood bears fruit and the sources of the streams flow . . ." (*AH* IV. 18, 4 [SC 100:608]). There is a twofold assumption underlying this question of his: (1) the eucharistic bread and wine *are* the body and blood of Christ (in some unspecified sense; the "how" is not his question) and (2) there is a connection between the identity of that bread and wine with Christ and Christ's role as Word by whom creation came to be. The incarnate one links creation and redemption in such a way as to make possible his own saving presence in the fruits of creation.

Irenaeus's next question about his opponents is even more telling. He asks: "Again in what way do they say flesh which has been nourished by the body and blood of the Lord will go into corruption and not have part in life?" (*AH* IV. 18, 5 [SC 100:610]). The assumption underlying this question is that the incarnate one being risen, when his risen flesh feeds human flesh the latter has the possibility of sharing in his risen life. This is a sound reflection of the teaching of John 6 although Irenaeus does not cite that chapter here. Rather, he goes on to say:

> For we offer to him those things which are his own, proclaiming appropriately the communication and union of flesh and spirit. For just as the bread which is

from the earth, receiving the invocation of God, is now not common bread, but eucharist, constituted from two things, earthly and heavenly, so our bodies receiving the eucharist are no longer corruptible, having the hope of resurrection (*AH* IV. 18, 5 [SC 100:610]; see also V. 2, 3 [SC 153:34]).

The parallel is clear: as bread receives word to become Eucharist, so through the medium of Eucharist flesh receives spirit to enable humans to share in the risen life. The concern is not with *how* the reception occurs, but with *the fact that* it occurs. This conception of Eucharist, while still theologically somewhat naïve, is dynamic and respectful of the diverse elements joined sacramentally. It will exert immense influence in shaping patristic sacramental theology from the second century through the time of Augustine.[18]

Turning to the broader context of the offering of gifts, Irenaeus notes that offering is made not because God needs human gifts, but to thank God and to sanctify creation. God, in turn, accepts good actions so as to give humankind God's own gifts. The word of the Lord introduced here serves as a reminder that the final judgment will be based on humans' use of the goods of creation for others, those others being surrogates for God in the divine eyes: "I was hungry, and you gave me food . . ." (Matt 25:34-36). It is normal that earthly things serve as figures of heavenly things, for the same God made them. Casting a look at the Gnostics, Irenaeus remarks that to think that heavenly and spiritual things are in their turn figures of other heavenly things and of another Pleroma, and that God is the image of another Father "is to wander from the truth" (*AH* IV. 19, 1 [SC 100:616]).

Conclusion: *AH* IV. 19, 1b-3

God is absolutely incomprehensible in greatness; how is it that anyone can imagine a god beyond God, or accept a god who is not perfect and does not embrace all things? But, says Irenaeus, anyone who speaks in a manner worthy of God proclaims that "God contains and sustains all things, including us" (*AH* IV. 19, 3 [SC 100:622]).

CHAPTER SEVEN: SUMMARY

Irenaeus uses a variety of arguments drawn from the words of Christ to defend the unity of the two testaments. Throughout the interrelationships among the nature of God, the nature of salvation, and the nature of the human person become more apparent. The two testaments are one because of the one Word, who speaks through them both, and the one Creator-Father who is the God of both and the Creator of humankind. That one God is the one revealed to the patriarchs. Christ came to fulfill the Law of the Old Testament, and in doing so brings forth the New Testament (in whose light the Old is known *as* Old). God offers the two testaments to enable the gradual maturation of humanity into salvation. The Law given by God in the Old Testament served to educate humankind in its growth into freedom. With the Gospel that Law is abrogated, somewhat as the Eucharist abrogates the sacrifices of the Law. The One God of Law and Gospel, of sacrifices and Eucharist, remains the absolutely incomprehensible Creator, unknown according to greatness, but made known out of love for humankind.

Throughout this first part of *AH* IV Irenaeus has taken a stance within the gospel, choosing to show the connections between the two testaments from the perspective of the coming of Christ. The argument pivots on the words of Christ; "perspective" here refers to the place from which the argument is made, in this case the world of the gospel. The perspective will change in Part Two.

NOTES

[1]This follows Bacq's more detailed outline (*De l'ancienne à la nouvelle alliance selon S. Irénée* 417–421, with summary explanation on 41–48).

[2]Irenaeus uses the term "substance" to refer to identity of origin by contrast with the differences in origin among the Gnostic classes of humans. The Latin reads: *demonstrat ex una substantia esse omnia, id est Abraham et Moysen et prophetas, etiam ipsum Dominum qui resurrexit a mortuis* (SC 100:404). See also *AH* IV. 9, 1, reading *unius igitur et ejusdem substantiae sunt omnia, hoc est ab uno et eodem Deo* (SC 100:476). The usage implies common nature, human beings and God both having a spiritual nature. "Substance" is applied to things having a common nature and differing by size and quality in *AH* IV. 9, 2: *Plus autem et minus non in his dicitur quae inter se communionem non habent et sunt contrariae naturae et pugnant adversum se, sed in his quae ejusdem sunt substaniae et communicant secum, solum autem multitudine et magnitudine differunt* (SC 100:480). It is important to avoid reading into either *substantia* or *natura* implications of later developments in trinitarian and christological thought.

[3]The psalm verses quoted by Irenaeus are:

> Long ago you laid the foundation of the earth,
>   and the heavens are the work of your hands.
> They will perish, but you endure;
>   they will all wear out like a garment.
> You change them like clothing, and they pass away;
>   but you are the same, and your years have no end.
> The children of your servants shall live secure;
>   their offspring shall be established in your presence
>   (NRSV Ps 102:25-28 [LXX 101:26-29]).

[4]In Latin the underlined section reads: *homo vero rationabilis, et secundum hoc similis Deo, liber in arbitrio factus et suae potestatis, ipse sibi causa est ut aliquando quidem frumentum, aliquando autem palea fiat.* The original Greek is not extant.

[5]Irenaeus also invokes the prophet Daniel who adored the Lord God "because he is the living God" (Dan 14:25).

[6]Here the Greek text is not extant; the Latin of *AH* reads: *Nemo cognoscit Filium nisi Pater, neque Patrem quis cognoscit nisi Filius, et cui voluerit Filius revelare.* The texts of Matthew and Luke do not give an object; the clause in question reads *kai hōi ean boulētai ho huios*

apokalupsai. Modern exegetes assume that the Father is the object of the revelation. Thus the NAB translation is "and anyone to whom the Son *wishes to reveal him.*" On the basis of the immediate context and of parallel passages elsewhere Adelin Rousseau argues that Irenaeus holds that the Son reveals himself and in so doing also reveals the Father. Thus the French reads *voudra les révéler.* See SC 100:206, note marked "p. 439, n. 1."

[7]It is a question of the substitution of the aorist *egnō* for the present *epiginōskei.*

[8]For comment on this substitution and references to studies of Matt 11:27 in *AH,* see SC 100:207–208, note marked "p. 439, n. 2."

[9]Rousseau develops his justification for accepting the Armenian over the Latin in a closely argued, lengthy, and convincing note (SC 100:212–219, note marked "p. 465, n. 1").

[10]On this subject see Karl Rahner, "Theos in the New Testament," *Theological Investigations* 1.79–148.

[11]The SC numeration is Matt 5:21-22, 27-28, 33-34, 37.

[12]This appears to be an echo of a word occurring in Luke 15:25. Rousseau (SC 100:234, note marked "p. 545, n. 1") signals the context as the story of the prodigal son; the older brother, returning from the field during the celebration, hears the *symphōnian,* the "sound of music." Ysabel de Andía (*Homo Vivens. Incorruptibilité et divinisation de l'homme selon Irénée de Lyon* [Paris: Études Augustiniennes, 1986]) notes that Irenaeus uses this metaphor to signify the economy (pp. 55, 302, 355) as well as the consonance between the thought of the Church and the Eucharist (p. 240). D. Singles (*Le temps du salut chez S. Irénée* [Lyon: Profac, 1980] part 2, especially 43–46) focuses on "the symphony of the cosmos" as one figure Irenaeus uses (together with those of "the millennium" and "recapitulation") to express how the human being, faced with finitude, comes to a mastery of time.

[13]See below, p. 132.

[14]Scholars have examined whether Irenaeus has utilized a collection of "Testimonia" as source for *AH* IV. 17, 1-5, a section that draws on the same biblical references as parallel passages in Barnabas and Clement of Alexandria. In his first appendix Bacq reviews the scholarship, the sources, and the Irenaean material (*De l'ancienne à la nouvelle alliance* 299–313).

[15]David N. Power, *Irenaeus of Lyons on Baptism and Eucharist: Selected Texts with Introduction, Translation and Annotation.* Alcuin/GROW Liturgical Study 18 (Bramcote, Nottingham: Grove, 1991), offers convenient access to the pertinent texts.

[16]He cites 1 Sam 15:22: "Has the LORD as great delight in burnt offerings and sacrifices, as in obeying the voice of the LORD? Surely, to obey is better than sacrifice, and to heed than the fat of rams" (NRSV) and the following similar texts: Pss 40:6; 51:18-19; 50:9-13, 14-15 [LXX 39:7; 50:18-19; 49:9-13, 14-15]; Isa 1:11, 16-18 [LXX 1:10, 16-18].

[17]The citations, illustrative of the kind of life the people were meant to pursue, describe: walking in God's ways rather than offering holocausts or sacrifices (Jer 7:21-25); God's pleasure in kindness, justice, and uprightness rather than in sacrifice (Jer 9:24); God as not honored with sacrifice from those coming before God in sin (Isa 43:23-24); God approving of the lowly (Isa 66:2); that neither vows nor sacred meat alone turn people from their injustice (Jer 11:15); that the fasting God prefers is setting free the oppressed, sharing bread with the hungry, sheltering the homeless, clothing the naked (Isa 58:6-9); God ordering Israel to render true judgment, to show kindness and compassion to one another, to care for the widow, the orphan, the alien, and the poor (Zech 7:9-10) and to speak the truth, plotting no evil and loving no false oath (Zech 8:16-17); God directing that humans should refrain from evil and do good, seek after peace and follow it (Ps 33:13-15).

[18]Since the Reformation this passage, particularly the phrase *ex duabus rebus constans* (extant Greek, *ek duo pragmaton sunestēkuia*), has been invoked to witness to diverse accounts

of *how* the Eucharist becomes the body of Christ, each involving the attribution of a later position to the second-century author. Following the work of A. D'Alès ("La doctrine eucharistique de saint Irénée," *RSR* 13 [1923] 24–46) and of H. D. Simonin ("A propos d'un texte eucharistique de S. Irénée," *RSPhTh* 23 [1940] 281–292), D. Van den Eynde ("Eucharistia ex duabus rebus constans: S. Irénée, Adv. Haereses, IV. 18, 5," *Anton.* 15 [1940] 13–28), concluded to the absence of *any* position on that question in this text. This is worth noting as a milestone toward both a more sympathetic historical understanding of the text and mutual ecumenical understanding among the Christian churches.

CHAPTER EIGHT

Vision, Life, and Light

Adversus haereses IV. 20–35

Irenaeus continues to rest his argument on the words of Christ, but in this part of *AH* IV he changes the perspective from which he works. Instead of looking from the New Testament back to the Old he looks from the Old Testament toward the New in an effort to show that the Old Testament prophets foresaw the events of the New Testament. In his view this is the case, and the fact that it is so is a further indication that the God of the prophets and the God of the Gospel are one and the same. He proceeds by reviewing his understanding of prophecy, devoting Section One (*AH* IV. 20–22, 1) to prophecy and vision, while Section Two (*AH* IV. 22, 2–25) focuses on the New Testament interpretation of Old Testament prophecy. Then, standing with his contemporaries in the post-New Testament Church, he argues for the authoritative interpretation of the Scriptures. To illustrate this he offers two ecclesial readings of the Scriptures: Section Three (*AH* IV. 26–32) presents the exegesis of a presbyter and Section Four (*AH* IV. 33) that of a spiritual disciple. Throughout these presentations he further develops his teaching on the human person and salvation. In Section Five (*AH* IV. 34–35) he contrasts his teaching on these topics with that of the Marcionites and Valentinians.

It is not only the desire to establish the continuity between Old and New Testaments that makes prophecy central to Irenaeus's concerns. The Christian community at Lyons was apparently uneasy about "the new prophecy" of Montanism, an ecstatic form of Christianity that was itself not wholly at home in the Church of the late second and early third centuries.[1] The unease concerning Christian prophecy can only have been exacerbated by Gnostic leaders who presented themselves as visionary prophets.[2] Prophecy has been linked to vision from antiquity,[3] and the problem posed by prophecy and prophetic visions has always been to recognize the true prophet. All of these factors make more urgent Irenaeus's desire to teach the meaning of prophecy and, within that, to give a definitive understanding of prophetic vision.

Part 2, Section 1: *AH* IV. 20–22, 1. Prophecy and Vision

As he turns to ch. 20 Irenaeus has just completed a reflection on the transcendence of God, inspired by Old Testament passages like the Isaian verse "the heavens are measured out in the palm of his hand" (Isa 40:12).[4] There in a poetic vein he had asked: "How can we ever know God, when we do not comprehend the fullness and the greatness of God's hand?"[5] He opens the first meaning unit by repeating the question in declarative form and offering an answer: the God whose greatness defeats human knowing attracts humans by divine love. In the act of obeying God human beings learn the existence of God, who is the Creator of all things, including themselves and their world. Genesis 2:7 makes plain that God alone—and no one else—formed the human person. In fact, the only help needed was that of the Hands of God.[6] Irenaeus ends *AH* IV. 20, 1 with an announcement of the text to be commented on, remarking that God made all things "from Godself." [7]

In *AH* IV. 20, 2 Irenaeus begins with a citation of the announced text from *Shepherd of Hermas,* which affirms that there is only one God who created all things from nothing, who contains all and is contained by no one.[8] Irenaeus continues with a commentary. The one God is the Father, who delivered all things to the Son.[9] Then in *AH* IV. 20, 3 Irenaeus further identifies the Son. The Son, who is the Word, was always with the Father, as was Wisdom, who is the Spirit, to whom Irenaeus attributes the wonderful text of Prov 8:22-31.[10]

Now in *AH* IV. 20, 4a Irenaeus repeats the citation with which he opened this unit, affirming again that there is only one God who by the Word and Wisdom made and adorned all things. The God unknown according to greatness is known according to love. The content of *AH* IV. 20, 1-4a thus forms one unit of meaning. The pre-given, the Rule of Faith, affirms the unity of the one God, the Father, with the Creator, but allows roles for the Word and Wisdom. Working within the Rule of Faith, Irenaeus develops his thought by announcing and then citing a principal text, here from *Shepherd of Hermas,* for commentary, commenting on it with the use of other texts that are linked allusively, and he ends with an inclusion, repeating the original text cited.

The second meaning unit includes *AH* IV. 20, 4b-8a. That one same Word who worked in creation spoke through the prophets. Through the prophets the Word proclaimed in advance God's deeds for humanity: God would be seen by them and mix with them. This intimate presence of God among humankind would be a saving presence rooted in love.

The Gnostics, like many people in the second century, balked at the notion of the Supreme God "being seen." Their unease with this idea led them, as Irenaeus remarks, to say that "the Father of all remaining invisible, the one seen by the prophets was another" (*AH* IV. 20, 5 [SC 100:636]). The problem is, he thinks, that the Gnostics do not understand what prophecy is. In fact, both he and the Gnostics are concerned to reconcile the vision of God with the divine incomprehensibility. He explains his solution in a passage that relates prophetic words to the vision of God: "For a prophecy is the prediction of things to come, that is, the foretelling of things which will happen later. Therefore the prophets announce that God will be seen by humans, as the Lord says: 'Blessed are the pure of heart, for they shall see God' (Matt 5:8)" (*AH* IV. 20, 5 [SC 100:638]). But he notes that the experience of Moses confirmed that in respect to God's greatness and wondrous glory "no one shall see God and live" (Exod 33:20). So the question that has preoccupied Irenaeus is only intensified: "How do we know God? How do we see God?" He must answer this question if he is to offer an alternative to the Gnostic position. In doing so he begins the development that will culminate in his statement that "the glory of God is the living human, and the life of the human is the vision of God."

First of all for emphasis he repeats that human beings do not see God in the divine greatness and glory. In this sense God is truly incomprehensible. Rather, "According to his love, and kindness, and because he can do all things, even this, he grants to those who love him, that is, to see God."[11] The sense seems to be: "the all-powerful God enables his lovers to see him, not insofar as God is great and glorious, but rather as God is loving and kind." This implied statement is strengthened by the way in which Irenaeus continues: human beings do not see God by their own powers; rather, when God pleases, God is seen by humans. The selection of those to receive the vision, as well as the time and manner, is at the divine discretion.

Irenaeus continues his commentary, spelling out different ways in which God is seen. These differ in kind through time, and also according to which of the Three (God, Spirit/Wisdom, or Word/Son) is acting. As to time, in the past God has been seen "prophetically" through the Spirit. Now in the present God is seen "adoptively" through the Son. In the future God will be seen "paternally" in the kingdom of heaven. Furthermore, Spirit, Son, and Father play distinct roles in this seeing. The Spirit prepares human beings in the Son of God, and the Son leads them to the Father. What of the Father? The Father "gives incorruption for life eternal, which comes to every one from the fact that she sees God."[12] Prophetic seeing is a preparatory seeing under the guidance of the Spirit. Adoptive seeing happens through the agency of the Son, and here Irenaeus intends the incarnate Son. Paternal seeing has to do with the state of glory, where the Father gives eternal incorruption, the final gift to those who see God.

Father, Son, and Spirit are the agents who enable each of these three stages of the vision of God. The point merits emphasis; for Irenaeus it is God's activity that is central in the three stages. Irenaeus's approach is through description of the divine activity in the economy rather than through description

of the stages of mystical ascent to God. The result in either case is union with
God; Irenaeus's concern is with the divine role in effecting this union. Union
with God is a consequence of the divine revelatory activity. This principle distinguishes the Irenaean position from platonic, Gnostic, and later patristic
teaching on the ascent of the soul.

At the heart of the Irenaean teaching lies the notion that incorruption comes
from seeing God,[13] but one may well ask why incorruption should follow from
the divine vision. Irenaeus's meaning seems to be: as see-ers of light are in
light, so see-ers of God are in God. The see-ers of light who are in light share
in light's brightness *(claritas);* in a similar way the see-ers of God who are in
God share in the divine splendor *(claritas).* In both cases the splendor is vivifying. To enable such a vivification the invisible God became visible; the incomprehensible became comprehensible.[14] The statement reflects one of the
strongest and most beautiful presentations Irenaeus makes of the incarnation
in *AH* III. There he wrote: "Therefore he recapitulated humanity in himself,
the invisible becoming visible, the incomprehensible being made comprehensible, the impassible becoming capable of suffering, and the Word being made
a human being, summing up all things in himself . . . ."[15] So what Irenaeus
is saying in *AH* IV. 20, 5 is that the Word was made human in order to vivify
human beings. How important is the sort of life the Word gives? It is impossible to live apart from that life. Evidently the life he refers to is other than
physical and is the true life of humans. Entry into that life is by participation
(participatio) with God, a participation involving knowing God and enjoying
God's goodness. According to God's love God is known in such participation,
and human beings in turn enjoy the goodness of God in the same participation.

Now in *AH* IV. 20, 6, still continuing his commentary on "Blessed are the
pure of heart, for they shall see God," Irenaeus begins to explore the stages of
entering into participation. To grasp what he is about to do it is necessary to
keep in mind two points already made. First, in his outline of the movement
into the vision of God Irenaeus has portrayed a three-stage process: prophetic,
adoptive, and paternal. Second, he develops these stages in the context of his
overall goal in *AH* IV. His goal is to establish the unity of the two covenants,
and—in this the middle section of the book—to illustrate that unity by showing that the Old Testament is a prophecy of the New.

First, invoking Deuteronomy, Irenaeus restates the content of *AH* IV. 20, 5:
"Therefore 'human beings shall see God that they may live,' being made immortal by that sight and attaining even unto God."[16] Then he reminds his readers that he has already explained how the prophets declared this truth in figure.
Some among them saw the prophetic Spirit and that Spirit's works poured out
in all kinds of gifts; others saw the coming of the Lord and the way he did the
will of the Father both in heaven and on earth; still others saw the glories of
the Father adapted to the ones who saw. In all the prophetic seeings, Irenaeus
insists, the one God was revealed. How so?

Irenaeus uses texts of both the Old Testament (Hos 12:10) and the New Testament (1 Cor 12:4-7) to make a theological point. He cites Hosea 12:10 thus: "it was I who multiplied visions, and I have been presented through the hands of the prophets."[17] In Irenaeus's judgment Paul offered a similar idea in 1 Cor 12:4-7 which refers to diversities of gifts but one Spirit, diversities of ministries but one Lord, and diversities of operations but one God. The direct relation between the texts is simply the echoing of similar ideas. The multiple visions of Hosea become the diversities of gifts of 1 Corinthians; for Irenaeus the work of the prophets in Hosea has become the work of the Spirit in Paul. We have here an instance of association, on the order of "linking words." It is important to Irenaeus to make the connection in order to affirm clearly that the God known to the Old Testament prophets is the same proclaimed in the New Testament. What the Spirit reveals prophetically and in figure is not a different God from the God shown adoptively in the Son. Both in the prophetic seeing and in the adoptive seeing it is the one Word of God who shows the Father to the ones who accept the guidance of the Spirit.

Now Irenaeus moves to join this unit of meaning with the previous one. He repeats that as to power and greatness God is invisible to God's creatures. Yet God is not unknown, for all learn through the Word that there is only one God, the Father, who made all things (*AH* IV. 20, 6, citing John 1:18).

It begins to appear that, in Irenaeus's judgment, what unites the two testaments is the similar actions of the one same God who consistently works in the same way for human salvation. If human beings submit to the guidance of the Spirit, the Word shows them the Father, so fulfilling what has always been the role of the Word. He has prepared the way to explain the roles of Son, of Spirit, and of prophetic visions in bringing humankind to the lifegiving vision of God. In the remainder of *AH* IV. 20 he accomplishes this task.

Irenaeus opens *AH* IV. 20, 7 by remarking that the Son who was with the Father from the beginning has from the beginning been the revealer of the Father. The prophetic visions, the division of gifts, his own ministries, and the glorification of the Father have been unfolded by the Son to profit humankind. All has been done to show God to the human race, and to show or present the human race to God, while guarding the invisibility of the Father. On the one hand God is protected from the contempt that can follow overfamiliarity; at the same time God is shown to human beings in multiple ways lest, lacking God, the human person should cease to be. Obviously ceasing to be is to be avoided! Interestingly enough, Irenaeus holds it should be avoided, not for the sake of humans themselves, but rather because it is to the glory of God that human beings "live." What is at issue clearly is a very particular kind of "be-ing."

Now comes the text that has been the center of concern in the present discussion: *gloria enim Dei vivens homo, vita autem hominis visio Dei,* that is, "the glory of God is the living human being, and the human person has true

life only in the vision of God." In fact, Irenaeus immediately adds that if revelation through creation gives life, how much more does the revelation through
the Word give life![18]

There has been revelation through creation, a creation that is the work of
the One God and so reveals its Maker. To the extent that creation shows its
Maker to all who live on earth it is lifegiving to them. Irenaeus continues: if
there is some lifegiving vision of God in creation, how much more is there in
the vision presented in the incarnate Word! Life depends on the vision of God.
To be fully alive a human being must look on God; the human person turned
toward God in this seeing *is* the glory of God. The fullness of the seeing, and
so of life, comes through the incarnate Word. Such being the case, Irenaeus
continues, moving to *AH* IV. 20, 8, since the prophets signify the future, and
in the future humans will look on God, it is necessary that those predicting the
future should themselves see God. But how do the prophets look on God, and
how do they communicate what they see? The Irenaean response is that the
prophets look on God not directly, but "as the Spirit suggests," and they communicate what they receive in word, in vision, in conversation, and in acts.[19]

The second unit of meaning in *AH* IV. 20 closes here with a repetition and
elaboration of the work of a prophet. The major text, "Blessed are the pure of
heart, for they shall see God" (Matt 5:8) has been announced, cited, and commented on, in an interpretation that joins the verses, "In that day we will see,
because God will speak to humankind and it will live" (Deut 5:24), and "No
one has ever seen God. It is God the only Son, who is close to the Father's
heart, who has made him known" (NRSV John 1:18). The prophetic seeing
was a true seeing, although incomplete. The next unit of meaning will be concerned with the relation of the vision of the prophets to the coming of Christ.

As Irenaeus develops these ideas through the remainder of the chapter three
things become clear: in his view the prophets saw in vision the forthcoming
life of Christ; they proclaimed in word his forthcoming words; and they enacted deeds that would be his, at the same time announcing all of this prophetically. The balance of *AH* IV. 20 illustrates this insight from the prophets (that
is, the Old Testament), giving for each text both a literal and a prophetic interpretation and finally illustrating how the Old Testament texts are showings
of future deeds of God, deeds accomplished in the New Testament.

Here Irenaeus himself quite explicitly allows for two levels of meaning for
a text; one begins to suspect that it is not multiple meanings to which he objects, but rather any meaning contrary to the Rule of Faith. It will be helpful,
therefore, to examine in similar detail the next unit of meaning in *AH* IV. 20.

The third meaning unit is centered on the text of John 1:18. (That text thus
also serves to link this unit with the previous one.) The text is appropriate to
use in the interpretation of Old Testament prophecies since prophecies are
seeings of God, and any seeing of God is through the Word. The text itself—
no one sees the Father except through the Son—confirms this belief.

Remarking that prophets contemplate the "economies" of the Word's reca-pitulation, Irenaeus begins the unit with a series of interpretations of Old Tes-tament visions of God. Moses' vision (Exod 34:6-7) is interpreted on the literal level as indicating the invisibility of God, but at the same time on a prophetic level as indicating that "human beings shall see him in the last times, in the depth of a rock, that is, in his coming as a human being *[homo]*."[20] Elijah's experience of the still, small voice (1 Kings 19:11-12; Isa 42:3) is in-terpreted on the literal level as teaching the prophet to act more gently, and on the prophetic level as pointing out the Lord's coming as a human being *(homo),* following the Law, in a mild and tranquil way, neither breaking the bruised reed nor quenching the smoking flax.[21] Lest the force of these prophetic ex-periences prove deceptive, the final words in Ezekiel's account of the chariot of God are recalled: "This was the appearance of the likeness of the glory of God"(Ezek 2:1). Even here the prophet did not see God directly.

What Moses and Elijah and Ezekiel saw, Irenaeus writes in the beginning of *AH* IV. 20, 11, were likenesses of God's glory. How then did the prophets see God? The prophetic seeing, like the New Testament seeing, is through the Word. All the life-giving seeing of God, whether in the incarnate Word of the New Tes-tament or in the prophetic vision of the Old Testament, is through the agency of the one Word of God. That the one Word operates in both testaments to effect the seeing of God is a profound argument for the unity of the two testaments. So Irenaeus repeats "no one shall see God and live"; then he goes on to say: "His Word, as he himself willed it, and for the benefit of those who beheld, showed the Father's brightness, and explained his purposes . . . ; not in one figure, nor in one character, did he appear to those seeing him, but according to the reasons and effects aimed at in his dispensations . . ." (*AH* IV. 20, 11 [SC 100:660]). It is through the Word that the prophets see, according to the Father's will, and they see in multiple ways, depending on the purpose of the vision. Irenaeus then goes on to illustrate his point from the two apocalyptic books, Daniel in the Old Testament and Revelation in the New, making clear the multiple ways in which the Word enabled the seers to envision God and God's works, ways that correspond with the multiple working out of the "economies."[22]

The third unit of meaning focuses on John 1:18; Irenaeus builds toward it through his presentation of the series of Old Testament prophetic visions, all of which in his view receive fullness of meaning only in the light of the revealing Word. That same revealing Word enables diverse forms of vision, as Irenaeus suggests is clear from accounts in Daniel and Revelation. The *inclusio* is marked by two references to the economies of the Word that the prophets contemplate.

In addition to visions, there are the prefigurative deeds both of prophets and of patriarchs. Irenaeus examines prefigurative deeds of prophets in *AH* IV. 20, 12, interpreting each, as one might expect, in light of a word from the New Testament. Old Testament texts include Hosea marrying the prostitute (Hos 1:2) taken in light of the word of Paul on the unbelieving woman sanctified by her believing spouse (1 Cor 7:14); Hosea naming his children "the one who has not obtained mercy" and "not my people" (Hos 1:6-9) in the light of Paul's lines about how they who were not a people became a people, and they who had not obtained mercy did so (Rom 9:25-26); Moses marrying the Ethiopian, whom he made an Israelite (Exod 2:21) taken with Rom 11:17, referring to the grafting of a wild branch into the olive tree; Rahab hiding the spies (Josh 2:1), the spies taken as figures of Father, Son, and Holy Spirit, and she herself understood in light of Matt 21:31 about the tax collectors and prostitutes who go first into the kingdom of heaven.

Irenaeus examines the prefigurative deeds of the patriarchs in *AH* IV. 21, not by first turning to the Old Testament texts but rather by reviewing Paul's understanding of the significance of their acts. So, for example, Abraham's faith prefigures that of the believing Gentiles (Gal 3:5-9), and Rebecca's childbearing foretells the two peoples, slave and free (Rom 9:10-13).

In these sections Irenaeus reveals his understanding of the prophetic experience and illustrates another facet of his exegetical method. For him the prophet's experience is rooted in what alone gives meaning to all human life, the vision of God. In the case of the Old Testament prophet that vision may be very imperfect, but it is nonetheless real. In the vision the prophet "sees" more clearly some immediate aspect of daily life around which there is teaching, but the vision also is a "seeing" of an aspect of the divine economy still to unfold, and in this sense is predictive.

The deeds of prophets and patriarchs, Irenaeus writes, prefigure and predict coming things. They "accustom his heirs to obey God . . . and to presignify future things" (*AH* IV. 21, 3 [SC 100:684]). Because for those living after Christ's coming these deeds do signify what has now already come in Christ, the deeds of the giants of old are best interpreted in the light of the New Testament. One has the sense of prophets and patriarchs straining forward toward what is complete in Christ, while Christians, rooted in the New Testament, remain with an eye and an ear cocked toward them, the predecessors, whose experience enables Christians to appreciate the gift that is theirs.

The fulcrum around which the perspective shifts is the coming of Christ. Irenaeus remarks:

> In the same way that in the beginning through the first man we were all reduced to slavery, being indebted to death, so in the end through the most recent man, all, who from the beginning were his disciples, being purified and washed from death, have come into the life of God: for he who washed the feet of the disciples sanctified and led into purification the whole body (*AH* IV. 22, 1 [SC 100:686]).

Christ is the one whose life and death gives meaning to the Old Testament, and also the one whose present deeds announced another life to come for all those who believe in him.

PART 2, SECTION 1: SUMMARY

The prophets made known the coming of the Word in flesh, proclaiming in advance that God will be seen by humankind. What will be seen is not the immeasurable greatness of God but the saving presence of God made accessible as gift to humanity through divine love. The vision of God is granted differently at different stages of salvation history; the vision itself is a form of participation in God basic, even essential, to genuine human life.

Because prophets are used by the Spirit to make known the future in which humans will see God prophets themselves experience visions of God, and the visions can have multiple meanings. In addition, prophets as well as patriarchs perform prefigurative deeds. The prophets' experiences are best interpreted in light of these prefigured deeds, and so in light of the New Testament.

Part 2, Section 2: AH IV. 22, 2–25.
New Testament Interpretation of Old Testament Prophecies

Christ himself, according to Irenaeus, teaches how to value the Old Testament in the pericope about the fields white for the harvest when he mentions that one sows and another reaps. Irenaeus attributes the labor of sowing to the patriarchs and prophets, whose work made it possible for succeeding generations who were well instructed by the Scriptures to welcome readily the coming of Christ. It is from this vantage point that he interprets a cluster of New Testament passages, in each case explicitly applying an Old Testament prophecy to a New Testament event.[23] From Joseph the spouse of Mary through Paul the apostle, New Testament figures reap the harvest already sown by their predecessors in the faith. Such being the case the Gentiles who accepted the Word without previous knowledge of the Old Testament manifest a more generous faith than those who were first so instructed. All of this raises questions about how the Scriptures should be read, and it is to this topic that Irenaeus now turns. It will not be surprising to find that he connects the question of how the Scriptures are read to the question of who should interpret them.

Part 2, Section 3: AH IV 26–32. Exegesis of a Presbyter[24]

One who reads the Scriptures rightly, Irenaeus claims, will find a word about Christ who is the treasure hidden in the figures and parables of the Scriptures. And this "right way to read"? He writes:

> Therefore if anyone reads the Scriptures in the manner we are going to demonstrate—for so the Lord discussed with his disciples after his own resurrection from the dead, showing them from the Scriptures themselves that "it was necessary for Christ to suffer and then to enter into his glory" and "in his name the remission of sins will be preached in the whole world"—that one will be a perfect disciple, "like the master of a house who brings forth from his treasure new things and old" (AH IV. 26, 1 [SC 100:716]).

What is going to be taught is the kind of scriptural interpretation Christ taught the apostles after his resurrection. No higher warrant could be offered for the method, and it is probably not unintentional that the connection of the method with Christ's post-resurrection teaching parallels the setting of the Gnostic revelation dialogues.[25] Irenaeus himself referred to the Gnostic notion of Christ's post-resurrection teaching in *AH* I (*AH* I. 30, 14).

Having claimed the authority of post-resurrection teaching for his own position Irenaeus immediately places the handing on and interpretation of that teaching among the presbyters who are the successors of the apostles, noting that with the episcopal succession they received "the charism of certain truth."[26] He is critical of those presbyters who separate themselves from the succession (*AH* IV. 26, 2) as well as of a group he describes as hypocrites:

> those who are believed by many to be presbyters but serve their passions and do not set the fear of God as commander in their hearts, who drive the others into outrage and who are filled with pride because of their first places, who do evil in secret and say: "No one sees us"; they will be rejected by the Word (*AH* IV. 26, 3 [SC 100:720]).

Clearly not all presbyters are living up to a high standard according to which even secret misbehavior is reprobate. (This standard is not unreasonable if one thinks of ideals of the gospel and expects presbyters to be worthy proclaimers of that gospel; however, enforced uncritically it has led to separatism.) In any case Irenaeus's advice is plain. One ought to turn away from such presbyters and attach oneself to those who belong to the presbyteral order and who manifest healthy teaching and irreproachable conduct (*AH* IV. 26, 4 and 5).

This opening provides a striking setting for the exegesis of the presbyter forming the heart of this section, *AH* IV. 27–32. Irenaeus introduces this exegesis by testifying that "I heard this from a certain presbyter who heard it from the apostles whom he had seen,[27] and from their disciples." He uses the examples of David and Solomon to show that the one God does not approve of sin even in the case of illustrious persons. If this is the case for them, for whom Christ had not yet suffered, how much more can be expected of Christians over whom, Christ having died, death has no more dominion! (*AH* IV. 27, 1-2).

The sins of the whole people were recorded, the presbyter writes, both for the correction of believers and that these latter might know that the same God who was offended is the one who is offended by so-called believers today (*AH* IV. 27, 3–28, 2). Whether the story be the hardening of Pharaoh's heart, the despoiling of the Egyptians, or the case of Lot and his daughters, the presbyter reads the Old Testament not as evidence of an alien God but as evidence of the one same God who is the God of the New Testament (*AH* IV. 28, 3–32, 1).

By introducing this exegesis Irenaeus lays claim to the existence not only of a succession of authoritative teachers (as he did in *AH* III. 1–5), but also to the existence of an actual succession in scriptural interpretation among these teachers. The highly attested presbyteral teaching is thus truly an "ecclesial teaching," the burden of which, Irenaeus points out, is that the first testament had for its purpose to bring its recipients to the service of God and to prefigure the realities of the Church (*AH* IV. 32, 2).

PART 2, SECTION 3: SUMMARY

There is, according to Irenaeus, a "right reading" of the Scriptures that is the kind of interpretation Christ taught the disciples after his resurrection. This interpretation is handed on by the presbyters who are the successors of the apostles. Such presbyters cling to the succession and live piously both in public and in private. It is such presbyters to whom the believer ought to attach herself. Irenaeus crowns this teaching with examples he presents as an actual succession of scriptural interpretation handed on by the succession of authoritative teachers. For him there exist not only ecclesial authorities but an ecclesial exegesis.

Part 2, Section 4: *AH* IV. 33. Exegesis of a Spiritual Disciple

Irenaeus uses the verse "A truly spiritual disciple judges all, but is judged by no one" (1 Cor 2:15) to frame a second ecclesial exegesis, that of "a spiritual disciple." The verse occurs three times in *AH* IV. 33: at paragraphs 1, 7, and 15, dividing the chapter into three units in typical chiastic organization. The first unit (*AH* IV. 33, 1-7a) reviews those whom the spiritual disciple judges: the Gentiles, the Jews, the followers of Marcion and of Valentinus, the Ebionites, the docetists (although that term does not appear), false prophets, makers of schisms, and all those who are outside the Church. The last unit (*AH* IV. 33, 10-15) illustrates the spiritual disciple's exegesis of the word of the prophets.

The central unit (*AH* IV. 33, 7b-9) outlines the "true gnosis" held by the spiritual disciple, whose faith is triadic in form: it comprises faith in the all-powerful God, in the Son of God, Our Lord Jesus Christ (including his roles in creation and in the economy), and in the Spirit of God, who gives knowledge of the truth and teaches each generation the economies of Father and Son (*AH* IV. 33, 7b), Irenaeus remarks: "True gnosis[28] is the doctrine of the Apostles, and the ancient society[29] of the Church in the whole world, and the character of the body of Christ according to the successions of the *episkopoi* to whom they hand on the Church in each place" (*AH* IV. 33, 8 [SC 100:820]). He holds that this true gnosis comes to his day in the preservation of the Scriptures without addition or subtraction, and in the preservation of a "legitimate and diligent" reading of them, an explanation he further describes as "without danger and without blasphemy." Finally, true gnosis includes the gift of love, a gift more precious than knowledge. Because of its love for God, the Church everywhere and always sends a multitude of martyrs to the Father, a phenomenon he insists is supported only by the Church (*AH* IV. 33, 8-9).

Part 2, Section 5: *AH* IV. 34–35. Contra Marcionites and Valentinians

This last section of the second part of *AH* IV addresses first the Marcionites and then the Valentinians. To the followers of Marcion Irenaeus says:

> Read carefully the gospel which has been given to us by the Apostles and read the prophets carefully, and you will find the whole work and all the teaching and the whole passion of our Lord foretold in them. But if it enters your mind that you should say: "what new thing did the Lord do by his coming?" know that he brought every novelty in bringing himself, who had been announced (*AH* IV. 34, 1 [SC 100:846]).

The prophets were faithful servants, and what they said came to pass; Christ accomplished what they predicted, fulfilling the Law. There is no other God than the God of the prophets, to whom the Scriptures bear witness (*AH* IV. 34, 2-5).

To the Valentinians and "the rest of the falsely named Gnostics," Irenaeus writes: "We say that it is highly unreasonable to reduce the Father of the universe to such poverty as if he did not have his own instruments through which those things which are in the Pleroma might be purely announced" (*AH* IV. 35, 1 [SC 100:862]). After all, Irenaeus wants to know, whom would the Father fear so that he could not act freely without mingling himself with a fallen spirit? Would he fear saving too many because they would understand the truth? Was he incapable of preparing the foretellers of the Savior? Point by point he rejects his opponents' opinions, pointing to the disagreements among their leaders in the interpretation of single texts (*AH* IV. 35, 2-4). By contrast Irenaeus and his community have the words of the Lord as the "Rule of Truth" (that is, Rule of Faith), concerning which they all say the same thing, knowing one God who sent the prophets and, more recently, God's Son (*AH* IV. 35, 4).

PART 2, SUMMARY

Life worthy of the name depends on the vision of God, and the fullness of seeing (and so of life) comes through the incarnate Word. Irenaeus understands prophecy as a phenomenon rooted in vision and involving both a teaching and a predictive moment. God imparts the gift of vision differently in the two testaments. The Spirit enabled humans to see God in the Old Testament in a prophetic manner; in the New Testament the Son enables humans to see God in an adoptive manner; in the kingdom of heaven the Father will enable humans to see God in a paternal manner. Through it all the one God of both testaments works to reveal the divine plan for the human race. Thus there is continuity between the words and deeds of the prophets and the events and teaching of the New Testament.

The Scriptures are preserved and read by the Church, which introduces the question of "right reading." Within the Church it is the presbyters who preserve the authentic tradition of scriptural interpretation, a tradition based on the post-resurrection teaching of Jesus. Such a tradition founds true gnosis, which includes both the Scriptures and interpretation, as well as the great gift of charity, and is clearly not, in Irenaeus's opinion, the possession of either Marcionites or Valentinians.

NOTES

[1]Eusebius refers to the brethren in Gaul who, when dissension arose about the persons in the Montanist movement, "formulated their own judgement, pious and most orthodox, concerning them, subjoining various letters from the martyrs who had been consecrated among them, which letters while they were still in prison they had composed for the brethren in Asia and Phrygia, and also for Eleutherus, who was then bishop of the Romans, and so they were ambassadors for the sake of the peace of the churches" (*Hist. eccl.* 5.3.4 [Loeb 1] 443).

[2]Irenaeus mentions that Mark the magician and his women associates engaged in prophecy (*AH* I. 13, 3); he also refers to Mark's visionary experience (*AH* I. 14, 1). Hippolytus mentions Valentinus's vision in which he saw the Logos as a child (*Ref.* 6.42.2).

[3]Felicitas D. Goodman, "Visions," in Mircea Eliade, ed., *The Encyclopedia of Religion* 15 (New York: Macmillan, 1987) 282–288, reviews the phenomenon of visionary experience across religious traditions. Gerald T. Sheppard and William E. Herbrechtsmeier, "Prophecy: An Overview," in ibid. 12. 8–14 provide a similar study of prophecy, and Robert R. Wilson, "Biblical Prophecy," in ibid. 12. 14–23 reviews prophecy in the Bible.

[4]So Irenaeus recalls the text, which the NRSV renders "who has measured the waters in the hollow of his hand and marked off the heavens with a span . . .?"

[5]*AH* IV. 19, 2-3 (SC 100:618–622). In the ancient world the notion of the limits of human ability to speak of God was a commonplace, denoted by the "incomprehensibility" of God. In the Gnostic literature see, for example, *Ap. John* 2:33–4:10; *Tri. Trac.* 52:34–53.5; *Allogenes* 60:29–61:22. G. L. Prestige, *God in Patristic Thought* (2nd ed. London: S.P.C.K., 1969) 5–6, gives examples from the Pythagorean theory of numbers (Hippolytus, *Ref.* 1.2.6) as well as from Clement of Rome (*1 Clem.* 33:3) and Clement of Alexandria (*Strom.* 5.11; 71.5).

[6]*AH* IV. 20, 1 (SC 100:626), citing Gen 2:7 and 1:26.

[7]*Ipse a semetipso substantiam creaturarum et exemplum factorum et figuram in mundo ornamentorum accipiens* (*AH* IV. 20, 1 [SC 100:626]).

[8]*AH* IV. 20, 2 (SC 100:628), citing *Hermas, Man.* 1. See Philippi Bacq, *De l'ancienne à la nouvelle alliance selon S. Irénée* 166, n. 2 for discussion of Irenaeus's knowledge of the *Shepherd of Hermas;* what alone is certain is that Irenaeus knew the passage he cites here.

[9]Further texts cited: Mal 2:10; Eph 4:6; Matt 11:27; Acts 10:42; Rev 3:7; 5:3; 5:12; 5:9; John 1:14; 1 Pet 2:22; Col 1:18.

[10]*AH* IV. 20, 3 (SC 100:632). He also cites Prov 3:19-20.

[11]*AH* IV. 20, 5 (SC 100:638).

[12]Ibid. 638–640.

[13]Ysabel de Andía's work *(Homo vivens. Incorruptibilité et divinisation de l'homme selon Irénée de Lyon)* critically examines Irenaeus's notion of incorruptibility as human participation in the divine spirit, a participation that is itself the gift of God. See especially ch. 12, "Vision et incorruptibilité," 321–332.

[14]*AH* IV. 20, 5 (SC 100:640).

[15]*AH* III. 16, 6 (SC 211:312–314).

[16]*AH* IV. 20, 6 (SC 100:642), citing Deut 5:24.

[17]*Ego visionis multiplicavi et in manibus prophetarum assimilatus sum* (*AH* IV. 20, 6 [SC 100:644]). Here Irenaeus's citation differs from the received text. The NRSV reads: "I spoke to the prophets; it was I who multiplied visions, and through the prophets I will bring destruction."

[18]*AH* IV. 20, 7 (SC 100:648).

[19]*AH* IV. 20, 8 (SC 100:650).

[20]*AH* IV. 20, 9 (SC 100:654).

[21]*AH* IV. 20, 10 (SC 100:658).

[22]He cites Dan 3:92; 2:34-35; 7:13-14; Rev 1:12-16; 1:17; 1:17-18; 5:6-7; 19:11-16.

[23]Passages to which he refers are: Joseph's dream about Mary's pregnancy, in which the angel cites Isa 7:14 (Matt 1:18-24); Christ's use of Isa 61:1 to announce his own mission (Luke 4:16-23); Philip's explanation of Isa 53:7-8 to the eunuch (Acts 8:26-39); the early apostolic preaching that the prophecies have been fulfilled (Acts 4:18 and 21), and multiple instances from Paul.

[24]Known as the "Treatise of the Presbyter," this section has been the focus of much source-critical study, reviewed in Bacq's second appendix (*De l'ancienne à la nouvelle alliance,* 343–362). What must be kept in mind here, as elsewhere in *AH* IV, is that while Irenaeus did use sources he wove them into his own scheme, as Bacq has conclusively shown.

[25]Pheme Perkins, *The Gnostic Dialogue: The Early Church and the Crisis of Gnosticism* (New York: Paulist, 1980), notes: "Gnostic authors focus on the elements of commissioning in the canonical resurrection stories for the settings of their dialogues, since they claim that the preaching mandated by the Lord was gnosis, not the doctrine of their opponents" (p. 38); see all of ch. 3, "The Narrative Setting of the Gnostic Dialogue."

[26]See IV. 26, 2, quoted above at the end of Chapter Two. I agree with Bacq, *De l'ancienne à la nouvelle alliance,* who holds that in the context *charisma* refers simply to the doctrine of the apostles "received" by the bishops with succession in the episcopate. The apostolic origin of the doctrine also explains the certainty of the charism. See p. 202, n. 2, where Bacq also reviews the various positions on the meaning of this text to 1978.

J. D. Quinn, "Charisma veritatis certum. Irenaeus, Adversus haereses IV. 26, 1," *TS* 39 (1978) 520–525, notes that importance was attached to this text when its terminology was adopted by the First and Second Vatican Councils "to articulate their teaching on the episcopal and papal magisterium [DS 3071 and *Dei Verbum* no. 8]." But Quinn is aware that the language is that of Irenaeus's Latin translator, who supplied his later understanding of the presbyterate-episcopate as endowed through ordination with a prophetic gift that imparted certainty to the teaching of revelation. Such was not the position of Irenaeus.

[27]The Latin is *ab his qui Apostolos viderant.* Rousseau corrected the French here from the Armenian and the parallel text at IV. 32, 1, and it is this reading I follow, accepting his justification. See SC 100:263, note marked "p. 729, n. 1."

[28]The Greek is extant: *gnōsis alēthēs.* SC 100:818.

[29]The extant Greek is *to archaion tēs ekklēsias systēma.* SC 100:818.

CHAPTER NINE

Human Freedom

Adversus haereses IV. 36–41

Irenaeus depicted the Law and the Gospel as stages in a continuous and developing story of salvation in Part 1 of *AH* IV; he showed that human beings are created with a corresponding capacity for growth that enables them to respond to God's invitations and come to maturity. As he examined the work of prophecy in Part 2 he stressed the lifegiving role of the vision of God in salvation history. He introduced his understanding of the existence of an authoritative ecclesial reading of the Scriptures that both presents and protects the true gnosis. Such gnosis includes not only right teaching but right living, the life of charity.

In the discussion in Part 3 of the recognition of the one God of both covenants he will make apparent the role of human freedom in the divine economy. This shortest part of *AH* IV is unique in *Adversus haereses* because only here does Irenaeus give an extended treatment of the gospel parables. In *AH* I he showed his familiarity with various Gnostic interpretations of some of these parables.[1] Now he himself supplies an interpretation of a number of them, an interpretation that will of course be consonant with the Rule of Truth. His work falls into the expected three sections, the first treating one sole God as author of the vocations of Israel and of the Gentiles (*AH* IV. 36). The second section presents the Law of Liberty (*AH* IV. 37–39), and the third treats one sole God, judge of all (*AH* IV. 40–41, 3), with *AH* IV. 41, 4 forming the conclusion of the entire book.

One Sole God, Author of the Vocations of Israel and of Gentiles. *AH* IV. 36

In the preceding section Irenaeus had addressed the Marcionites and the Valentinians, who continue to color his thoughts for he begins this section by

reminding his readers that the prophets taught only one God, the Father of the
Lord (*contra* Marcion); they did not teach various substances, but one Creator
of this world, that same Father (*contra* Valentinus). He interprets the parables
allegorically, in a style close to what moderns might consider homiletical.
Much of what he writes here resonates with a certain familiarity to modern
ears, in part because of the very nature of the parable as a literary form designed to awaken engagement by disclosing the ambiguity within the familiar.[2]

After retelling the entire parable of the wicked tenants (Matt 21:33-43) Irenaeus focuses his interpretation on the master of the house (*paterfamilias*), the
father who, when the tenants refuse to give the fruit from his rented vineyard
to his servants, sends his own son. For Irenaeus the master and father is the
one God (*AH* IV. 36, 1). In addition, he identifies the vineyard with the human
race, the servants with the prophets, and the son with Christ[3] (*AH* IV. 36, 2).
He writes: "It is one and the same God the Father, who planted the vineyard,
who led out the people, who sent the prophets, who sent his Son, who gave
the vineyard to other farmers who will return fruit to him in its time" (*AH* IV.
36, 2 [SC 100:886]). This reading of the parable spans the sweep of salvation
history.

He next turns to the parable of the marriage of the king's son (Matt 22:1-
14) in which there is one king who, according to Irenaeus, is God. The servants rejected while delivering his invitation are the prophets. Irenaeus uses
words of Jeremiah (Jer 35:15 and 7:25-28) to ratify this interpretation, noting
that "the same God who called us from everywhere through the apostles formerly called the ancients through the prophets" (*AH* IV. 36, 5 [SC 100:900]).

The wedding garment, Irenaeus writes, is the works of justice with which
human beings must be clad if the Holy Spirit is to rest on them. It is, of course,
the one God who invites to the feast who also will decide who is to be cast
out; again words like 1 Cor 10:5 ("God was not pleased with most of them")
support this interpretation, as they do each further step in the reflection on the
parable (*AH* IV. 36, 6).

Irenaeus next turns to a series of parables, in each of which he simply focuses on one figure or aspect. Thus in the parable of the prodigal son (Luke
15:22-32) the key figure he identifies is the father who represents the one
Father, God; similarly, in the parable of the workers sent to the vineyard (Matt
20:1-16) Irenaeus points to the one master of the household who represents
the one God (*AH* IV. 36, 7). He further attests that the prayer of the tax collector merits praise over the prayer of the Pharisee (Luke 18:10-14) not because the tax collector prays to another God than the Pharisee but because the
tax collector prays to the same God with humility. In the parable of the two
sons sent to the vineyard (Matt 21:28-32) Irenaeus focuses again on the one
father. When he turns to the parable of the barren fig tree he reads the fruit as
the people: thus, reading "for three years I have come looking for fruit on this
fig tree, and still I find none" (NRSV Luke 13:7), he thinks of how the Lord,

using the prophets, searched in vain among the people for the fruit of justice
(*AH* IV. 36, 8).

The call of the people to justice is itself the work of the one God, a point
Irenaeus amplifies in the next text he chooses, Jesus' lament over Jerusalem:
"Jerusalem, Jerusalem, you who kill the prophets and stone those who are sent
to you, how often I longed to gather your children, as a hen her chicks under
her wings, and you were not willing! Behold your house is left to you, desolate" (Matt 23:37-38). He reads this text to show that the one God chose the
patriarchs, visited them in the prophets, and called "us" by his own coming.
The phrase, "I longed to gather your children . . . and you were not willing"
provides the connection to the significant consideration of human liberty Irenaeus offers in the middle section of this last part of *AH* IV.

PART 3, SECTION 1: SUMMARY

The parables can be interpreted to refer to the whole history of salvation,
Old as well as New Testament. God, the author of both covenants, is to be
understood in the parable of the wicked tenants as the master of the house who
sent his own son. The son is Christ, the vineyard is the human race, and the
servants are the prophets. Irenaeus interprets other parables in a similar way,
regularly insisting on the works of justice proper to those on whom the Holy
Spirit would rest.

The Law of Liberty. *AH* IV. 37-39[4]

Each of the gospel parables in the last group examined indicates the role of
human choice in response to God's invitation. This prepares the way for a consideration of human liberty, a consideration important in its own right and as
an element in Irenaeus's confrontation of the Gnostics.

In his world view the question of human liberty is related to the question of
the nature of God. Human freedom is a prerequisite if God is to be just in re-
warding and punishing human behavior. In this approach human freedom is
the correlate of divine justice. If, however, humans require freedom to come
to perfection that might imply that the Creator was unable to make humanity
perfect from the beginning. Human freedom could become, from this vantage
point, the correlate of a form of divine impotence.

Irenaeus has tended to stress the enslaved condition of humanity after the
sin of Adam and contrast with it the liberty won by Christ.[5] Redeemed humanity in the image of God is in the condition of needing to spend life growing toward the fullness of the likeness to God. This requires the exercise of
free choice in charity.

The Gnostics are both more and less optimistic about the human condition.
They are more optimistic in that they do not view the race as harmed by the

primal sin of an ancestor. Evil, for the Valentinians, is part of the structure of the universe, rooted in cosmic events outside human scope. Some, at least, of the human race are free and able to affect their own fate. Yet even for them gnosis does not obviate sin, which remains a possibility to be dreaded.

Continuing his exposition of right belief supported by right exegesis, Irenaeus addresses three topics in this section: why God made humanity free; why God did not make humanity perfect from the beginning; and the necessity for the knowledge of good and evil.

Why a Free Humanity? God made men and women free, in Irenaeus's view, because of divine justice. If humans were by nature good or evil it would be impossible to reward or punish them justly. He supports his case from the Scriptures, remarking that the prophets were sent to remind humankind of their duties, and citing numerous sayings of the Lord[6] and of Paul[7] to confirm human freedom (*AH* IV. 37, 1-4).

According to Irenaeus those good by nature and not by will could scarcely enjoy what they had not won (*AH* IV. 37, 6). This is why the Lord said "the kingdom of heaven has suffered violence, and the violent take it by force" (Matt 11:12) and why Paul describes himself as an athlete struggling for the crown (1 Cor 9:24-27). So Irenaeus remarks, "What comes to us freely is not loved in the same way as that which is found only with great difficulty" (*AH* IV. 37, 7 [SC 100:940]). God has arranged things to allow for human maturation, so that human beings might come to see and know God (*AH* IV. 37, 7).

Why a Perfectible Humanity? Some object that God could have saved an immense amount of bother by making all creatures perfect from the beginning. Irenaeus holds that they do not realize that the very meaning of "creature" excludes this possibility. By definition a creature receives its beginning of existence from another, and so is inferior to its maker. The newly created (in a view quite typical of Irenaeus) are like little infants who are not used to exercising perfect conduct (*AH* IV. 38, 1).

There is here a reflection of his teaching in the *Proof,* where the newly created Adam is described as "a little one," "a child" who had "his discretion still undeveloped, wherefore he was easily misled by the deceiver." Adam and Eve together are described as "childlike"[8] and embracing "with the innocence of childhood" (*Proof* 12 and 14). The point is not physical but moral childhood.

The Lord kept in view this aspect of the human condition in coming among humankind. Irenaeus writes: "He came to us not as he was able, but as we were capable of seeing him" (*AH* IV. 38, 1 [SC 100:946]). He came not in glory but as a human infant. And why? "So that, nourished as it were by the breast of his flesh and accustomed through such a lactation to eat and drink the Word of God, we might be able to contain in ourselves him who is the bread of immortality, who is the Spirit of the Father" (*AH* IV. 38, 1 [SC 100:946, 948]). The impotence was not on God's side but on the side of humanity, Irenaeus insists. God arranged things so that over the centuries humanity might mature into the ability to rest in submission to God. With that submission comes incorruptibility, and to remain in incorruptibility, says Irenaeus, is the very glory of the Uncreated One. It is this that the vision of God will procure (*AH* IV. 38, 3).[9]

If the true life of the human person is the vision of God, one must ask of what sort humans are that only the sight of the divine brings them alive. Even in this area it is important to keep in mind the difference between the Irenaean approach and that of the Gnostics. Theodotus, a disciple of Valentinus, illustrates the Gnostic approach in his list of key questions: "Who were we? What have we become? Where were we? Whither have we been cast? Whither do we hasten? From what have we been set free?"[10] Reflection oriented by such questions takes as its starting point the human dilemma. The accent is on the human being and the movement of thought is philosophical.

Not so for Irenaeus. His point of departure is the conviction that the human situation is under the Hand—or the Hands—of God. The movement of thought is theological. His exploration of the meaning of the human person employs the biblical language of image and likeness. For him, as for his predecessor Philo and his contemporary Clement of Alexandria,[11] the Son is the true image of God, and humans are the image of the Son (*Proof* 22). Underlying this is his conviction that image is according to nature (*AH* II. 7, 3).

In the Irenaean schema the image in the person is in the flesh. This sense of image corresponds to form, and form inheres only in matter. Both the Gnostics and the later Alexandrian Fathers hold that the image is in the spiritual part of the human being. Irenaeus rejects this possibility explicitly (*AH* II. 7, 6 [SC 294:176]. *AH* II. 19, 6 [SC 294:192–194]).[12]

Consequently the image of God in the human being must exist in matter, that is, in the flesh itself. Orbe points out that in this view the Incarnate Son is the positive image of the Father, the concrete and circumscribed form of the unformed God, positively reflecting God's personal attributes in the form of human flesh, adapted to the design of the economy of salvation. The human being, or its characteristic element, the *plasma,* is the positive image of the Word understood as the concrete soteriological expression of the economy he serves.[13] But image so understood retains its role as revealer of the archetype; the human as human and in its flesh is revelatory of the divine. The very Hands of God modeled human beings in the divine image (*AH* IV. 20, 1 [SC 100:626]). Since the divine is by definition formless, and image as form requires a material substratum, the archetype of the image of God in humankind is the incarnate Son (*Proof* 22; *ACW* 16, 61).[14] Once more Irenaeus has called attention to the centrality of the Incarnation. In fact, Jacques Fantino points out that "the Son reveals the human form through His incarnation, and He also manifests that the human person is indeed in His image."[15]

The image is thus present, and present as humanity's proper form. But this form calls for works appropriate to it. This points to another basic human endowment. As to be human is to bear the divine image in the flesh itself, so too to be human is to be free. This leads to consideration of the divine likeness. Fantino has demonstrated that Irenaeus utilizes two meanings of likeness, depending on whether in the fourth-century Latin likeness *(similitudo)* translates *homoiōtēs* or *homoiōsis*.[16] (For convenience here "similitude" will stand for *homoiōtēs,* and "likeness" for *homoiōsis*.)

Irenaeus identifies freedom of choice with the first sense of human likeness to God, the *homoiōtēs* (here "similitude") (*AH* IV. 37, 4 [SC 100:932]). Human beings are free to do good or evil, to believe or not, and even "to accept or to refuse that gift of the Spirit which is the likeness *(homoiōsis),* which alone is able to make [the human person] pursue conduct pleasing to God."[17] There is a similitude to God in human freedom. This strong affirmation of human liberty is at the same time a clear rejection of the Gnostic notion of predetermined natures (*AH* IV. 37, 2 [SC 100:922–924]).

The Need to Know Good and Evil. To be created free, and so perfectible, is the condition of humanity according to Irenaeus. Related to this is the need to know both good and evil that is built into the structure of the human person. Irenaeus uses the analogy of the senses to explain this. The tongue acquires the experience of sweet and bitter by tasting. The eye in seeing learns to distinguish white from black, and the ear distinguishes sounds by listening. So the spirit (here *mens*) acquires by experience of both the knowledge of good, and learns to obey God. By penitence the spirit rejects disobedience because it is bitter and evil. Having experienced the contrary of the sweet and good, never will one want to taste disobedience again. This may sound extraordinarily optimistic, but the outlining of ideals often does. In fact Irenaeus is insistent on discernment through experience of both good and evil. He states sharply: "If anyone repudiates the knowledge of both and the double sense of perception, secretly that one kills herself[18] as human" (*AH* IV. 39, 1 [SC 100:964]). One could hardly express it more strongly.

This is followed by a passionate series of questions:

> How will you be God who have not yet been made human? In what way will you be perfect, you who have scarcely been made? How will you be immortal, who in your mortal nature have not obeyed the Maker? It is necessary first to guard your human rank, then only will you become a participant in the glory of God. For you did not make God, but God made you (*AH* IV. 39, 2 [SC 100:964, 966]).

As Irenaeus explains it this requires that one offer a supple heart to the creating Artist who will reveal the docile person's hidden beauty and bring that one to completion. The resisting person's imperfection will be self-made (*AH* IV. 39, 2-3). God prepares for each the proper rewards (*AH* IV. 39, 4).

Both the image of the incarnate Son in the body and the similitude of the divine and paternal freedom belong to human beings as human beings. Yet something more is needed for the mortal to be conquered, for human corrupt-ibility to be swallowed up in incorruptibility, for human beings to receive the knowledge of good and evil, and so to become the image *and* likeness of God. Human beings are without the likeness. For Irenaeus the Spirit effects the like-ness. Until it is there the human person is not whole. Irenaeus develops this concept in *AH* V, to be met in due course.

PART 3, SECTION 2: SUMMARY

In the Irenaean view the human person carries the image of the Son of God in his or her flesh and bears the similitude to God in the gift of freedom. Being free, the human person is, as it were, morally incomplete but perfectible. Ex-periential knowledge of good and evil is an essential component enabling dis-cernment and choice of the good. (A little later he comes to the role of the likeness to God.) Such an understanding of human liberty is not just consis-tent with but even essential to the picture of God and the divine economy pre-sented thus far.

One Sole God, Judge of All. *AH* IV. 40-41, 3

The one God the Father, Irenaeus writes in this final section of *AH* IV, pre-pares good things for those who hope for communion with God and persevere in obedience to God. For the devil and the apostate angels that same God pre-pares eternal fire. That same one God will separate the human race on the day of judgment (Matt 25:32-46), like a shepherd separating the sheep from the goats, in the language of the parable (*AH* IV. 40, 1).

Irenaeus also introduces here the parable of the weeds and the wheat (Matt 13:40-43) and identifies the enemy who sowed the wheat with the serpent cursed by God, who is at enmity with the posterity of the woman (Gen 3:15). This enemy the Lord has recapitulated in himself, being born of a woman and trampling underfoot the head of the serpent (*AH* IV. 40, 2-3).

The serpent is the devil, for whom the eternal fire was prepared, and the weeds are the children of evil, both the devil and the children of evil being creatures of God (*AH* IV. 41, 1). If this is so, Irenaeus asks, in what sense are the "children of evil" children of the devil? He distinguishes two kinds of fil-iation. One is that of the child by nature, who is the work of the one who pro-duced that child. The other is the child by instruction, who has been formed by the word of the teacher. According to nature all human beings are children of God, for all were made by God. According to obedience and teaching only those who obey God and do God's will are God's children. Those who do not are the children and angels of the devil (*AH* IV. 41, 2).

In the human family parents deny their rebellious children who do not in-herit from their parents according to nature. So too with God, says Irenaeus.

Those who do not obey God are denied by God. They have ceased to be God's children and have no part in their heritage. This is what it means that the Lord calls those who trust in the devil and do his works "the angels of evil and children of the devil" (*AH* IV. 41, 3).

CHAPTER NINE: SUMMARY

Through exegesis Irenaeus has continued to show the oneness of salvation history and the correlations among the nature of God, the nature of salvation, and the nature of the human person. He reads the gospel parables to refer to the whole of salvation history, Old Testament as well as New. Figures like the giver of the wedding banquet represent the God who seeks out each human being across the ages, hoping—indeed, expecting—to find each one clad in the wedding garment of justice.

Nevertheless, humans are free to respond as they wish. In the Irenaean view the human person carries the image of the Son of God in the flesh and bears the similitude to God in the gift of freedom. Being free, the human person is, as it were, morally incomplete but perfectible, and meant to mature into the ability to rest in submission to God, which brings incorruptibility and a participation in the glory of God. Experiential knowledge of good and evil is, in this view, an essential component enabling discernment and choice of the good.

Continuing to use the parables, Irenaeus shows that God prepares good things for those who hope for communion with God and persevere in obedience to God. The devil, the apostate angels, and those who disobey God will be denied by God and have no part in their heritage.

NOTES

[1]Earlier we reviewed his account of Gnostic exegesis of the parables of the rich young man and the woman using yeast (*AH* I. 8, 3; ch. 2, n. 10 above), the woman cleaning her house, and the lost sheep (both in *AH* I. 8, 4; ch. 2, n. 11 above). Antonio Orbe, *Parábolas Evangélicas en San Ireneo* 1 and 2 (Madrid: Biblioteca de Autores Cristianos, 1972) has made readily available to Spanish readers the history of both orthodox and heterodox interpretations of this material prior to Irenaeus.

[2]It is significant that John R. Donahue, *The Gospel in Parable: Metaphor, Narrative, and Theology in the Synoptic Gospels* (Philadelphia: Fortress, 1988) begins with a chapter, "How Does a Parable Mean?" that treats the parable as text, as narrative, and as context.

[3]Orbe comments on Irenaeus's exegesis of the entire passage: *Parábolas* 1.243–270.

[4]Bacq devotes his fourth appendix (*De l'ancienne à la nouvelle alliance* 363–388) to this section, which contains a theology of the development of the human person that has been seen as a contradiction of the theology of recapitulation found in *AH* III. He reviews the history of the scholarship, evaluates it, and examines the theology with attention to all the related passages and concludes that the two theologies articulate well with each other. Contrasting *AH* IV. 38, 3 with *AH* III. 18, 1, he writes:

A notre sens, cette opposition est factice, car, d'un passage à l'autre, les points de vue sont différents. En III, 18, 1, en effet, Irénée parle de l'incarnation du Seigneur: c'est son humanité à lui qui est "à l'image et à la ressemblance de Dieu" et c'est donc en lui que nous retrouvons, comme en raccourci, ce que nous avions perdu en Adam. Encore faut-il que "l'image et la ressemblance" deviennent nôtres, et c'est précisément le pointe de vue adopté en IV, 38, 1: il s'agit là, non plus de l'humanité du Seigneur, mais de la multitude des hommes qui sont récapitulés en elle: nous ne sommes pas encore, nous devenons "à l'image et à la ressemblance de Dieu," et nous ne recevrons la plénitude de cette perfection qu'au terme de notre histoire. Mais cette croissance est rendue possible grâce à la récapitulation opérée par le Christ. La théologie de la croissance et de la récapitulation ne s'opposent donc pas l'une à l'autre. Elles abordent le même mystère selon deux points de vue différents et complémentaires (p. 381).

[5]See *AH* III. 18, 7.

[6]Irenaeus quotes Matt 5:16; Luke 21:34; 12:35-36, 43; 12:47; 6:46; 12:45-46; Matt 24:48-51.

[7]Irenaeus quotes 1 Cor 6:12; 10:23; Eph 4:25, 29; 5:4, 8; Rom 13:13; 1 Cor 6:11.

[8]By the fourth century this idea had entered Christian iconography. In the upper left register of a sarcophagus the Trinity (represented by three identical males depicted conventionally as philosophers) draws a tiny but physically mature Eve from the side of an equally miniature but physically mature and recumbent Adam. In the next panel, the temptation scene, the two are full size, presumably having "grown" through the knowledge of good and evil. Plate 268 (Christian Sarcophagus in the Lateran Museums, Rome) in André Grabar, *Christian Iconography: A Study of Its Origins*. The A. W. Mellon Lectures in the Fine Arts. Bollingen Series 35 (Princeton: Princeton University Press, 1961).

[9]Irenaeus is recalling the content of *AH* IV. 20, 5.

[10]Clement of Alexandria, *Exc. Theod.* 78.2.

[11]Philo, *Leg. all.* III. 96 and II. 4; Clement, *Prot.* 10, 98, 4 and *Strom.* VII. 3, 16, 5. See Antonio Orbe, *Antropología de San Ireneo* (Madrid: La Editorial Catolica, S.A., 1969) 107–110.

[12]See Jacques Fantino, *L'Homme image de Dieu chez saint Irénée de Lyon* (Paris: Cerf, 1986) 87–89.

[13]Orbe, *Antropología* 116.

[14]See Fantino, *L'Homme* 103–106.

[15]Fantino, *L'Homme* 105.

[16]Fantino, *L'Homme* 106–118, especially 117. In the course of developing his thesis Fantino surveys the history of the notion of image prior to Irenaeus (pp. 4–44), and reviews the notion of the Son, image of the Father, in second-century literature (pp. 145–151). He also includes three useful appendices listing the occurrences of *imago* and *similitudo* in Irenaeus, the citations of Irenaeus in patristic literature, and the interpretation of image and likeness after Irenaeus.

[17]Fantino, *L'Homme* 105.

[18]He has already defined the life of the human person as obedience to God and death as disobedience to God; see *AH* IV. 39, 1, lines 2–5 [SC 100:960].

Conclusion to Part Four

Adversus haereses IV. 41, 4

Irenaeus recognizes that he has written a long book, and wryly admits it. He explains that, as the Lord has used many words to proclaim the one Father, Creator of the world, so he himself has used many proofs to refute those held in numerous errors, so that by the very abundance of proof they may come to the truth and be saved. However, he knows he still has not touched the letters of Paul, and his presentation of the words of the Lord is incomplete. This will be the material of his next book. There today's readers will find what may be a surprising, and perhaps even a refreshing valuation of the flesh.

PART FIVE

The Salvation of the Flesh

Introduction to Part Five

"The fruit of the work of the Spirit is the salvation of the flesh."
(*AH* V. 12, 4)

The incarnation of Christ is pivotal throughout this fifth and final book of *Adversus haereses*. It serves as a hinge on which turns each step of the argument. The accent is on the flesh common to the Incarnate One and humanity; through Christ's assumption of flesh humanity is saved in all that it is, most especially in its flesh. The book's theme is thus the salvation of the flesh. The purpose of Part Four is to follow Irenaeus as he develops this theme, showing the centrality of the incarnation (and so of human flesh) to the completion of salvation history.

Characteristically, Irenaeus has organized the book in triptychs.[1] Discussions of the resurrection of the flesh, with attention to Paul's epistles (Chapter Ten) and of the events of the end time, based primarily on Daniel and Revelation (Chapter Twelve) frame the central part (Chapter Eleven) in which three events from the life of Christ capsulize the story of salvation while at the same time establishing the identity between the Father and the Creator. The organization thus follows a chiastic pattern. In addition, the exegesis continues the antignostic bent of the earlier books as the presence of the Valentinians continues to stimulate the writer's powers of rebuttal.

In fact not only their presence but the request of some other person in authority together with his own responsibility for "the word" seem to be holding Irenaeus to his task. Addressing the recipient of the work, he speaks of "obeying your order, since it is for the ministry of the word that we have been established" (*AH* V, Preface [SC 153:12]). Considering earlier references to the addressee,[2] it is likely that the obedience in question is in fact compliance with a request, perhaps made by another Church leader, rather than with a true command.[3] More interesting than the phrase "obeying your order" is the clause "it is for the ministry of the word that we have been established." The context demonstrates that the "we" is an editorial plural. Irenaeus affirms that he has responsibility for service of the word like the responsibility of the apostles (Acts 6:4). While scholars remain divided as to what this phrase reveals about Irenaeus's position in the Church,[4] the implications are consistent with what we have suggested earlier: he knows himself to have a leader's responsibility in the Church and he behaves as one holding the bishop's office, although he never ascribes that title to himself.[5]

It is a similar dedication to the word that he urges on his addressee and all his readers. So dedicated, they will be able to refute all the heretics with the help of faith and "following the sure and true Teacher, the Word of God, Jesus Christ our Lord, who on account of his immense love was made what we are, so that we might become what he is" (*AH* V, Preface [SC 153:14]). This final line of the preface sounds a dominant theme that recurs throughout *AH* and traces its own path in Christian history,[6] occurring in another form in Athanasius: "God became a human that humans might become God" (*De Inc.* 54).

NOTES

[1]For discussion of the plan of *AH* V, see SC 152:166–191.

[2]A comparison with the other prefaces shows that *AH* II, Preface, 1 is addressed simply to a friend, and *AH* I, Preface, 2–3, is addressed to a friend having some responsibility for teaching the word; the friend is described as having "ordered" Irenaeus to do this work in III, Preface, and in IV, Preface, 1. It is worth noting that the *Proof,* ch. 1 is addressed to a friend for whose spiritual well being and teaching Irenaeus shows concern.

[3]See Antonio Orbe, *Teología de San Ireneo. Comentario al Libro V del "Adversus haereses."* 3 vols. (Madrid: La Editorial Catolica, 1985–1988) 1. 41. Hereafter cited as Orbe, *Comentario,* with appropriate volume number.

[4]See Orbe, *Comentario* 1.42.

[5]See above, ch. 1, n. 7.

[6]Orbe, *Comentario* 1.50–51 lists the occurrences, traces the history of the concept, and comments on the meaning of the text with relevant bibliography.

CHAPTER TEN

The Resurrection of the Flesh

Adversus haereses V. 1–14

Carrying forward the theme of incarnation, Irenaeus opens his argument with the thesis that the resurrection of the flesh is a consequence of the incarnation (*AH* V. 1, 1–V. 2, 3). To those who consider that fleshly weakness precludes such a resurrection he offers his second argument, that resurrection of the flesh is the work of the power of God (*AH* V. 3, 1–V. 5, 2). Aware of the key role of Paul in the understanding of the resurrection, he turns in a third section (*AH* V. 6, 1–V. 8, 3) to exegesis of Pauline texts on the resurrection, with section four (*AH* V. 9, 1–V. 14, 4) reserved for the important text "flesh and blood cannot inherit the kingdom of God" (1 Cor 15:50).

Resurrection of the Flesh Postulated by Incarnation. *AH* V. 1, 1–V. 2, 3

Casting his argument in terms of teaching and learning, Irenaeus moves from creation to communion in new creation through growth that includes resurrection. He begins with limpid clarity: "We would not have been able to know the things of God unless our Teacher, being the Word, were made one of us" (*AH* V. 1, 1 [SC 153:16]). Irenaeus holds that there are two reasons for the incarnation: from God's side only the Word can reveal the Father; from the side of humankind they come to know only when they see their Teacher and hear his voice. It is in imitating his actions and carrying out his words that humans have communion with him. From him human beings receive growth in likeness to him. They had been alienated from their God but the Word ransomed them by his blood. Thus Irenaeus writes:

> Therefore, the Lord having redeemed us by his blood, and given his soul for our
> soul and his flesh for our flesh, and poured out the Spirit of the Father for the

union and communion of God and humanity, having brought God down to humankind through the Spirit while having raised humankind to God through his own incarnation, and firmly and truly in his coming having given us incorruptibility through communion with him, all the doctrines of the heretics perish (*AH* V. 1, 1 [SC 153:20]).

As this dense but beautiful text illustrates, Irenaeus views the saving work of Christ as including not only his death but also the incarnation itself, which in itself elevated the human race and, making it one with him, destined the race for incorruptibility. Irenaeus then summarizes the arguments against the incarnation made by all those who refuse to accept that the Son entered flesh as one of them. The very reality of the incarnation, he holds, disproves all arguments against it (*AH* V. 1, 2–2, 2).

Earlier Irenaeus pointed to the link the incarnation establishes between the creative Word and the things of creation, a link that makes Eucharist possible (*AH* IV. 18, 4). He returns to that argument, turning it now so as to say that unless flesh were saved the bread and wine would not be a communion in Christ's body and blood (*AH* V. 2, 2). But if human flesh is nourished by such a gift, the Gnostic teaching that flesh is incapable of the gift of God that is eternal life is overturned. Irenaeus invokes several analogies: just as grain, buried, will rise multiplied by God's Spirit, and just as bread and wine, touched by God's Word, become Eucharist, so human beings, nourished by the Eucharist and hidden in the ground, will rise for the glory of God (*AH* V. 2, 3, amplifying *AH* IV. 18, 5). So the incarnation makes the Eucharist possible, and participation in the Eucharist prepares human beings for resurrection.

SECTION 1: SUMMARY

In this section Irenaeus shows that the incarnation is a means of the divine revelation and that it serves to join humanity to God. He sees that if one grants the literal truth of the incarnation one cannot simultaneously accept any Gnostic teaching that assigns negative value to the flesh, whether belonging to Christ or to other human beings. Finally, because the incarnation makes Eucharist possible it enables humanity to be nourished on the body and blood of Christ and so to be capable of incorruptibility. The incarnation thus makes resurrection possible for human beings.

Resurrection of the Flesh, Work of the Power of God. *AH* V. 3, 1–V. 5, 2

Human flesh is weak by nature. Paul, who suffered from "a thorn in the flesh" and asked God to remove it, was told: "My grace is sufficient for you, for power is made perfect in weakness" (2 Cor 12:7-9). Irenaeus remarks that for a person to experience his or her own weakness is by no means evil; rather such experience is good because it teaches knowledge of one's own nature.

How else can one learn that God is by nature powerful while humans are by nature weak if not by experiencing both? There is more than an echo of Irenaeus's conviction of the importance of experiencing both good and evil, which we saw in *AH* IV. 39. The experience of both, he holds, produces true knowledge of God and of the human person and increases one's love for God. In turn God's power will give more abundant glory to those who love God more (*AH* V. 3, 1).

God's power is not understood by those who are fixed on the weakness of the flesh. The latter do not consider that the one who shaped the flesh and gave it life in the first place also has the power to raise it up. Irenaeus explains that whatever can participate in the creative wisdom of God can also share in the power of God (*AH* V. 3, 2). He says: "Flesh is therefore not excluded from the wisdom and the power of God; for God's power which offers life is completed in weakness, that is in flesh" (*AH* V. 3, 3 [SC 153:48]). Irenaeus goes on to argue that if temporal life makes human bodily members living, how much more powerful will eternal life be! (*AH* V. 3, 3).

By contrast, Irenaeus writes, those who imagine another Father than the Creator make him weak, useless, and negligent since they say human bodies are unable to be vivified by him. That bodies are capable of life is evident; if they live by another than by the Father, the one by whom they live is the more powerful (*AH* V. 4, 1 and 2).

The heretics read the Scriptures, Irenaeus writes, and they know that the Scriptures illustrate the vivifying power of God. Irenaeus points to the ancients who lived long lives (Pss 23:6; 91:16 [LXX 22:6; 90:16]), to Enoch who was translated in his body (Gen 5:24), and to Elijah who was taken up in his body (2 Kings 2:11). The very Hands of God that had modeled these bodies took them up, according to the teaching of "the presbyters," to the place of Paradise from which Adam had been expelled. There, the presbyters say, those who have been taken up will remain until the final consummation (*AH* V. 5, 1).

The Hand of God[1] accomplished equally astonishing things in the flesh of Jonah (Jonah 1–2) and of the three young men in the fiery furnace (Daniel 3). Irenaeus explains that this is because God does not submit to creatures, but creatures to God. Unbelievers, he claims, will not reduce to nothing the fidelity of God (*AH* V. 5, 2).

SECTION 2: SUMMARY

In this section Irenaeus affirms that human flesh is weak by nature while God is powerful; experiential knowledge of both these givens opens human beings to the truth of their own nature and God's, and nurtures their love of God. Those who focus too narrowly on the weakness of human flesh overlook the strength of the one who shaped that flesh and first gave it life. The Scriptures themselves give witness to the vivifying power of God.

Pauline Texts on the Resurrection of the Flesh. *AH* V. 6, 1–V. 8, 3

Irenaeus has argued that the incarnation makes resurrection possible for human beings, and that the vivifying power of God can effect the resurrection of weak human flesh. He now begins his interpretation of Pauline texts on the resurrection of the flesh.

Irenaeus quotes Paul as saying "we speak wisdom among the perfect" (1 Cor 2:6). He notes that in Paul "the perfect" designates those who have received the Spirit of God together with the gift of tongues, like those whom Irenaeus knows in whom the gift of tongues is part of the prophetic charism. Such ones Paul calls "spiritual." The Spirit, Irenaeus emphasizes, does not suppress the flesh. Rather, he writes, "when the Spirit mingling with the soul, is united to the modeled work [*plasmati,* that is, the flesh] the human being is made spiritual and perfect on account of the effusion of the Spirit, and this is the one who is made according to the image and likeness of God" (*AH* V. 6, 1 [SC 153:76]). By contrast, where the Spirit is not present that one remains physical and carnal, "being imperfect, having the image in the modeled work [that is, the flesh], but not assuming the likeness through the Spirit" (*AH* V. 6, 1 [SC 153:76]).

It is, then, in this section that Irenaeus returns to the notion of the "likeness" of God. He holds that the Spirit effects the likeness in the human person. Until the likeness is there, the human person is not whole. In language that echoes Paul he identifies the person without the likeness as not "perfect." Perfection requires the likeness, and the likeness is connected with the Spirit. According to Irenaeus human perfection is not proper to the flesh alone, or to the soul alone, or to the Spirit alone. Rather, as 1 Thess 5:23 shows, "it is the mingling and union of all of these that effects the perfect human being" (*AH* V. 6, 1 [SC 153:78]).

The question is whether Irenaeus intends Spirit or spirit. In some places Irenaeus speaks as if the spirit in human composition is in fact the Spirit of God.[2] The perfect then are those who possess the Spirit. For example, he speaks of human beings receiving "a certain portion of His Spirit, for our perfection and preparation for incorruption, little by little accustoming us to choose and to bear God" (*AH* V. 8, 1 [SC 153:92]). In other places there seems to be a clear distinction between Spirit and the human spirit. He refers to the idea that "our substance, that is, the union of flesh and spirit, receiving the Spirit of God, makes up the spiritual person" (*AH* V. 8, 2 [SC 153:96]). What are we to make of his teaching about the "spirit" in the human person?

IRENAEUS ON "SPIRIT" IN THE HUMAN PERSON

In the overall context of the first part of *AH* V Irenaeus is presenting Paul's teaching on resurrection. He intends to affirm the value of the flesh and is concerned to retain the Pauline tripartite division of the human person, cited by him from 1 Thess 5:23. His analysis of other Pauline passages (Eph 1:13; 2 Cor 5:4; Romans 8—all in *AH* V. 8, 1) convinces him that the Spirit dwelling with human beings is the pledge of salvation that renders them spiritual in the present time.

A look ahead to *AH* V. 9 will show that Irenaeus repeats that the complete human being is composed of three things: flesh, soul, and spirit. He then explains that it is the role of the Spirit to save and form the person. The *flesh* (not the soul) is saved and formed. The soul is "between these two." When the soul follows the Spirit it is raised up by it; when it sympathizes with the flesh it falls into earthly desires (*AH* V. 9, 1 [SC 153:106–108]). In Irenaeus's opinion the presence of the Spirit brings true life to the flesh. The capacity of the soul to follow either Spirit or flesh inserts a dynamism into the human constitution, allowing the possibility of growing unto God (*AH* V. 9, 3 [SC 153:112–114]). The importance of capacity for growth is a fundamental Irenaean insight.[3]

This raises the issue of the relation between true life as described here and fullness of life as described in the analysis of *AH* IV. 20. Irenaeus himself does not explicitly relate the two pictures he draws, but the relation of the two to one another is readily discernible. The picture portrayed in *AH* IV. 20 depicts, first of all, the movement of the economy of salvation. The one God draws all human beings to Godself. The one same God creates all through God's two Hands, the Word and Wisdom, the Son and Spirit. The same one God reveals Godself to humankind through the Son that they might live. That revelation began in the Old Testament, prophetically in the Spirit. It comes to another visibility in the New Testament in the Son. It will be completed in the resurrection (and so in the millennial kingdom)[4] when humans are in God and receive of the divine splendor. That gradual coming to the vision of God is the call of the race.

It is also the call of the individual person. Each human being is called to fullness of life in the vision of God. The broad lines of the movement for each are traced in a parallel fashion. One begins bearing God's image in his or her very physicality. I would suggest that prior to conversion to Christ one sees God "prophetically" along the lines of the Old Testament seeing described by Irenaeus. During the postconversion earthly life one sees God "adoptively," as Irenaeus has shown us. On a daily basis this works out as the Irenaean anthropology describes it in *AH* IV. 37–39 and V. 6, 1–V. 9, 3. Individuals sense the struggle between the "flesh" and the "spirit." Through experience and under the guidance of the Spirit they learn to "choose life." It is God's dearest hope that ultimately in the resurrection each will come to the "paternal vision," the face-to-face seeing of glory. Then truly each one will be fully alive to the glory of God.[5]

AH V. 9, 1-14, 4. Interpretation of 1 Cor 15:50:
"Flesh and blood cannot inherit the kingdom of God."

Two second-century exegetical traditions clash over the interpretation of this text: the Gnostic[6] and the antignostic[7] readings of Paul. Irenaeus says that all the heretics use this text to show that "the thing modeled by God" cannot be saved. In her review of Gnostic exegesis of Paul, Elaine Pagels confirms that the Valentinians consider this verse to be "decisive evidence against the Church's claim of bodily resurrection."[8]

Irenaeus's exegesis begins with a description of the "perfect" human being and develops an understanding of the relationship between flesh and spirit. The heretics insist that flesh cannot enter the kingdom, he claims, because they do not understand that three things constitute a perfect human being: the Spirit, who saves and forms; the flesh, which is saved and formed; and the soul, which is between these two. One who does not have the lifegiving Spirit is truly dead. By implication it is the one without that Spirit who really cannot enter the kingdom (AH V. 9, 1). But, Irenaeus teaches, those who fear God and believe in the coming of the Son establish the Spirit in their hearts; these are justly called "spiritual." The Lord himself witnesses that "the flesh is weak" but "the Spirit is willing" (Matt 26:41). According to Irenaeus, when Spirit mingles with flesh the more powerful absorbs the weaker. A person who experiences this mingling is no longer carnal but spiritual, thanks to the communion in the Spirit, that very communion that enabled the martyrs to despise death. This kind of union of flesh and Spirit makes the living human being: living by participation in the Spirit, a human being by virtue of the flesh (AH V. 9, 2).

Without the Spirit the flesh is dead; as Paul says, "As was the earthly one, so also are the earthly," in Rufinus's Latin, *"qualis terrenus, talis et terreni"* (AH V. 9, 3 [SC 153:112], quoting 1 Cor 15:48). With the Spirit the flesh *as* flesh becomes like Spirit; Paul also says, "Just as we have borne the image of the earthly one, we shall also bear the image of the heavenly one" (1 Cor 15:49). The earthly one, Irenaeus writes, is the modeled work, the *plasma;* the heavenly one is the Spirit. With the Spirit we are able "to walk in newness of life" (Rom 6:4). So the apostle urges Christians to conserve the Spirit of God by faith and a chaste life lest losing the Spirit they lose the kingdom of heaven. It is in this sense, Irenaeus writes, that flesh *alone* is not able to inherit the kingdom of God (AH V. 9, 3).

Flesh may not inherit, he says, but it is inherited as the Lord taught: "Blessed are the meek, for they will possess the earth as an inheritance" (Matt 5:5). Irenaeus writes: "In the kingdom the earth, from which comes the substance of our flesh, will be possessed as an inheritance" (AH V. 9, 4 [SC 153:116]). Reflecting the marriage customs of his day, Irenaeus compares the flesh to the woman, who does not "espouse" a husband but "is espoused" when her husband comes and takes her to his home. So flesh cannot possess the kingdom as an inheritance, but can be possessed in the kingdom by the Spirit. If the Word does not inhabit a person, and if the Spirit of the Father does not come to him or her, if a person leads a vain life, then that person will be nothing but flesh and blood and cannot inherit the kingdom of heaven. This, Irenaeus says, is what Paul means by "flesh and blood cannot inherit the kingdom of God" (*AH* V. 9, 4).

Irenaeus interprets the parable of the wild olive branch grafted onto the olive tree (Rom 11:17-24) to illustrate what happens when humans, like the tree, receive the graft of the word of God, and like the branch do not stop being what they are, but bear better fruit. By contrast, a wild tree that rejects a graft is useless and burned. So the human who does not receive the graft of the Spirit remains unable to inherit the kingdom of God (*AH* V. 10, 1-2). To this he adds an entire tissue of texts (1 Cor 15:50, 53; Rom 8:8-13) focused on what it means to live not in the flesh, but in the Spirit (*AH* V. 10, 3).

Irenaeus clarifies how life in the flesh differs from life in the Spirit, following Paul (Gal 5:19-23) who also teaches (1 Cor 6:9-11) that the unjust will not inherit the kingdom of God. One may perform the works of the flesh or the works of the Spirit. The baptized are expected to use their bodies to accomplish the works of the Spirit. The baptismal bath does not wash away the flesh or the image in the flesh; what it removes is the former life of vanity (*AH* V. 11, 1-2).

The flesh is capable of both corruptibility and incorruptibility, of death and of life, although only of one of these at a time (*AH* V. 12, 1). To understand the ramifications of life for God one must distinguish between the "breath of life" (Gen 2:7) that makes a person psychic and the "vivifying Spirit" (1 Cor 15:45) that makes the person spiritual. Not everyone has the Spirit, but those who receive it find life (*AH* V. 12, 2). Paul teaches: "Kill in your members whatever is earthly: fornication, impurity, passion, evil desire, and greed (which is idolatry)" (Col 3:5). Irenaeus rightly maintains that it is not the body but its evil acts that are to be killed (*AH* V. 12, 3). He points out that Paul also says: "to live in the flesh is the fruit of a work" (Phil 1:22),[9] indicating that the apostle does not contemn the flesh itself. In his opinion the Pauline text means "the fruit of the work of the Spirit is the salvation of the flesh" (*AH* V. 12, 4 [SC 153:154]). Christ's healing miracles (*AH* V. 12, 6) and his resurrection miracles (*AH* V. 13, 1) are further evidence that flesh will be saved.

The heretical reading of "flesh and blood will not enter the kingdom of heaven," Irenaeus holds, not only misunderstands Paul (*AH* V. 13, 2) but also overlooks the very next lines of the same epistle which he gives as:

> It is necessary that the corruptible must clothe itself with immortality. For when this mortal dons immortality, then will be accomplished the word that is written: "Death is absorbed in victory. Death, where is your sting? Death, where is your victory?" (*AH* V. 13, 3 [SC 153:170], quoting 1 Cor 15:53-55).

Irenaeus comments that death is conquered when flesh escapes its power; he cites a number of Pauline texts in the same vein,[10] stressing that 1 Cor 15:50

must be read in agreement with all of Paul's writings, including especially the next verses of 1 Corinthians 15 (*AH* V. 13, 3-5).

Finally, Irenaeus notes a language clue to Paul's meaning. Paul uses the very same words, "flesh" and "blood," that occur in the verse "flesh and blood cannot inherit the kingdom of heaven" when he speaks of our Lord Jesus Christ. Paul does this, Irenaeus claims, to emphasize the Lord's humanity and the salvation of human flesh. As he puts it: "If flesh were not to be saved, the Word of God would not have been made flesh, and if account were not required of the blood of the just, the Lord would not have had blood" (*AH* V. 14, 1 [SC 153:182]). But the Lord does recapitulate in himself all those just whose blood was shed from the beginning; an account is required because in their flesh and blood they are saved. The Lord came through this economy, in the substance of human flesh and blood, recapitulating the race in himself to save humans in their entirety (*AH* V. 14, 2). With this Irenaeus concludes his exegesis of "flesh and blood cannot inherit the kingdom of heaven."

TWO EXEGETICAL TRADITIONS

The major difference between Irenaeus's exegesis and the Valentinians' is that Irenaeus sees flesh, soul, and Spirit as components of one human being; the dynamic interplay of these components, possible because of the godlike freedom of the human, eventuates in entry into the kingdom or loss of it. By contrast, the exegesis of the Valentinians known to Irenaeus understands fleshly, psychic, and pneumatic as denoting three kinds of persons. The dynamism has to do with what "seed" was sown, and so what is raised up, as well as with the psychics putting off body and soul. Pagels summarizes Valentinian comment on this passage:

> The gnostics claim that it was the psychic apostles—whose understanding was (and remained) merely "literalistic"—who proclaimed Christ's bodily resurrection. Paul alone, they claim, as "apostle of the resurrection," taught the pneumatic doctrine of resurrection: that "flesh and blood cannot inherit the kingdom of God, nor can corruption inherit incorruption." Nothing that is psychic, nothing that comes from the demiurge, can enter into the kingdom of God the Father. Instead, "what is corruptible must put on incorruption" and "what is mortal must put on immortality" (1 Cor 15:53). Heracleon cites this verse to show that the psychic, "corruptible" in body and "mortal" in soul (cf. Matt 10:28), can only receive salvation after he has "put off" the psychic "garments" of body and soul.[11]

There are clearly two quite different second-century traditions of interpretation of the Pauline material. This section of Irenaeus represents a stage in the struggle for dominance of the antignostic tradition familiar today to many in the usual interpretation of the Christian Church.

Irenaeus closes the section as well as Part 1 of *AH* V with an exhortation. He urges his "most beloved friend" who has been "ransomed by the flesh of our Lord and acquired by his blood" to hold to the fleshly coming of the Son of God, to confess him God and cling to his humanity, and to utilize the proofs from the Scriptures so as to overthrow easily all the heretical opinions (*AH* V. 14, 4).

CHAPTER TEN: SUMMARY

The salvation of the flesh is the predominant theme of *AH* V. The nature of "saved flesh," in Irenaeus's judgment, will be to rise, so Irenaeus has opened Part 1 of *AH* V with a consideration of the resurrection of the flesh. In *AH* V. 1, 1–V. 2, 3 Irenaeus shows that the resurrection is itself in direct relation to the incarnation. In fact his first line of argument is that the resurrection of the flesh is a consequence of the incarnation. He reasons that the incarnation is a means of divine revelation and serves to join humankind to God. Because the incarnation makes Eucharist possible it enables humans to be nourished on the body and blood of Christ and so to be capable of incorruptibility. In this way the incarnation makes resurrection possible for human beings.

In *AH* V. 3, 1–V. 5, 2 Irenaeus suggested that the resurrection of the flesh is a work of the power of God. Those who focus too narrowly on the weakness of human flesh overlook the strength of the one who shaped that flesh and gave it life. In *AH* V. 6, 1–V. 8, 3 Irenaeus turns to Pauline texts on the resurrection of the flesh. Here he examines the role of the spirit in the human person. In his reading of Paul the perfect are those who have received the Spirit of God. It is the Spirit who effects the likeness of God (as distinct from the image). In his opinion the presence of the Spirit brings true life to the flesh. The capacity of the soul to follow either Spirit or flesh, or—in the language Irenaeus used in *AH* IV, the gift of freedom of choice that is the person's similitude to God—inserts a dynamism into the human constitution, allowing the possibility of growing unto God. Finally Irenaeus devotes Section 4 to an interpretation of the text "flesh and blood cannot enter the kingdom of heaven," relating this text to the understanding of the human person and the dynamism of salvation presented in the preceding sections.

NOTES

[1]The free movement between "Hands of God" in *AH* V. 5, 1 and "Hand of God" in *AH* V. 5, 2 is typical; *AH* IV. 19, 2-3 treats of the grandeur of the Hand of God while *AH* IV. 20, 1 speaks of God with whom are always God's Hands, the Word and the Wisdom, the Son and the Spirit.

[2]Orbe, *Comentario* 1, repeating his earlier opinion (*Antropología* 128–131), strongly affirms the Spirit reading on 274–275: "La identidad entre el *spiritus Dei* y el *spiritus hominis* la indica suficientemente el proprio Santo en V 6, 1, 23s: 'sed spiritus hominis aut spiritus Dei'; ibid., 52 ss: 'Perfecti igitur qui et *spiritum in se* perseverantem *habent Dei* et animas et corpora sine querela servaverint.'" He sees no need for the arguments Rousseau presents

for the Spirit reading in a series of notes on the text of *AH* V. 6, 1 through 7, 1 in SC 152:226–237.

[3]It is helpful to recall here his analysis of why humans were not made perfect from the beginning (*AH* IV. 38, 1-4 [SC 100:942–960]) and his comments on the "increase and multiply" of Gen 1:28 (*AH* IV. 11, 1-2 [SC 100:496–502]).

[4]See below, p. 165 and pp. 167–168. For further commentary see Orbe, "Visión del Padre e incorruptela según san Ireneo," *Gr.* 64 (1983) 199–240.

[5]Such a movement contains the outlines for a spirituality; my "Irenaeus: At the Heart of Life, Glory," in Annice Callahan, ed., *Spiritualities of the Heart: Approaches to Personal Wholeness in Christian Tradition* (New York: Paulist, 1990) 11–22, sketches the Irenaean spirituality.

[6]Michel Desjardins (*Sin in Valentinianism* [Atlanta, Ga.: Scholars, 1990] 124–126) makes the case for a Gnostic reading of the text. Valentinian use of Paul is evident in such Nag Hammadi documents as *Gos. Truth, Treat. Res., Tri. Trac., Pr. Paul, Gos. Phil.,* and *Interp. Know.,* which are among the sources used by Elaine Pagels in *The Gnostic Paul: Gnostic Exegesis of the Pauline Letters* (Philadelphia: Fortress, 1975).

[7]Antignostic readings include the Pastoral Letters, the *Adversus haereses* of Irenaeus, and the *Adversus Marcionem* and *Adversus Valentinianos* of Tertullian.

[8]Pagels, *The Gnostic Paul* 85. Her chapter on Valentinian exegesis of 1 Corinthians (pp. 53–94) offers a fine context for this section of *AH;* its detailed textual work defies summary.

[9]According to Rousseau both the *Papyrus of Iena* and the Armenian support this version of the Philippians text (SC 152:258, note marked "p. 155, n. 1").

[10]Here I paraphrase the content on which Irenaeus comments and give the texts he cites: Christ will change our lowly body to be like his glorious body (Phil 3:20-21); what is mortal will be swallowed up with life (2 Cor 5:4-5); you were bought with a price, so glorify God with your body (1 Cor 6:20); we carry in our body the death of Jesus so the life of Jesus may be manifested there (2 Cor 4:10-11); you are a letter from Christ written by the Spirit on human hearts (2 Cor 3:3); that I may become like Christ in his death (Phil 3:10-11); there is no resurrection if Christ has not been raised—but he has, the first fruits of those who have died (1 Cor 15:13-21).

[11]Pagels, *The Gnostic Paul,* 85–86.

CHAPTER ELEVEN

The Enfleshed Word, Crucified, En-Spirits Creation

Adversus haereses V.15–24

The same friend addressed in *AH* V. 14, 4, reading on, will learn that three events from Christ's life summarize the story of salvation while establishing the identity of the Father and the Creator. The God in question is the one of whom the prophets spoke, and Irenaeus pauses to call this to mind before continuing his development.

He begins the middle part of *AH* V with a "hinge" section, *AH* V. 15, 1. In the previous book he showed the continuity between the Old and the New Testaments, emphasizing the role of prophecy in both its teaching and its predictive moments, with particular attention to how the Old Testament prepared for the coming of Christ. The Scriptures, he claimed, show that the story of salvation is one, from Adam through Christ. The form salvation takes, he explained, is appropriate to the kind of beings humans are, the one same God having created them and planned for their salvation.

In the opening part of *AH* V Irenaeus has shown that according to Paul resurrection of the flesh appropriately completes human salvation. Now, as he moves on to another topic, Irenaeus pauses to show that Paul's resurrection teaching reflects the teaching of the prophets. He cites two passages from Isaiah[1] and an extensive extract from the Ezekiel passage about raising up the dry bones (Ezek 37:1-10, 12-14). He comments that these texts show the Creator God does three things with respect to our bodies:[2] he vivifies them, he will raise them, and he will give them incorruptibility. If this is what the Creator God does, then the Creator is the only God, and the good Father, contra the heretics (*AH* V. 15, 1). The passage thus serves hinge-like functions: it connects the content of *AH* IV with that of *AH* V and it also joins the teaching on the resurrection of *AH* V Part One (discussed in Chapter Ten) to the teaching on the Creator God of *AH* V Part Two (discussed in this chapter).

Three events from the life of Christ serve to capsulize the story of salvation while at the same time establishing the identity between the Father and the Creator. Section 1 (*AH* V. 15, 2–V. 16, 2) examining the healing of the man born blind (and reflecting how the creative Word modeled humanity from the earth) stands with Section 3 (*AH* V. 21, 1–V. 24, 4) considering the temptations of Christ (and reflecting the overthrow of the Devil) to frame Section 2 (*AH* V. 16, 3–V. 20, 2) treating the crucifixion of Christ (viewed as the recapitulation of Adam).

Healing of the Man Born Blind. *AH* V. 15, 2–V. 16, 2

This healing story differs from the others, Irenaeus writes, because in them the Lord healed with a word, for example: "You are made whole, now sin no more, lest something worse happen to you" (*AH* V. 15, 2 [SC 153:204], quoting John 5:14). Such a procedure shows that human maladies are due to the sin of disobedience, according to Irenaeus. By contrast the blind man was healed not by a word but by a deed, so revealing the Hand of God, which formed humanity from the beginning. Thus he interprets the verse: "Neither this man has sinned nor his parents, but that the works of God might be manifested in him" (*AH* V. 15, 2 [SC 153:204], quoting John 9:3). Since the work of God is the formation of the human person, whom God made from the mud of the earth, so the blind man was healed by an application of the mud of the earth. The creative Hand of the One God, the Word, performed both these acts (*AH* V. 15, 2).

As human beings were modeled in the womb by the Word according to the prophet (Jer 1:5) and Paul (Gal 1:15-16), so the same Word remodeled the eyes of the blind man. Sending the man to wash in the pool of Siloam symbolizes the bath of baptism that cleanses sinful humanity (*AH* V. 15, 3).

The Valentinians assert that humanity was not made from this earth but "from fluid and waste matter" (*AH* V. 15, 4 [SC 153:210]). They are wrong. Eyes, Irenaeus insists, come from the same earth as the rest of the body, and both are modeled by the same one. That one is the Word to whom the Father said "Let us make humankind according to our image and according to our likeness" (*AH* V. 15, 4 [SC 153:210], quoting Gen 1:26). According to Irenaeus even God's quest in the garden for the hidden, fallen Adam has its parallel in the Word who visits and inquires after the race (*AH* V. 15, 4).

On Irenaeus's reading this miracle shows that the Hand of God who modeled Adam from the earth is the same one who modeled all human beings, and there is one God whose voice has been present to the modeled work from beginning to end. So he writes:

> It is not necessary now to seek another Father beyond this one, or another sub-
> stance of our plasma beyond that proclaimed and shown by the Lord, or another
> Hand of God beyond this one that from beginning to end formed us and shaped
> us for life and is present to his formation and perfects it according to the image
> and likeness of God (*AH* V. 16, 1 [SC 153:214]).

Humans have one Father, and are of the substance of the earth as the Lord has shown, formed by the one Hand of God. That Hand formed them, shaped them for life, remains present to them, and perfects them. Irenaeus asserts that the truth of this became apparent in the Incarnation. While it used to be said that we were in the image of God, it was not then apparent that this was true because then the Word, in whose likeness human beings were made, was invisible, so the image could be missed. Now it is different: "When the Word of God was made flesh, it confirmed two things: it showed the image true, he himself being that which was his image, and it established[3] the likeness, making humanity like to the invisible Father through the Visible Word" (*AH* V. 16, 2 [SC 153:216]). Jesus Christ, the Son, Word and image of God, is the visible image who makes visible the invisible God. Since humans are the image of the Son, the appearance of the Son in flesh made visible the one in whose image they are, and established the likeness to the Father.

SECTION 1: SUMMARY

In the first section of Part Two Irenaeus has shown that the healing of the man born blind shows unity between the work of creating Adam and that of healing the blind man. The creating Hand of God was at work in both, and the voice of God has been present to the created work in both cases; creation is under the one God.

The Crucifixion. *AH* V. 16, 3–V. 20, 2

Irenaeus notes that as the original disobedience happened "through the wood," so the healing obedience is "through the wood." The replication indicates that the one whose law was transgressed in the beginning is the Father whom Jesus announces. Thus the second Adam reconciles humankind with the God whom they offended in the person of the first Adam (*AH* V. 16, 3).

And who is this God? According to the Valentinians the true God and Father is the Bythos;[4] according to Irenaeus the Demiurge himself is Father as to his love, Lord as to his power, and Maker and Former as to his wisdom. These titles are all proper titles of the one Creator God.[5] This is not an unknowable God but one known through the prophets, and one against whom humankind has sinned (*AH* V. 17, 1).

Because that same God sent the Only-Begotten Son to save humanity the Son worked miracles to bring the unbelieving to glorify his Father, as the crowd did after the healing of the paralytic. Irenaeus notes that when Jesus performed that miracle he said: "so that you may know that the Son of Man has power to forgive sins" (*AH* V. 17, 2 [SC 153:226], quoting Matt 9:6). The voice of forgiveness is the voice of God; thus the very voice of God from which humanity originally had received the commandments echoes in this episode (*AH* V. 17, 2). When the Lord forgave the sins of the paralytic he not only healed the man but also revealed himself as Son of God become Son of Man. Irenaeus points out that David foretold that the coming of the Lord would effect the remission of sins,[6] a remission that occurred by the wood of the cross (*AH* V. 17, 3). He invokes the story of Elisha and the lost axe (2 Kings 6:1-7) as prefiguration that what was lost by the wood would be recovered by economy of the wood (*AH* V. 17, 4). Irenaeus stresses that the Lord realized this economy not by means of an alien creation but by means of his own creation. Creation could never have borne him if it were the fruit of ignorance and of a defect. As it is, at the invisible level creation is borne by the Father while at the visible level it bears his Word (*AH* V. 18, 1).

The heart of this section on the crucifixion is as follows:

> While the Father at once carries the weight of creation and of his Word, the Word, sustained by the Father, gives the Spirit to all, as the Father wills: to some, according to their creation, he gives what is of creation, which is made; to others, according to their adoption, he gives what is from God, which is generated (*AH* V. 18, 1 [SC 153:238–240]).

Rousseau and Orbe agree in reading the second half of this text thus: "to some, according to their creation, he gives the spirit of creation, which is made; to others, according to their adoption, he gives the Spirit proceeding from God, which is generated." The precision that introduces "spirit of creation" and "Spirit of God" is called for by the construction of the text. Irenaeus does not stop to explain *how* the Spirit of filiation that is generated (*"quod est generatio"*) is communicated to believers. Having set up his parallel, he moves on.

He writes these lines under the influence, as it were, of the vision of the cross. For him the Father remains the invisible of the Son and the Son is the visible of the Father (*AH* IV. 6, 6). So on the invisible plane, as one looks at the cross both creation (represented by the wood) and the Son (enfleshed on the wood) are sustained by the Father. Sustained by the Father, the Son pours out the Spirit.[7] The Spirit is given to all, but differently. Some receive simply the spirit of creation, while others receive the Spirit of God (*AH* V. 8, 2). This is completely consistent with what we saw above in Part One. For Irenaeus theology in its etymological sense of word about God, as well as the special theologies of creation, anthropology, and soteriology meet at the cross of the Incarnate One. He finds scriptural warrant for his position in Eph 4:6: "there is one God who is above all and through all and in us all," thus cited three times in this section (*AH* V. 17, 4 and V. 18, 2 [twice]), and in the prologue of John (*AH* V. 18, 2).

As a summary of this section Irenaeus sets up a pattern of recapitulation that includes creation and the Savior, Mary and Eve, Adam and Christ, and the serpent and the dove. The creation borne by the Lord has in turn borne him. The Savior's obedience on the wood has reversed the disobedience enacted on the wood. Mary's obedience has reversed Eve's disobedience, the virgin Mary becoming advocate for the virgin Eve. (Irenaeus establishes a strong parallel: as the human race was bound together *[adstrictum est]* in death by a virgin, so it was unbound *[solutum est]* by a virgin. Mary's obedience countered Eve's disobedience.)[8] The sin of the First Made *(protoplasti)* is healed by the First Born *(primogeniti)*. The prudence of the serpent is vanquished by the simplicity of the dove *(AH V. 19, 1)*.

By way of contrast to this summary of the saving recapitulation Irenaeus then summarizes the errors of those who are "ignorant of the economy" and "blind to the truth." Some of them posit another Father than the Creator. Some consider matter a product of the angels, or say it is formed by itself, or hold that it is the fruit of a defect and of ignorance. Some hold in contempt the manifest coming of the Lord, rejecting the incarnation. Some deny the virgin birth. Some hold neither soul nor body is capable of eternal life, but only the "inner human person," that is, the intellect, which alone is perfectible. Still others say the soul can be saved but not the body. Irenaeus mentions that he has described all of these positions in *AH* I and has shown their inner inconsistencies in *AH* II *(AH V. 19, 2)*.

He then remarks that all of these people are much later than "the bishops *(episcopi)* to whom the apostles handed on the Church, as we have made clear in the third book" *(AH V. 20, 1 [SC 153:252])*. He again contrasts Gnostic diversity with ecclesial uniformity, a uniform tradition that is dispersed as widely as the Church. The light of God, he maintains, has been confided to the Church, which is the lamp bearing the light of Christ *(AH V. 20, 1)*. The heretics bring grief to the presbyters, not seeing how the simple but religious people understand their blasphemous sophistry. (Once again the reader catches a glimpse of the Gnostics as a kind of intellectual Christian group posing a pastoral problem to Church leadership.) It is important to avoid their opinions and take refuge in the Church, a Church "planted as paradise in this world." Christ has inducted into the Church "those who obey his preaching, recapitulating in himself all things that are in the heavens and on earth" *(AH V. 20, 2 [SC 153:260]*, quoting Eph 1:10).

SECTION 2: SUMMARY

In the second section of Part Two Irenaeus reflects on the crucifixion as part of the recapitulation effected through the life, the work, the death, and the resurrection of Christ. Thus the crucifixion reconciles humanity with the One God whose laws it transgressed in the beginning; salvation is under the one God.

Temptation of Christ. *AH* V. 21, 1–V. 24, 4

Irenaeus inserts the account of the temptations into the saving recapitulation effected by Christ to make clear that the One God is Lord of the Law, and the Word of God, made a member of the human race, is the destroyer of the enemy of that race. He begins by showing the parallels between the characters in the Genesis account of the temptation of Adam and Eve (in part as interpreted by Paul in Galatians) and the gospel accounts of the temptation of Christ. The serpent, the woman, and the man are recapitulated by the devil and "the man born of woman," that is, the Lord and his mother (*AH* V. 21, 1). Irenaeus writes: "Because one and the same modeled us in the beginning and sent his Son in the end, the Lord fulfilled his commandment, 'being made from woman,' and destroying our adversary, and completing humanity according to the image and likeness of God" (*AH* V. 21, 2 [SC 153:264–266]). Because the Demiurge, the Father, and the Lawgiver are one the Lord could effectively recapitulate the beginning so as to right the wrong, and—in the process—destroy the enemy. He did this by fulfilling the commandments of the Father.

Like Moses and Elijah the Lord fasted forty days, and then, as any human being would be, he was hungry. Irenaeus explains that in the beginning the devil used food to lead a human being who was not hungry into transgressing God's command; in the end, when "the man" was hungry, the devil could not turn him away from the food that comes from God. The Lord used the Law to repulse him, saying: "It is written, 'One does not live by bread alone'" (*AH* V. 21, 2 [SC 153:268], quoting Matt 4:4).

Irenaeus notes that, having been repulsed by the Law, the devil set out to use the Law in his next effort. He tempted the Lord to throw himself down from the pinnacle of the Temple, urging that it would be to the Lord's advantage since the Scriptures said that if he were son of God the angels would bear him up. The Lord responded with another word from the Law: "it is also written, 'Do not tempt the Lord your God'" (*AH* V. 21, 2 [SC 153:270], quoting Matt 4:7). Irenaeus remarks that the Lord in his visible humanity acted as one bound by the Law affecting humanity. His humility destroyed the serpent's pride.

Repulsed a second time, the devil, Irenaeus explains, brought into play all his skills in lying. He promised the Lord all the kingdoms of the earth and their glory in return for his worship. The Lord answered: "Leave me, Satan! It is written, 'The Lord your God you shall adore and him alone shall you serve'" (*AH* V. 21, 2 [SC 153:272], quoting Matt 4:10). Irenaeus comments that the Lord stripped the devil, giving him his true name: Satan, meaning Apostate. The Lord conquered Satan, destroying Adam's transgression by his own observance of the Law of God.

The Lord God to whom Christ gave witness in these events is the God of the Law. This is so, according to Irenaeus, both because these things had been predicted by the Law and because it was by the Law that the Lord destroyed the devil. In this way the one who unjustly made humanity captive was him-self justly taken captive. Humanity escaped its captor's power through God's mercy, who gave it salvation through Christ (*AH* V. 21, 3). If there were an-other Father beyond the Demiurge whom the Law lauds as God, the Lord would not have been able to destroy the Apostate by means of the Creator's words and commandments (*AH* V. 22, 1).

As to human beings, they have been saved, and it is by the very same com-mandments that the Lord teaches them what they should do. In applying the story to his own day Irenaeus gives some straightforward advice, undoubtedly thinking of situations with which he is familiar. Certainly they are perennial situations in the Christian community. He writes that the hungry, following the example of the tempted Christ, should pay attention to the nourishment God gives.[9] Those lifted up by charisms[10] or confident in their works of justice or ornamented with outstanding ministries should neither be proud nor tempt God. Like Christ, lifted up to the top of the Temple, they should be humble. Nor should anyone be impressed by money or fame or good appearances any more than Christ was so impressed. Instead each one should remember that it is necessary to adore the Lord God and serve God alone. After all, the devil does not have the power to give the things he promises (*AH* V. 22, 2).

In fact, the devil has been a liar from the start. He lied in telling Adam and Eve that they would not taste death if they ate of the forbidden tree. The fact is quite different: "Together with the food they took death to themselves, be-cause they ate in disobedience: truly disobedience to God brought death. Be-cause of this from this [moment] they were handed over to it, being made debtors of death" (*AH* V. 23, 1 [SC 153:290]). In order to follow Irenaeus in the exegesis of this passage it will be helpful to consider his interpretation of death.

IRENAEUS ON DEATH

It is common among second-century writers to consider the death resultant from sin as moral death.[11] That is, they recognize in addition to physical death an ethical or moral death. To grasp what Irenaeus introduces here it is neces-sary to realize that he interprets the death[12] referred to in Gen 2:17 in a man-ner consistent with his teaching on the nature of the human person in *AH* V and with his teaching on human freedom in *AH* IV. 37–39.

There he set up two sets of equations: good = obedience to God = life, and evil = disobedience to God = death (*AH* IV. 39, 1). Yet as he developed that section it was clear that good and evil must both be experienced, and over a period of time, simply because one is human and so not perfect from the be-ginning. Indeed, to repudiate the capacity for both good and evil is to kill one-self as human. The Irenaean understanding of "life" and "death" in relation to good and evil, and to sin, will bear further examination.

Clearly for him the complete human being is a union of flesh, soul, and Spirit, so that the human without the Spirit of God is incapable of life in the kingdom of God. That is, those without the Spirit are dead (*AH* V. 9, 1). What is essential is life according to the Spirit rather than life according to the flesh (*AH* V. 9, 4). Life according to the Spirit is equated with the divine life, and so with incorruptibility and glory.

Irenaeus distinguishes between physical death and death as a consequence of sin. Death in the second sense has to do not with the presence of sin in the soul but with the *ultimate consequences* of sin for the human composite. Those who live according to the flesh are finally excluded in their totality, in flesh and in soul, from the kingdom. They are claimed by corruptibility. By contrast, those who live according to the Spirit enjoy incorruptibility and so glory, as Orbe writes, "*en la sustancia del polvo.*"[13] It is this that marks Irenaeus off from his contemporaries; he does not distinguish between physical death and moral death, but between physical death and the total, final death of the human composite. Sin causes that death.

Earlier Irenaeus was seen to consider disobedience to God as death for humans. It is in the context of his anthropology that one can grasp the sense in which he understands this to be true. The *act* of disobedience, taken in itself, is not death. It is the *cause* of death. How is that so? Those who disobey follow the flesh and not the Spirit. But only the Spirit leads to life and incorruptibility. Therefore disobedience causes death because it excludes human beings from eternal life. Such is the significance Irenaeus assigns to the death referred to in Gen 2:17.

Our consideration of Irenaeus's understanding of death interrupted the discussion of his explanation of the death incurred by Adam and Eve in the Genesis story (*AH* V. 23, 1). Continuing his presentation, Irenaeus remarks that not only do the same Genesis verses (Gen 2:16-17) speak of the death of Adam and Eve, but they mention that Adam and Eve will die "on the day" they eat. Irenaeus then attends to the meaning of "day": "Because of this from this time[14] they were handed over to death, being made its debtors" (*AH* V. 23, 1 [SC 153:290]). The very day on which they ate, Irenaeus holds, was incorporated into the recapitulating saving death of Christ. His passion was on the eve of the Sabbath, so the sixth day of the week, paralleling the sixth day of creation when humankind was created (*AH* V. 23, 2). While "day" as the sixth day of creation seems to be his preferred reading Irenaeus notes that "day" can be understood in several ways. His point is that whichever reading one applies to "day," God is true and the devil is a liar and a homicide.

He concludes his exegesis of the temptation of Christ by returning to the devil's final offer to the Lord: "All these [kingdoms of the earth] have been given to me, and I give them to you." Irenaeus supplies a series of texts to illustrate that power over the kingdoms of this world belongs to God (*AH* V. 24, 1).[15] Because humanity apart from God falls fearlessly into all kinds of trouble

God imposes on the race fear of human authority. God's intent is to introduce a certain kind of justice and moderation toward one another. That is why Paul teaches that authority bears the sword (Rom 13:4) and why magistrates act as they do (*AH* V. 24, 2). In fact they are ministers of God, established by God, and the claims of the devil are lies (*AH* V. 24, 3). The Word of God, having conquered the devil as a man, will in the end submit the devil to a man.

CHAPTER ELEVEN: SUMMARY

Thus with an account of the defeat of the devil Irenaeus completes a compact review of salvation history under the aegis of interpretation of three events in Christ's life. The move serves him well. It joins creation to redemption through the person of the Word become a man. The Word of the Father as Hand of God in creation illustrates the identity of Father and Creator; the same Word made flesh reaches out his hand to give vision to the blind man. The one same Word enfleshed completes the recapitulation of Adam in the crucifixion; at the cross not only are the two testaments joined as the new Adam reverses the deed of the old Adam but Irenaeus's positions on creation, anthropology, and soteriology are also brought together. Finally, the temptation accounts serve as capstone to the recapitulation wrought by the Word made flesh, as the devil who destroyed humanity is in turn defeated by a human being, the enfleshed Word. The events of the end time will complete his defeat. Irenaeus turns to those events in Part Three, our chapter twelve.

NOTES

[1]Irenaeus writes: "'The dead will rise and those who are in the monuments will spring up, and those who are in the land will rejoice: for the dew which is from you is health for them.' And again 'I will comfort you, and in Jerusalem you will be comforted, and you will see, and your heart will give thanks, and your bones will arise like herbs, and the hand of the Lord will be known to those who worship him'" (*AH* V. 15, 1 [SC 153:196], citing Isa 26:19 and 66:13-14).

[2]Antonio Orbe, *Teología de San Ireneo, Comentario al Libro V del "Adversus Haereses"* 2.18–19, gives a simple reading more helpful than Rousseau, SC 152:268–272.

[3]"Established" translates the Greek *katestēse*, extant in a fragment, which corresponds to the Latin *constituit*. In choosing this reading I agree with Orbe, *Comentario* 2.103 rather than Rousseau, SC 152:277, note marked "p. 217, n. 1." Rousseau is guided by the Armenian in replacing the Greek with *apokatestēsen*, and so uses the Latin *restituit*. As Orbe remarks, "There can be no restoration of the likeness without a first and definitive installation of the Spirit . . . in the flesh of Jesus, following upon his glorious resurrection *in Forma Dei*."

[4]Orbe, *Comentario* 2.121, cites fragments of Numenius which illustrate that the Valentinian split between the Father and the Demiurge is rooted in Numenius (and *not* directly in Plato).

[5]Orbe, *Comentario* 2.121, locates the origin of this grouping in Justin and Theophilus.

[6]Irenaeus quotes Ps 32:1-2 thus: "Blessed are those whose iniquities have been forgiven and whose sins have been covered. Happy the person to whom the Lord does not impute sin" (*AH* V. 17, 3 [SC 153:228–230]).

[7]This "economic" sending of the Spirit by the Son, wholly consistent with the New Testament, is at the basis of the later Latin development in trinitarian theology postulating the intra-trinitarian sending of the Spirit by Father and Son (however that "and" might be understood). See Yves M. J. Congar, *Je crois en l'Esprit Saint, III: Le Fleuve de Vie coule en Orient et in Occident* (Paris: Cerf, 1980). English: *I Believe in the Holy Spirit, 3: The River of the Water of Life (Rev 22:1) Flows in the East and in the West,* translated by David Smith (New York: Seabury, 1983), "The Filioque as Professed by the Latin Fathers and the Councils Before it Became a Subject of Disunity," 49–56.

[8]Orbe, *Comentario* 2, has extensive notes, pp. 263–278.

[9]In light of the rest of Irenaeus's teaching (e.g., see above ch. 4, n. 18) this should be read not as a cynical refusal of bread to the poor nor as an equally callous direction to the hungry poor to be satisfied with pious reflection, but rather as the suggestion that for a Christian bodily hunger should serve as a reminder of the need for heavenly sustenance as well.

[10]Earlier, in *AH* II. 32, 4 (SC 294:340–342) Irenaeus, as a proof that the Lord alone is the Son of God, lists the works yet being done in his name: exorcisms, visions, prophecies, healings, and raising the dead. As each one receives, so each gives for the benefit of all, whether within or without the Church. The reception and use of gifts for the welfare of others seems to have been an accepted part of life. Similarly, in *AH* V. 6, 1 (SC 153:74) he mentions the many "brothers" in the Church who have gifts of prophecy, of tongues, and possibly of interpretation (since they manifest human secrets and explain the mysteries of God).

[11]See Antonio Orbe, *Antropología de San Ireneo* 476–477.

[12]In this material I adhere closely to Orbe, *Antropología,* ch. 15, "San Ireneo y la muerte," especially pp. 450–457, and *Comentario* 2.463–502.

[13]*Antropología* 451.

[14]The SC text has *propter hoc ex eo;* Orbe, *Comentario* 2.479 and 497, attending to the parallel passages, suggests that the phrase be understood as *propter hoc exinde.*

[15]Prov 21:1; 8:15-16; Rom 13:1, 4, 6.

CHAPTER TWELVE

The Just, Risen in the Flesh, Enjoy the Millennial Kingdom

Adversus haereses V. 25, 1–V. 36, 3

As Christ recapitulated Adam in the time of salvation, so the Antichrist will recapitulate the works of evil in the end time. This material forms Part 3, Section 1 (*AH* V. 25, 1–30, 4). When all have had the opportunity for salvation there will be the judgment, followed by the resurrection of the just, which forms the topic of Part 3, Section 2 (*AH* V. 31, 1–36, 2). In a brief third section (*AH* V. 36, 3) Irenaeus both connects his teaching on the kingdom with the argument of *AH* V and recalls his major antignostic themes. Irenaeus intends to show in Part 3 of *AH* V that in its end, as in its beginning and throughout its course, all creation is under the dominion of the one God, the Creator and Father.

The Antichrist. *AH* V. 25.1–30.4

Irenaeus uses the interpretation of 2 Thessalonians 2 and of several passages from Revelation to frame this section which falls into a three-step presentation: (1) the Antichrist will come as the recapitulation of evil (*AH* V. 25, 1–25, 5); (2) every possibility of human beings coming to salvation having been offered, God will judge justly both those who reject God and those who believe (*AH* V. 26, 1–28, 1); (3) the Antichrist comes willingly as the recapitulation of the apostasy (*AH* V. 28, 2–30, 4).

In his initial depiction of the Antichrist Irenaeus portrays one who will have all the power of the Devil. He writes: "He will come not as a just king or as lawful, in subjection to God, but as impious and unjust and without law, as an apostate and iniquitous and a homicide, as a thief, recapitulating in himself the apostasy of the devil" (*AH* V. 25, 1 [SC 153:308]). The picture is starkly awesome and, as one would expect of Irenaeus, rooted in the Scriptures. When the apostle[1] describes how the Adversary, the Son of Perdition, will seat himself in the temple of God, showing himself as God (2 Thess 2:3-4) Irenaeus says Paul is writing about the Antichrist (*AH* V. 25, 1). The phrase "temple of God" is the apostle's own, and means that the Temple at Jerusalem was built at the direction of the true God. Neither Paul nor the other apostles, Irenaeus maintains, practice the "double teaching" the Gnostics attribute to them, having one teaching for the simple and another for the initiates.[2] Therefore, he holds, it is in the true God's place that the Adversary will sit, as the Lord taught (Matt 24:15-17) when he described "the desolating sacrilege" (*AH* V. 25, 2).

Irenaeus cites numerous texts as speaking of the same Evil One, including the reference to "another" in Jesus' words about himself: "I have come in my Father's name, and you do not accept me; if another comes in his own name, you will accept him" (John 5:43). He also identifies the Evil One with the wicked judge of Jesus' story (Luke 18:6), while other texts like the one about the devastation of that time (Dan 8:11-12) and the angel Gabriel's explanation of Daniel's visions (Dan 8:23-25) are applied to the description of the end time itself (*AH* V. 25, 3-4). According to Irenaeus all of this not only teaches about the coming apostasy but also makes clear that there is only one and the same God the Father who was announced by the prophets like Daniel and heralded by Gabriel both to Daniel and to Mary (*AH* V. 25, 5).

Irenaeus cites texts (*AH* V. 26, 1) that suggest that when the Antichrist comes the earthly kingdom will be divided (Rev 17:12-14; Matt 12:25; Dan 2:33-34, 41-42) and God will sustain one kingdom that will never be destroyed (Dan 2:44-45).

Through Daniel God made known in advance what the Son confirmed: Christ, the Son, will confute those who do not admit the prophets sent by the one Father. Irenaeus writes:

> Therefore those who blaspheme the Demiurge—whether in their own words and openly as those who are of Marcion, or according to the overturning of meanings like those who are from Valentinus and all who are falsely said to be Gnostics—will be known to be organs of Satan by all who honor God (*AH* V. 26, 2 [SC 153:332]).

Irenaeus notes that Justin had said that before the coming of the Lord, Satan dared not blaspheme God as he did not yet know his own condemnation. Earlier the prophets spoke only in figure. But from Christ he knows his eternal destiny. He and his followers, like other lawbreakers, impute their apostasy not to themselves but to the Lawgiver (*AH* V. 26, 2).

Satan's position, according to Irenaeus, misunderstands the Father. If the Father did not judge it would be either because the Father has no concern about human actions or because he approves of all that humans do. In either case Christ's coming would be superfluous. But Christ comes, Irenaeus says, to separate and judge. If his coming will work a judgment it is clear that the Father has created all human beings, each possessing the capacity for decision and free will (*AH* V. 27, 1).

God will give to each, Irenaeus states, what each has chosen. Those who love God will enter into communion with God, "which is life and light and the enjoyment of those goods that are with God." Likewise anyone who chooses to separate from God, God will permit to be separate. In such cases "it is not that God punishes them by taking Godself from them, but rather the punishment follows from the fact that they are desolate of all good" (*AH* V. 27, 2 [SC 153:344]). Irenaeus strongly defends the role of human freedom in human destiny. Human beings choose good or the absence of good, and all else follows from that (*AH* V. 27, 2). The Word of God will then assign to each an appropriate place according to the choice made (*AH* V. 28, 1). The central notion of this sub-section on the Antichrist thus has revolved around a defense of the justice of God's judgments.

Irenaeus returns to the framing text from 2 Thess 2:10-12 where the writer says the Worker of Errors is sent because "they did not welcome God's love." In this examination of the text Irenaeus stresses the willingness of the apostate's actions. By his own choice the apostate seats himself in the Temple of God to be adored as Christ. Because the Antichrist acts willingly he will be justly thrown into the fire. There is a symmetry between the judgment of the Antichrist and of humans, just judgment in both cases depending on an underlying freedom of action.

There is a second symmetry, this time between Christ and Antichrist; each is a recapitulator. Christ recapitulates all of human history, setting it right, whereas Antichrist recapitulates all evil, continuing it as evil. Irenaeus turns to Revelation 13, a description of the coming of the Antichrist; he claims that the number[3] of the Beast, 666,[4] recapitulates all the apostasy of the six thousand years (*AH* V. 28, 2).

He makes the connection through Ps 90:4 (LXX 89:4), which speaks of a thousand years as a day in God's eyes. This offers a transition from an ordinary day to the millennium, or Day of the Lord. Since creation took place in "six days," it took six thousand years. Because the creation story is not only an account of past things but also a prophecy of the future, this then means that the end of all things will happen in the six thousandth year (*AH* V. 28, 3).[5]

For this reason, according to Irenaeus, during all this time human beings, modeled in the beginning by the Hands of God, become the image and likeness of God. There was a first stage of incomplete creation that is continued and completed as humans grow according to the image and likeness, the weeds being thrown away and the wheat stored in the granary. Tribulation is necessary for those who are saved, to prepare them for the feast of the King

(*AH* V. 28, 4). In earlier books, Irenaeus says (recalling, among other things, what he wrote in *AH* IV), he has explained why God permitted this to be so, and he has shown that all events like this are for the good of the ones who are saved, making their free will mature in view of immortality and rendering them more apt for eternal submission to God. After all, creation is arranged to benefit human beings as it was made for them, and not the reverse (*AH* V. 29, 1). All evil, then, works for the good of the just, and the very number of the name of the Antichrist indicates that he recapitulates all evil in himself (*AH* V. 29, 1).

Irenaeus considers whether from the number of his name one can arrive at the name itself of the Antichrist. He summarizes the reasons he has already given why 666 is, in fact, the number of that name: (1) the Scriptures, in all the oldest copies, assign this number; (2) those who saw John give this number; (3) by the theory of number symbolism 666 is the most apt number (*AH* V. 30, 1). He suggests three names: Euanthas, which is meaningless and so not possible, Lateinos, which designates "those who reign now," or Teitan, which he considers most possible, although he finally is unwilling to commit himself to a firm pronouncement that this will be the name of the Antichrist (*AH* V. 30, 3).

It may be asked why John revealed the number and not the name. Irenaeus replies that the number was given so that people can be on guard, but not the name (he says "he killed the name"), since it is unworthy to be recorded by the Holy Spirit! (*AH* V. 30, 4).

SECTION 1: SUMMARY

This section presents the Antichrist. Irenaeus writes that he will come as the recapitulation of evil, a true Son of Perdition. With his coming the earthly kingdom will be judged; God will give to each what each has freely chosen. The Antichrist too, having also acted freely, will be justly punished. Irenaeus's consideration of the texts of Revelation here brings him to speak about the millennial kingdom and the number of the name of the Antichrist.

Resurrection of the Just. *AH* V. 31, 1–V. 36, 2

Throughout *AH* V the salvation of the flesh remains a preoccupation of Irenaeus. In this final section he is concerned with resurrection. First he outlines the mistaken opinions of some believers as well as of the heretics. Such people, he claims, do not value the thing modeled by God and do not accept the salvation of the flesh. In their view after death they will ascend beyond the heavens and even beyond the Demiurge to the Mother, or to the imagined Father. They do not understand that the Lord, in his resurrection, set a model valid for all. Thus they misunderstand the resurrection teaching of the prophets (Pseudo-Jeremiah), the gospels (Matt 12:40), Paul (Eph 4:9), David (Ps 86:13 [LXX 85:13]), and John (John 20:17). All these texts affirm the resurrection of the Lord, according to Irenaeus (*AH* V. 31, 1). Because "a disciple is not above the teacher, but every perfect disciple will be like the teacher" (Luke 6:40), what happened to the Lord will happen to his disciples. They will rise after a period of time, and after that those who are worthy will be taken up to heaven (*AH* V. 31, 2).

Irenaeus understands this repetition of the Lord's pattern to mean that after the resurrection of the just will come the period of the kingdom of God on earth.[6] He sees entry into the kingdom as the beginning of incorruptibility. The coming of the kingdom is thus a first phase of the end time. In the kingdom those who are worthy will gradually come to know God.[7] His sense of fairness and fittingness comes to the fore as Irenaeus argues that it is only just that the righteous should receive the reward of their suffering in the same world in which they suffered (*AH* V. 32, 1).

He finds scriptural warrant for his opinion in a number of passages, beginning with the promises made to Abraham of a posterity who will inherit the earth. Abraham's posterity, according to Irenaeus, is the Church, and the heritage will be the millennial kingdom of God (*AH* V. 32, 2). It is to this kingdom that the Lord himself referred when at the Last Supper he told the disciples that he would not drink wine again until he drinks with them in the kingdom of his Father. Certainly they will need their bodies to drink, so in addition this passage supports the resurrection of the body (*AH* V. 33, 1).[8]

There will come a time when the just, risen from the dead, will reign, and when all creation, freed and renewed, will bear abundant fruit. Irenaeus claims the Lord as warrant for this teaching, tracing its succession: he himself received it from the presbyters, who knew John, who knew the Lord (*AH* V. 33, 3). In addition[9] to their anonymous teaching he has access to that of Papias, who was both a disciple of the Lord's disciple, John, and a friend of Polycarp (*AH* V. 33, 3).

The great prophecies describing the time when the lion and the lamb will lie down together and a little child will lead them (he cites Isa 11:6-9 and 65:25) can, according to Irenaeus, be applied quite literally to the time of the kingdom. He explicitly objects to metaphorical interpretations of this material, insisting that God will ultimately reestablish the original order of creation so that the beasts will again live in harmony and obey humankind (*AH* V. 33, 4). He takes an equally literal approach to the prophecies of the resurrection (Isa 26:19; Ezek 37:12-14) and the regathering of Israel (Ezek 28:25-26). Each creature will reach its maturity as God has planned it (*AH* V. 34, 2). Since, however, the Church is the posterity of Abraham these prophecies will be fulfilled in the time of the New Covenant (*AH* V. 34, 1 and 3). It is then that Jerusalem will be rebuilt (*AH* V. 34, 4). This position is a logical consequence of the Irenaean doctrine of recapitulation.

Irenaeus next (*AH* V. 35) levels a strong critique at allegorical interpretation of any eschatological Scriptures.[10] If one accepts allegorical interpretation of such material one eliminates the millennial kingdom and at the same time introduces incongruencies that literal interpretation avoids. Irenaeus applies what can best be called a naïvely literal interpretation to a series of such texts (Isa 6:11; 13:9; 26:10; 6:12; 65:21; Bar 4:36–5:9). Then he develops an extended theological interpretation focusing on the relationship between the earthly and the heavenly Jerusalem. He continues to use the Baruch text on the return of Jerusalem's children (Bar 4:36–5:9), reading it in harmony with the lines from Isaiah in which God speaks of inscribing Jerusalem *"in manibus meis"* (Isa 49:16) as well as verses from Paul (Gal 4:26) and John (Rev 20:11) marking Jerusalem's high place.

Irenaeus summarizes his position on why none of these texts should be interpreted allegorically with a strong affirmation of the reality of the resurrection. God will truly raise humanity; humans will truly (not allegorically) rise from the dead. He writes: "As the human being truly rises, so he will truly exercise incorruptibility and grow and flourish in the time of the kingdom, that he might be made capable of the glory of the Father; then, all things being renewed, he will live in the city of God" (*AH* V. 35, 2 [SC 153:450]). He continues, pointing out that since human beings are real the translation that affects them must also be real. In fact, "neither the substance nor the matter of creation will be exterminated . . . but 'the figure of this world will pass,' that is, those things in which the transgression was done, for humans grew old in them" (*AH* V. 36, 1 [SC 153:452, 454]). So when humans have been made new, as the presbyters say, then, being worthy of heaven, they will possess the splendor of that city, "where they will see God, to the degree that they are worthy of seeing God" (*AH* V. 36, 1 [SC 153:456]). Irenaeus finally describes the ultimate progression: through the Spirit they will ascend to the Son, through the Son they will ascend to the Father, and then the Son will hand over his work to the Father. Here he returns to the text with which he was preoccupied in the opening sections of *AH* V, that of 1 Corinthians 15, and he concludes this penultimate section with the following citation:

> For he must reign until he has put all his enemies under his feet. The last enemy to be destroyed is death. [In the time of the kingdom the just man living on earth will forget to die.] . . . But when it says, 'All things are put in subjection,' it is plain that this does not include the one who put all things in subjection under him. When all things are subjected to him, then the Son himself will also be subjected to the one who put all things in subjection under him, so that God may be all in all[11] (*AH* V. 36, 2 [SC 153:460]).

At the end of the kingdom of the Son[12] there will be the ultimate return of all to the Father,[13] and so the final consummation.

Conclusion of Part 3 and of *Adversus haereses. AH* V. 36, 3

In a last closely worked section Irenaeus connects his teaching on the Kingdom with the argument of *AH* V and at the same time recalls his major antignostic themes. Appropriately as he draws his work to an end he comments on a concluding theme of Revelation, Christ's thousand-year reign described in Revelation 20. With this reign he associates the cup the Lord promised to drink in the kingdom (Matt 26:29). In addition he associates with the millennial kingdom the twofold resurrection (John 5:25, 28-29), the "seventh day" of Genesis (Gen 1:31-32), the psalmist's "day of rest on which the just will enter" (Ps 132:14, loosely associated with Ps 118:20 [LXX 131:14; 117:20]), and Paul's reference to the "liberation of creation" (Rom 8:19-21).[14] Here as elsewhere Irenaeus works from a verbal and thematic association of texts.

In all these texts and through all the activity therein described Irenaeus discerns the one unique Father, the sole Son, and the single human race in which God's mysteries are accomplished, the creature being made "concorporate"[15] with the Son and the Son who is the only-begotten Word descending into the creature. The oneness of God, the oneness of the Son, the oneness of the race, and the immensely positive role of bodiliness are all in evidence. The angels themselves would like to know the divine mysteries but remain unable to penetrate God's wisdom.[16] Irenaeus amplifies the nature of the mysteries of God in a fitting conclusion: "The first-begotten Word descends into the creature, that is into the 'plasma,' and is known by it, and again the creature knows the Word and ascends to him, surpassing the angels and becoming in the image and likeness of God" (*AH* V. 36, 3 [SC 153:464–466]). His final words stress the reality of the incarnation and the exaltation of the human in its very physicality unto the divine image and likeness. He ends *AH* V where he began, with the salvation of the flesh as a principal fruit of the incarnation.

NOTES

[1]Irenaeus attributes 2 Thessalonians to Paul.

[2]SC 152:322, note marked "p. 313, n. 2," and 152:280, note marked "p. 227, n. 1."

[3]J. Massyngberde Ford, *Revelation: Introduction, Translation and Commentary,* AB 38 (Garden City, N.Y.: Doubleday, 1975) 215–217, reviews the history of interpretation of this text and discusses the nature of number symbolism (a system dependent on assigning numerical value to letters, and popular among the Gnostics, as was evident in chapter 4).

[4]The figure is suitable for the Antichrist because 6 is 1 less than 7; 7 is the number of perfection. Ford comments:

> Christian readers would have noticed the contrast between the number of the beast, 666, and the number of Jesus, 888 (the sum of the Greek letters *Jesous*). In 888 could be seen superabundant perfection, the three-fold 7 + 1. On the other hand 666 indicates the three-fold failure to reach perfection, 7 – 1. This showed how precarious and how doomed to failure the reign of the beast must be.

The problem that has exercised exegetes is to know whether the author of Revelation had in mind a name whose letters total 666, and if so, what that name was. See Ford, *Revelation* 225–227.

[5]A clear indication of the millenarianism he will develop below.

[6]Such an understanding locates Irenaeus within early Western Christian millenarianism; for a study devoted to Irenaeus's millenarianism see Antonio Orbe, "San Ireneo y el régimen del milenio," *StMiss* 32 (1983) 345–372.

In Christian terms millenarianism refers to the expectation of a thousand-year reign of Christ prior to the Last Judgment. (The phenomenon is also known as chiliasm from the Greek for a thousand.) As Bettencourt notes ("Millenarianism," in *SM* 4 [1969] 43), in one form or another millenarianism was found in the Western Church as late as the second half of the fourth century. Millennial thought has been perduring and widespread in the history of religions; for an overview in cross-cultural context with extensive bibliography see H. Schwartz, "Millenarianism," in *The Encyclopedia of Religion* 9 (1987) 521–532.

[7]*Per quod regnum qui digni fuerint paulatim assuescunt capere Deum* (*AH* V. 32, 1 [SC 153:396]).

[8]Further texts he uses include: in *AH* V. 33, 2 the dinner given for the needy, who will repay the debt in the kingdom (Luke 14:12-13) and the hundredfold in the age to come (Matt 19:29); in *AH* V. 33, 3 Isaac's blessing of Jacob (Gen 27:27-29) with its consequences.

[9]Some would identify the teaching of the presbyters referred to in *AH* V, 33, 3 with that of Papias cited in *AH* V. 33, 4. Rousseau leans this way; note the tenor of the translation (SC 153:417): *"Voilà ce que Papias . . . ."* The original Greek in the fragment reads: *"tauta de kai Papias . . . ."* I follow Antonio Orbe who distinguishes the two; see *Teología de San Ireneo, Comentario al Libro V del "Adversus Haereses"* 3.416–431, especially 417 and 428.

[10]I follow Orbe, *Comentario* 3.489.

[11]NRSV translation of 1 Cor 15:25-28, with the Irenaean interjection concerning the just who will "forget to die."

[12]Orbe, *Comentario* 3.603–604, explains that for Irenaeus this means that in the vision of the Father the mediatorial role of Christ in the economy disappears. Humans, configured in their flesh to the flesh of Christ, and so inserted in the total Christ, enter into the glory of the Father. This takes place by the submission of the Incarnate Son (together with Adam and his offspring) to the Father and the uniform insertion of the total Christ into the glory and incorruptibility of God.

[13]Orbe (*Comentario* 3.605–611) discusses both the patristic commentary on the Pauline text (the general studies cited being E. Schendel, *Herrschaft und Unterwerfung Christi. 1 Kor 15, 24-28 in Exegese und Theologie der Väter bis zum Ausgang des 4. Jahrhunderts* [Tübingen, 1971] and B. Halvorsen, "La formation de l'Exégèse patristique de 1 Cor 15, 24-28," *AEPHE* 82 [1973/1974] 62–64); and on the Valentinian exegesis of *subiectio Filii.*

[14]All the scriptural texts beyond Rev 20:5-6 and Matt 26:29 are found in an Armenian fragment and not in the Latin manuscripts; Orbe (*Comentario* 3.616–617) notes the much more strongly millenarian cast introduced through Rousseau's incorporation of the Armenian.

[15]Latin *concorporatum*, Greek retroversion *sussōmon;* the awkward neologism reflects a primitive stage well before the development of a technical christological vocabulary.

[16]Rousseau sees here a play on *sapientia,* so that it denotes both the understanding deployed by God throughout the creative and redemptive processes and also the Wisdom or Spirit of God. If this is the case, then, as Rousseau suggests, there is a trinitarian allusion in this concluding passage. See SC 152:351, note marked "p. 465, n. 2." Such an allusion would not be unexpected.

Afterword

Guidebooks lead, not to conclusions, but to visits to new places or to new views of familiar territory. One highlight of the journey through *Adversus haereses* is insight into the living association of the Scriptures and the Rule of Faith, specifically insight into the vital, complex, and highly organized ways in which the Irenaean project concerns itself with right interpretation of the Scriptures. The Rule of Faith supplies his interpretive principle. In turn the Scriptures supply the explanation of the Rule of Faith, the *content* of which is understood as a "narrative creed" telling the theological story of Jesus Christ. The Rule of Faith and the Scriptures are in a dialogical relationship, each amplifying and correcting the insights of the other.

To deal with the transmission of the Rule of Faith Irenaeus invokes the vocabulary of tradition. The faith belongs to the universal Church; having been proclaimed by the prophets it was received by the Church from the apostles and their disciples. The Church that accepted the faith guards, preaches, and teaches it, transmitting it as if possessing a single mouth. Thus Irenaeus outlines a clear dynamism around the Rule of Faith. The function of the Rule is to unify the Church wherever it is found. In Irenaeus's view it works to create unity in such a way that human limitations do not impede it. Dissident interpretations are to be rejected.

Thus for Irenaeus the Scriptures belong to the Church in such a way that *any valid reading must be congruent with the faith of that community.* It is in this sense that for Irenaeus there is only one "right reading," and so it becomes critically important for him to reject false interpretation. The whole of *Adversus haereses* is an exercise organized toward exegesis under the Rule of Faith. In Book One, designed to denounce Gnostic teaching, the movement is from one Gnostic system and its exegesis (always criticized, as we have seen, by contrast to the "right" exegesis) through comparison with orthodox unity to multiplicity of Valentinian Gnostic ancestors, remote and immediate. The dominant role of the Rule of Faith is apparent when Irenaeus compares the

Gnostic positions to the Rule of Faith at *AH* I. 10 and 22, supported by right exegesis of the Scriptures.

Irenaeus planned Book Two to refute Gnostic teaching; here the Rule of Faith serves to supply him with the understanding of God against which he measures the Gnostic understanding of the Deity, which he finds wanting and rebuts. As he attacks Gnostic exegesis, Irenaeus presents what he views as conditions for the right use of the Scriptures, in which he explores the role of theology. In Books Three through Five, his "proof from the Scriptures," Irenaeus interprets the Scriptures according to the Rule of Faith in order to complete the overthrow of the Gnostics.

Throughout *Adversus haereses* Irenaeus reveals himself as a highly disciplined thinker. His exegetical method offers a key to the organization of his work. It involves two literary processes: first, announcement of a word of the Lord, citation of it, and commentary on it. This process supplies external unity to his work. The second process consists in joining the words of the Lord to one another, so supplying internal unity to his developing argument. The resultant structure is chiastic.

The formal unity supplied by this method supports a unified content: the explanation of the Rule of Faith or the meaning of belief in the One God, Father, Son, and Spirit with, as we have seen, implications for the understanding of Church, human person, and human destiny. To proclaim this content is Irenaeus's task as leader of the Church, a task shaped by the context of the times in which he lived. That context includes the presence within the Christian community of Valentinian Gnostics. Irenaeus sees this group as adversaries to be opposed. But who are they?

Another highlight of the journey was to notice that study of *Adversus haereses,* especially *AH* I, enables us to catch a glimpse of the "face of the adversary." The book's triadic organization includes a summary of the Valentinian myth, a contrast between the Church's unity and Valentinian diversity in doctrine, practices, rites, and exegeses, and a review of Valentinian ancestry attentive to the link between belief and life. Even on Irenaeus's presentation, (that is, the presentation of someone opposed to the Valentinians), the Valentinian mythology appears to be complex and internally consistent; it betrays an intelligent understanding of the religious questions of the day. From the perspective of Irenaeus the central problem with this mythology is that it is supported by an interpretation of the Scriptures that works from a different theological principle than that used by the community led by Irenaeus. The Valentinians display rich diversity in expressions of the myth and in forms of ritual; such diversity contrasts with the emerging common Christian experience. In addition, not only do these thinkers use a different principle to support their exegesis but they also make use of a wider variety of scriptural texts than those in use in the Church. When one considers the ancestry of the Valentinians one encounters questions about the link between doctrine and practice.

The many shadings of Gnostic mythology support quite diverse life choices, including encratism. The Valentinian Gnostic face that presents itself is intelligent, probably educated, creative, and unafraid of the challenges of diversity, whether in the Scriptures or in rite, in myth or in life choices. It is also the face of one at home with women's leadership.

A third highlight of the journey was to discover Irenaeus himself, who appears as a man deeply immersed in the Scriptures, which he uses skillfully to defend the Rule of Faith received from the Church. In doing so he reveals himself as one who assigns a high value to the material world. He views the primal sin as a misstep rather than a fall into the abyss; it is part of the moral education of the race. He stresses the inclusion of all in Christ through the doctrine of recapitulation. Notably (in light of criticisms that have been made of him), he makes no remarks about "wanton women," nor does he attack Gnostic women's roles in leadership. In all of these ways he is in harmony with the popular understanding of his famous line: "The glory of God is the human person, fully alive."

But Irenaeus understands that fullness of life in ways popular understanding alone does not penetrate. For him fullness of human life is in the vision of God: "the life of the human person is the vision of God." Participation in that vision is in two ways: first, by the race in a manner that evolves across salvation history. Thus God was seen then, in the Old Testament, in a prophetic manner through the mediation of the Spirit. God is seen now, in the time following the New Testament, in an adoptive manner through the mediation of the Incarnate Son. God will be seen in the future, that is, in the resurrection, in a paternal manner through the gift of the Father. The three periods correspond to a progressively fuller revelation.

In an individual life a similar pattern unfolds. The Spirit prepares each person for the Son, and the Son then leads that one to the Father, who delights in giving each one the vision of God. The vision of God results in a share in the divine life, and so—for mortal humans—a share in what Irenaeus calls "incorruptibility."

The two testaments are the work of One God who nonetheless utilizes the Hands of God, that is, the Word and the Wisdom, or the Son and the Spirit, to accomplish the divine work: thus *AH* IV. All of the Scriptures witness to that One God, as the first half of *AH* III makes clear, and the gospels teach that Jesus Christ is the Son of God incarnate. The incarnation is central to *AH* V, and itself postulates the resurrection of the flesh. Because of the flesh common to the Incarnate One and to humanity, humanity is saved in all that it is, including the flesh; the epistles of Paul support this teaching. The One God, Creator and Father, is witnessed to by the life and death of Christ and by the teaching of the Scriptures relative to the end time.

At the close of the journey the traveler may choose to compare what the journey revealed with the situation at home. Irenaeus claimed as the right and duty of the leaders of the Christian Church the interpretation of the Scriptures in a way consistent with the Rule of Faith contained in those same Scriptures. In doing so he played a central role in shaping Christian identity not only in the second century but for all the centuries since. The soteriological principle he used played a significant role in fourth- and fifth-century theology. His theology of image and likeness has relationships to that taught by the Greek Fathers.

Unfortunately not all that he taught has been as faithfully heeded as his position on the teaching authority or his contribution to christological thought. His emphasis on the positive value of the flesh, his penchant for attaching a minimum weight to the primal sin and a maximum weight to human freedom, and his insistence on the positive value of human history seem to have gone the way of his style of Scripture interpretation. It may not be possible or desirable to reclaim the latter, but what a pity to abandon his rich theology! In addition, the spirituality dependent on that theology deserves further study in itself, with attention to the context from which it emerged. Careful study of Irenaeus has the potential to inject the Christian Church with the fullness of life appropriate to a new millennium.

Feast of Saint Irenaeus
June 28, 1997

The Question of Irenaeus's Reliability

In a body of work so keyed to polemical response the question of the writer's reliability as a witness to his opponents' positions must be raised. The question is all the more acute because Irenaeus has long been a principal source for knowledge of Gnosticism. Nineteenth-century historical-critical scholarship recognized the polemical character of heresiological reports of opponents and so treated this material, including that of Irenaeus, as suspect. C. Schmidt[2] and E. de Faye[3] recognized the corroborative value of Gnostic material like that in the then newly discovered Codex Berolinensis 8502. F. Sagnard[4] was cautious about all but firsthand accounts; in his view Irenaeus can be trusted when writing about those of whom he has personal knowledge. What remained problematic was the use of secondary sources by Irenaeus as well as others.

Discovery of the Nag Hammadi library changed the situation. Frederik Wisse[5] has compared the writings of the heresiologists with the Nag Hammadi library and finds two major discrepancies that must be accounted for. The first is lack of significant overlapping in material and detail. One might expect in so large a collection to find some of the sources used by the heresiologists. In fact there are only five cases of clear agreement. Of these, three certainly and one possibly are with Irenaeus.[6] A second discrepancy is that the heresiologists name various sects, describing them in terms of characteristic traits and teachings as if each had developed its own distinct doctrines. The collection as a whole and individual writings within it contain ideas that according to the heresiologists are appropriate to different sects. This raises the question whether the sects were indeed as differentiated by doctrine as the ancient Church writers indicated.

In Wisse's own view the sections in which Irenaeus discusses Ptolemy (*AH* I. 1–8) and the Marcosians (*AH* I. 13–21) as well as *AH* I. 9–10 and *AH* I. 31, 3-4 are of the bishop's own composition and draw on his direct knowledge of the disciples of Ptolemy and Marcus. Wisse thinks the remaining passages describing Gnostic sects derive from an earlier catalog of heresies.[7] To such a source Wisse attaches the blame for describing Gnostics as "pathological systems builders" comprising numerous sects; this differs from what we read in the Nag Hammadi library.[8]

Pheme Perkins[9] attacks Wisse's position, maintaining that considerations of style and literary genre raise problems. Drawing on studies by W. R. Schoedel[10] and R. M. Grant,[11] she recalls that oral and rhetorical models greatly influenced ancient writers and shows how in *AH* I Irenaeus follows the model of a rhetorical refutation. (In 1981 Gerard Vallée[12] developed this insight but without attention to the reliability of Irenaeus's presentation of Gnostic thought.) What of Wisse's theory of an earlier heresiological source? In Perkins's judgment *AH* I. 11 and 12 are rightly ascribed to Irenaeus since each contains elements proper to the refutation. *AH* I. 29 and 30 are also ascribed to Irenaeus, in this case as a result of comparison of style and method between clear Irenaean materials and clear source material.

Elaine Pagels[13] has challenged the dependability of Irenaeus's accounts of Gnostic teaching in another passage, contending that in *AH* I. 7, 1 Irenaeus distorts the correct account preserved in Clement of Alexandria. In a review of her publications through 1977 Grant[14] finds minimal differences between the texts. He notes that this aspect of Pagels' position has been questioned by Schoedel and rejected by Ekkehard Muhlenberg. J. F. McCue[15] (1980) also questions the attack on Irenaeus's reliability. The issue remains controverted.

If read with attention to his goal and methodology the work of Irenaeus can yield a fair appreciation of the Valentinians. Study of the Nag Hammadi material has not thus far raised substantial challenges to this opinion.

NOTES

[1]With the exception of the final paragraph this was originally published as part of "Irenaeus" in David N. Freedman, ed., *ABD* 3 (Garden City, N.Y.: Doubleday, 1992) 457–461. Used by permission.

[2]"Irenaus und seine Quelle in Adversus Haereses I, 29," in *Philothesia. Paul Kleinert zum LXX. Geburtstage dargebracht* (Berlin, 1907) 315–336.

[3]*Gnostiques et gnosticisme. Etude critique des documents de gnosticisme chrétien* (2nd ed. Paris: Librairie orientaliste P. Guethner, 1925).

[4]*La gnose valentinienne et le témoignage de Saint Irénée* (Paris: J. Vrin, 1947).

[5]"The Nag Hammadi Library and the Heresiologists," *VigChr* 25 (1971) 205–223.

[6]Ibid. 217–218.

[7]Ibid. 212–215.

[8]Ibid. 218–219.

[9]"Irenaeus and the Gnostics: Rhetoric and Composition in *Adversus Haereses* book one," *VigChr* 30 (1976) 193–200.

[10]"Philosophy and Rhetoric in the *Adversus Haereses* of Irenaeus," *VigChr* 13 (1959) 22–32.

[11]"Irenaeus and Hellenistic Culture," *HThR* 42 (1949) 41–51.

[12]*A Study in Anti-Gnostic Polemics: Irenaeus, Hippolytus, and Epiphanius.* Studies in Christianity and Judaism 1 (Waterloo, Ont.: Wilfrid Laurier University Press, 1981).

[13]"Conflicting Versions of Valentinian Eschatology. Irenaeus' *Treatise* vs. the *Excerpts from Theodotus*," *HThR* 67 (1974) 35–53.

[14]Review of *The Johannine Gospel in Gnostic Exegesis* and *The Gnostic Paul*, by Elaine Pagels, *RStR* 3 (1977) 30–34.

[15]"Conflicting Versions of Valentinianism? Irenaeus and the *Excerpta ex Theodoto*," in Bentley Layton, ed., *The Rediscovery of Gnosticism* (Leiden: Brill, 1980) 404–416.

Bibliography

All citations of Irenaeus are from the critical edition unless otherwise noted. A citation such as *AH* IV. 20, 7 (SC 100:648) indicates *Adversus haereses,* Book IV, ch. 20, paragraph 7; where an SC number follows, it indicates Sources chrétiennes volume number (here, 100) and page (here, 648). The division into books is from Irenaeus; that into chapters comes from the manuscript tradition for books one through four, although succeeding editors have reorganized the chapters variously. The major differences in commonly used editions are between Harvey and Migne. The Sources chrétiennes edition follows Migne but indicates the corresponding Harvey numeration on every page. Translations throughout are my own unless otherwise indicated. This includes most biblical quotations, which I have translated from the text of Irenaeus. Those cases in which I have preferred to use the NRSV are marked.

PRINCIPAL SOURCES (WORKS OF IRENAEUS)

Irenaeus. *Adversus haereses.* J.-P. Migne, ed. Patrologia Graeca 7, cols. 437–1224, 1882. Reprint of Massuet's 1712 edition.

_____. *Libros quinque Adversus haereses.* William W. Harvey ed. Cambridge: Typus Academicus, 1857; repr. Ridgewood, N.J.: Gregg, 1965.

_____. *Adversus haereses. Contre les hérésies* 4, vols. 1 and 2. Adelin Rousseau, ed., with Bertrand Hemmerdinger, Louis Doutreleau, and Charles Mercier. SC 100. Paris: Cerf, 1965.

_____. *Adversus haereses. Contre les hérésies* 5, vols. 1 and 2. Adelin Rousseau, Louis Doutreleau, and Charles Mercier, eds. SC 152, 153. Paris: Cerf, 1969.

_____. *Adversus haereses. Contre les hérésies* 3, vols. 1 and 2. Adelin Rousseau and Louis Doutreleau, eds. SC 210, 211. Paris: Cerf, 1974.

_____. *Adversus haereses. Contre les hérésies* 1, vols. 1 and 2. Adelin Rousseau and Louis Doutreleau, eds. SC 263, 264. Paris: Cerf, 1979.

_____. *Adversus haereses. Contre les hérésies* 2, vols. 1 and 2. Adelin Rousseau and Louis Doutreleau, eds. SC 293, 294. Paris: Cerf, 1982.

_____. *Against Heresies* 1–5. Roberts and J. Donaldson, eds.; Grand, translator, in *Ante-Nicene Fathers* 1. Grand Rapids: Eerdmans, 1973; reprint of 1867 ed., 309–567; with fragments of lost works, 568–578.

_____. *Against the Heresies,* I. Translated and annotated by Dominic Unger, O.F.M. cap., with further revisions by John J. Dillon. ACW 55. New York: Paulist, 1992.

_____. *Proof of the Apostolic Preaching.* Joseph P. Smith, S.J., ed. ACW 16. New York: Newman, 1952.

_____. *Démonstration de la Prédication apostolique d' Irénée de Lyon.* L. M. Froideraux, ed. SC 62. Paris: Cerf, 1971.

SECONDARY WORKS

Abramowski, Luise. "Irenaeus, Adv. haer. III, 3, 2: Ecclesia Romana and omnis Ecclesia; and ibid., 3, 3: Anacletus of Rome," *JThS* n.s. 28 (1977) 101–104.

Aland, Barbara, et al, eds. *Gnosis. Festschrift für Hans Jonas.* Göttingen: Vandenhoeck & Ruprecht, 1978.

d'Alès, A. "La doctrine eucharistique de saint Irénée," *RSR* 13 (1923) 24–46.

_____. "Le mot *oikonomia* dans la langue théologique de saint Irénée," *REG* 32 (1919) 1–9.

Ammundsen, Vladamar. "The Rule of Truth in Irenaeus," *JThS* 13 (1912) 547–580.

Andia, Ysabel de. *Homo vivens. Incorruptibilité et divinisation de l'homme selon Irénée de Lyon.* Paris: Études Augustiniennes, 1986.

Audin, Amable. "Sur la géographie du Lyon-Romain: La population, les voies et les quartiers," *Revue de géographie de Lyon* (1952) 133–139.

_____. "Sur les origines de l'église de Lyon" in *L'homme devant Dieu. Mélanges offerts au Père Henri de Lubac. I: Exégèse et patristique.* Paris: Aubier, 1963, 223–234.

Bacq, Philippe. *De l'ancienne à la nouvelle alliance selon S. Irénée. Unité du livre IV de l'Adversus haereses.* Paris: Lethielleux, 1978.

Barnes, T. D. *Constantine and Eusebius.* Cambridge, Mass.: Harvard, 1981.

_____. "Eusebius and the Date of the Martyrdoms" in CNRS, eds., *Les martyrs de Lyon (177).* Paris: Éditions du Centre national de la Recherche scientifique, 1978, 137–143.

Bauer, Walter. *Rechtgläubigkeit und Ketzerei im ältesten Christentum.* Tübingen: Mohr/Siebeck, 1934. English: Robert A. Kraft and Gerhard Krodel, eds., *Orthodoxy and Heresy in Earliest Christianity.* Philadelphia: Fortress, 1971.

Benoît, André. "Irénée et l'hérésie. Les conceptions hérésiologiques de l'éveque de Lyon." *Aug.* 20 (1980) 55–67.

_____. *Saint Irénée. Introduction à l'étude de sa théologie.* EhPhR 52. Paris: Presses universitaires de France, 1960.

Berthouzoz, Roger. *Liberté et grâce suivant la théologie d'Irénée de Lyon.* Paris: Cerf, 1980.

Bianchi, U., ed. *Le origini dello gnosticismo*. Coloquio de Messina, April, 1966. Leiden: Brill, 1967.

Boulluec, Alain Le. *La notion d'hérésie dans la littérature grecque IIe–IIIe siècles. I: De Justin à Irénée*. Paris: Etudes Augustiniennes, 1985.

Bousset, Wilhelm. *Jüdisch-Christlicher Schulbetrieb in Alexandria und Rom, literarische Untersuchungen zu Philo, Clemens von Alexandria, Justin und Irenäus*. Göttingen: Vandenhoeck & Ruprecht, 1915.

_____. *Kyrios Christos: A History of the Belief in Christ from the Beginnings of Christianity to Irenaeus*. Translated by John E. Steel. Nashville: Abingdon, 1970.

Bowersock, Glen. "Les Eglises de Lyon et de Vienne; relations avec l'Asie" in CNRS, eds., *Les martyrs de Lyon*. Paris: Éditions du Centre national de la Recherche scientifique, 1978, 249–256.

Breck, John. "Biblical Chiasmus: Exploring Structure for Meaning," *BTB* 17 (1987) 70–74.

Brind'Amour, Pierre. "La Date du Martyre de Saint Polycarpe (le 23 Février 167)," *AnBoll* 98 (1980) 456–462.

Brown, Peter. *The World of Late Antiquity: AD 150–750*. London: Harcourt, Brace, Jovanovich, reprint 1978.

Brown, Raymond E. *The Birth of the Messiah*. Garden City, N.Y.: Doubleday, 1977.

Brox, Norbert. "Charisma veritatis certum (zu Irenäus Adv. haer. IV, 26, 2)," *ZKG* 75 (1964) 327–331.

_____. *Offenbarung, Gnosis, und gnosticher Mythos bei Irenäus von Lyon. Zur Charakteristik der Systeme*. SPS 1. Salzburg and Munich: Pustet, 1966.

_____. "Rom und 'jede Kirche' im 2. Jahrhundert. Zu Irenäus, Adv. haer. III, 3, 2," in W. von Brandmueller and R. Baumer, eds., *Festgabe Hubert Jedin zum 75. Geburtstag*. AHC 7. Paderborn: Schöningh, 1975, 42–78.

Clark, David J. "Criteria for Identifying Chiasm" *LingBibl* 35 (1975) 63–72.

Comby, Jean. *177–1977: Aux origenes de l'église de Lyon: Irénée*. Lyon: Faculté de théologie, 1977.

_____. *L'evangile au confluent. Dix-huit siècles de christianisme à Lyon*. Lyon: Chalet, 1977.

Congar, Yves M. J. *Je crois en l'Esprit Saint, III: Le Fleuve de Vie coule en Orient et in Occident*. Paris: Cerf, 1980. English: *I Believe in the Holy Spirit 3: The River of the Water of Life (Rev 22:1) flows in the East and in the West*. Translated by David Smith. New York: Seabury, 1983.

Desjardins, Michel. *Sin in Valentinianism*. Atlanta: Scholars Press, 1990.

Donahue, John R. *The Gospel in Parable: Metaphor, Narrative, and Theology in the Synoptic Gospels*. Philadelphia: Fortress, 1988.

Donovan, Mary Ann. "Alive to the Glory of God: A Key Insight in St. Irenaeus," *Theological Studies* 49 (1988) 283–297.

_____. "Insights on Ministry: Irenaeus," *TJT* 2 (1987) 79–93.

_____. "Irenaeus: At the Heart of Life, Glory," in Annice Callahan, ed., *Spiritualities of the Heart: Approaches to Personal Wholeness in Christian Tradition.* New York: Paulist, 1990, 111–122.

_____. "Irenaeus in Recent Scholarship," *SecCen* 4 (1984) 238–240.

Fantino, Jacques. *L'homme image de Dieu Chez Saint Irénée de Lyon.* Paris: Cerf, 1986.

Faye, Eugene de. *Gnostiques et gnosticisme. Etude critique des documents gnosticisme chrétien.* 2nd ed. Paris: Librairie orientaliste P. Guethner, 1925.

Filoramo, Giovanni. *L'attesa della fine: Storia della gnosi.* Rome: Laterza, 1983. English: *A History of Gnosticism.* Translated by Anthony Alcock. Oxford: Blackwell, 1990.

Ford, J. Massyngberde. *Revelation: Introduction, Translation and Commentary.* AB 38. New York: Doubleday, 1975.

Gilliard, Frank. "The Apostolicity of Gallic Churches," *HThR* 68 (1975) 17–33.

González Faus, J. I. *Carne de Dios. Significado salvador de la encarnación en la teología de San Ireneo.* Barcelona: Herder, 1970.

Grabar, André. *Christian Iconography: A Study of Its Origins.* The Andrew W. Mellon Lectures in the Fine Arts, 1961. BollS 35. Princeton: Princeton University Press, 1961.

Grant, Robert M. *After the New Testament.* Philadelphia: Fortress, 1967.

_____. "The Heresy of Tatian," *JThS* n.s. 5 (1954) 62–68.

_____. "Irenaeus and Hellenistic Culture," *HThR* 42 (1949) 41–51.

_____. Review of *The Johannine Gospel in Gnostic Exegesis* and *The Gnostic Paul,* by Elaine Pagels, *RStR* 3 (1977) 30–34.

Green, Henry A. *The Economic and Social Origins of Gnosticism.* SBL.DS 77. Atlanta: Scholars, 1985.

Greer, R. A. "The Dog and the Mushrooms. Irenaeus' View of the Valentinians Assessed," in Bentley Layton, ed., *The Rediscovery of Gnosticism.* 2 vols. Proceedings of the International Conference on Gnosticism at Yale, 1978. Leiden: Brill, 1978, 1.146–175.

Grillmeier, Aloys. *Christ in Christian Tradition* 1. Translated by John Bowden. 2nd rev. ed. Atlanta: John Knox, 1974.

Gross, Jules. *La divinisation du Chrétien d'après les Pères grecs.* Paris: Gabalda, 1938.

Halvorsen, B. *La formation de l'exégèse patristique de 1 Cor 15, 24-28.* AEPHE 82 (1983/1984) 62–64.

Harnack, Adolf von. "Der Presbyter-Prediger des Irenäus IV, 27, 1-32. 1; Bruckstücke und Nachklänge der ältesten exegetisch-polemischen Homilien," *Philotesia zu Paul Kleinert zum LXX. Geburtstage dargebracht.* Berlin, 1907, 1–38.

Harris, William V. *Ancient Literacy.* Cambridge, Mass: Harvard University Press, 1989.

Hay, D. M. *Glory at the Right Hand: Psalm 110 in Early Christianity.* SBL.MS 18. Nashville: Abingdon, 1973.

Hedrick, Charles W., and Rogert Hodgson, Jr., eds. *Nag Hammadi, Gnosticism, and Early Christianity.* Peabody, Mass.: Hendrickson, 1986.

Houssiau, A. *La Cristologie de saint Irénée.* Louvain: Publications universitaires de Louvain, 1955.

Jonas, Hans. *Gnosis und spätantiker Geist.* 2 vols. Vol. 1 Göttingen: Vandenhoeck & Ruprecht, 1934. Vol. 2 Göttingen: Vandenhoeck & Ruprecht, 1954.

_____. *The Gnostic Religion.* 2nd ed. Boston: Beacon, 1963.

Kasher, Rimon. "The Interpretation of Scripture in Rabbinic Literature," in Mulder and Sysling, eds., *Mikra: Text, Translation, Reading and Interpretation of the Hebrew Bible in Ancient Judaism and Early Christianity,* 560–577.

Kelly, J.N.D. *Early Christian Creeds.* 3rd ed. Longman: New York, 1972.

Keresztes, P. "The Massacre at Lugdunum in 177 AD," *Hist.* 16 (1967) 65–86.

Koschorke, Klaus. "Gnostic Instructions on the Organization of the Congregation: The Tractate *Interpretation of Knowledge* from CG XI" in Bentley Layton, ed., *Rediscovery of Gnosticism* 2:757–769.

Kretschmar, Georg. "Zur religionsgeschichtlichen Einordnung der Gnosis," *EvTh* 13 (1953) 354–361.

Kugel, James L., and Rowan A. Greer. *Early Biblical Interpretation.* LEC 3. Philadelphia: Westminster, 1986.

Langerbeck, H. *Aufsätze zur Gnosis.* Göttingen: Vandenhoeck & Ruprecht, 1967.

Lanne, E. "L'église de Rome 'a gloriosissimis duobus apostolis Petro et Paulo Romae fundatae et constitutae ecclesiae' (Adv. Haer. III, 3, 2)," *Irén.* 49 (1976) 275–322.

_____. "La règle de vérité. Aux Sources d'une expression de S. Irénée," in *Miscellanea C. Vagaggini,* 1980.

Lassiat, H. "L'anthropologie de Irénée," *NRTh* 100 (1978) 399–417.

Lawson, John. *The Biblical Theology of St. Irenaeus.* London: Epworth, 1948.

Layton, Bentley, ed. *The Rediscovery of Gnosticism.* Proceedings of the International Conference on Gnosticism at Yale, March 28–31, 1978. I: The School of Valentinus. Leiden: Brill, 1980. II: Sethian Gnosticism. Leiden: Brill, 1981.

Lindemann, Andreas. *Paulus im ältesten Christentum: Das Bild des Apostels und die Rezeption der Paulinischen Theologie in der frühchristlichen Literatur bis Marcion.* Tübingen: J. C. B. Mohr, 1979.

Loofs, F. *Theophilus von Antiochien Adversus Marcionem und die anderen theologischen Quellen bei Irenäeus.* TU 46, part 2. Leipzig: J. C. Hinrichs, 1930.

Les Martyrs de Lyon (177). Paris: Éditions du Centre national de la Recherche scientifique, 1978.

McCue, J. F. "Conflicting Versions of Valentinianism? Irenaeus and the *Excerpta ex Theodoto,*" in Bentley Layton, ed., *The Rediscovery of Gnosticism.* Leiden: Brill, 1980, 2:404–416.

Meyer, Ben F. *The Early Christians: Their World, Mission and Self-Discovery.* Wilmington, Del: Michael Glazier, 1986.

Mulder, Martin Jan, and Harry Sysling, eds. *Mikra: Text, Translation, Reading and Interpretation of the Hebrew Bible in Ancient Judaism and Early Christianity.* Philadelphia: Fortress, 1988.

Neusner, Jacob. *Midrash in Context: Exegesis in Formative Judaism.* Philadelphia: Fortress, 1983.

Nielsen, J. T. *Adam and Christ in the Theology of Irenaeus of Lyons.* Assen: Van Gorcum, 1968.

Nock, Arthur Darby. "Gnosticism," *HThR* 57 (1964) 255–279.

Ochagavia, Juan. *Visibile Patris Filius: A Study of Irenaeus' Teaching on Revelation and Tradition.* OCA 17. Rome: Gregoriana, 1964.

Orbe, Antonio. *Antropología de San Ireneo.* Madrid: Biblioteca de Autores cristianos, 1969.

_____. *Cristologia Gnostica: Introduccion a la soteriología de los siglos II y III, 1.* Madrid: Biblioteca de Autores cristianos, 1976.

_____. "La definición del hombre en la teología del s. II," *Gr.* 48 (1967) 522–575.

_____. *Hacia la primera teología de la procesión del Verbo: Estudios Valentinianos, 1.* AnGr 99. Rome, 1958.

_____. *Parabolas evangelicas in San Ireneo.* 2 vols. Madrid: Biblioteca de Autores cristianos, 1972.

_____. "La Virgen Maria abogada de la virgen Eva; en torno a s. Ireneo adv. haer. V, 19, 1" *Gr.* 63 (1982) 453–506.

_____. " San Ireneo adopcionista? En torna a adv. haer. III, 19, 1" *Gr.* 65 (1984) 5–52.

_____. "S. Ireneo y el régimen del milenio" in *Eschatology in Christianity and Other Religions.* StMiss 32 (1983) 345–372.

_____. *Teología de San Ireneo, Comentario al Libro V del "Adversus Haereses."* 3 vols. Biblioteca de Autores cristianos, serie maier, 25. Madrid: La Editorial Católica, 1985–1988.

_____. "Visión del Padre e incorruptela según san Ireneo." *Gr.* 64 (1983) 199–240.

Pagels, Elaine H. "Conflicting Versions of Valentinian Eschatology. Irenaeus' *Treatise* vs. the *Excerpts from Theodotus." HThR* 67 (1974) 35–53.

_____. *The Gnostic Gospels.* New York: Random House, 1979.

_____. *The Gnostic Paul: Gnostic Exegesis of the Pauline Letters.* Philadelphia: Fortress, 1975.

_____. *The Johannine Gospel in Gnostic Exegesis: Heracleon's Commentary on John.* SBL.MS 17. New York: Abingdon, 1973.

_____. "A Valentinian Interpretation of Baptism and Eucharist and its Critique of 'Orthodox' Sacramental Theology and Practice," *HThR* 65 (1972) 153–169.

_____. "The Valentinian Claim to Esoteric Exegesis of Romans as Basis for Anthropological Theory" *VigChr* 26 (1972) 241–251.

Pearson, Birger. "Use, Authority and Exegesis of Mikra in Gnostic Literature," in Mulder and Sysling, eds., *Mikra: Text, Translation, Reading and Interpretation of the Hebrew Bible in Ancient Judaism and Early Christianity,* 35–52.

Perkins, Pheme. *The Gnostic Dialogue: The Early Church and the Crisis of Gnosticism.* New York: Paulist, 1980.

_____. "Irenaeus and the Gnostics: Rhetoric and Composition in *Adversus Haereses* book one." *VigChr* 30 (1976) 193–200.

_____. "Ordering the Cosmos: Irenaeus and the Gnostics," in Hedrick and Hodgson, eds., *Nag Hammadi, Gnosticism, and Early Christianity,* 221–238.

Pétrement, Simone. *Le Dieu Séparé: Les origines du gnosticisme.* Paris: Cerf, 1984. English: *A Separate God: The Christian Origins of Gnosticism.* San Francisco: Harper, 1990.

Pietrella, E. "Caro et sanguis regnum Dei possidere non possunt (I Cor 15:50). I: L'exegesi gnostica ed ecclesiastica fini ad Ireneo. II: L'exegesi gnostica ed ecclesiastica in Tertullian" *Aevum* 49 (1975) 36–76.

Powell, D. "Ordo presbyterii," *JThS* n.s. 26 (1975) 290–328.

Power, David N. *Irenaeus of Lyons on Baptism and Eucharist: Selected Texts with Introduction, Translation and Annotation.* Alcuin/GROW Liturgical Study 18. Bramcote, Nottingham: Grove, 1991.

Prestige, G. L. *God in Patristic Thought.* 2nd ed. London: S.P.C.K., 1969.

Puech, Aimé. *Histoire de la littérature grecque-chrétienne depuis les origines jusqu'à la fin du IVème siècle. Vol. 1: Les IIe et IIIe siècles.* Paris: Les Belles-Lettres, 1928.

Puech, Henri-Charles, ed. *En quête de la Gnose.* 2 vols. Paris: Gallimard, 1978.

Quinn, J. D. "Charisma veritatis certum. Irenaeus, Adversus haereses IV, 26, 1," *TS* 39 (1978) 520–525.

Quispel, Gilles. *Gnosis als Welt-religion.* Zurich: Origo, 1951.

_____. "Der gnostische Anthropos und die jüdische Tradition," *Eranos Jahrbuch* 22 (1953) 354–361.

Rahner, Karl. "Theos in the New Testament," *Theological Investigations* 1. Translated by Cornelius Ernst. London: Longman & Todd, 1963, 79–148.

Reynders, Bruno. *Lexique comparé du texte grec et des versions latine, arménienne et syrique l'Adversus Haereses de saint Irénée.* CSCO 141, subsidia 5–6. Louvain: Orientaliste, 1954.

_____. "Paradosis: Le progrès de l'idée tradition jusqu'à S. Irénée," *RThAM* 5 (1933) 155–191.

Ries, J., et al, eds. *Gnosticisme et monde héllénistique. Actes du colloque de Louvain-la-Neuve (11–13 Mars 1980).* Louvain: Université catholique de Louvain, 1980.

Robinson, James M., general ed. *The Nag Hammadi Library in English.* 3rd rev. ed. San Francisco: Harper & Row, 1988.

Rordorf, W., and A. Schneider. *L'évolution du concept de tradition dans l'église ancienne.* TC 5. Bern and Frankfurt: Peter Lang, 1982.

Rudolf, Kurt. *Die Gnosis: Wesen und Geschichte einer spätantiken Religion.* GDR: Köhler & Amelang, 1977. English: *Gnosis.* Translated by R. M. Wilson. Edinburgh: T & T Clark, 1983.

Ruggini, Lellia Cracco. "Les structures de la société et de l'économie lyonnaises au IIe siècle, par rapport à la politique locale et imperiale," in *Les martyres de Lyon (177).* Paris: Éditions du Centre national de la Recherche scientifique, 1978, 65–92.

_____. "Nuclei immigrati e forze indigene in tre grandi centri commerciali dell' impero," *MAAR* 36 (1980) 55–76.

Safrai, Shmuel. *The Literature of the Sages, Part 2: Midrash, Aggada, Midrash Collections, Targum, Prayer.* Philadelphia: Fortress, 1987.

Sagnard, François. *La gnose valentinienne et le témoignage de Saint Irénée.* EPhM 36. Paris: J. Vrin, 1947.

Saxer, Victor. "L'authenticité du 'Martyre du Polycarp': Bilan de 25 ans de critique," *MEFRA* 94 (1982) 979–1001.

Schendel, E. *Herrschaft und Unterwerfung Christi. 1 Kor 15, 24-28 in Exegese und Theologie der Väter bis zum Ausgang des 4. Jahrhunderts.* Tübingen: J.C.B. Mohr, 1971.

Schmidt, C. "Irenäus und seine Quelle in Adversûs Haereses I, 29," in *Philotesia zu Paul Kleinert zum LXX. Geburtstage dargebracht.* Berlin, 1907, 315–336.

Schoedel, W. R. "Philosophy and Rhetoric in the *Adversus Haereses* of Irenaeus," *VigChr* 13 (1959) 22–32.

_____. "Theological Method in Irenaeus," *JThS* n.s. 35 (1984) 31–49.

Schoedel, W. R., and R. L. Wilken, eds. *Early Christian Literature and the Classical Intellectual Tradition. In honorem R. M. Grant.* ThH 53. Paris: Beauchesne, 1979.

Scholer, David M., ed. *Nag Hammadi Bibliography, 1948–1969.* Leiden: Brill, 1971.

Schottroff, Luise. "Animae naturaliter salvanda: zum Problem der himmlischen Herkunft des Gnostikers," in W. Eltester, ed., *Christentum und Gnosis.* Berlin: Topelmann, 1969, 65–97.

Segal, Alan F. *Two Powers in Heaven: Early Rabbinic Reports About Christianity and Gnosticism.* Studies in Late Antiquity 27. Leiden: Brill, 1977.

Sesboüé, Bernard. "La preuve par les Ecritures chez S. Irénée. A propos d'un texte difficile du livre III de l'Adversus haereses," *NRTh* 103 (1981) 872–887.

Simonin, H. D. "A propos d'un texte eucharistique de S. Irénée," *RSPhTh* 23 (1940) 281–292.

Singles, D. *Le temps du salut chez S. Irénée.* Lyon: Profac, 1980.

Sobosan, J. G. "The Role of the Presbyter. An Investigation into the Adversus Haereses of Saint Irenaeus," *DJTh* 27 (1974) 129–146.

Stock, Augustine, o.s.b. "Chiastic Awareness and Education in Antiquity," *BTB* 14 (1984) 23–27.

Sumney, Jerry. "The Letter of Eugnostos and the Origins of Gnosticism," *NT* 31 (1989) 172–181.

Trembley, R. *La manifestation et la vision de Dieu selon S. Irénée de Lyon.* MBTh 41. Münster (Westfalen): Aschendorff, 1978.

Turcan, Robert. "Les religions 'orientales' à Lugdunum en 177," in *Les martyrs de Lyon (177)*. Paris: Éditions du Centre national de la Recherche scientifique, 1978, 195–210.

Vallée, Gérard. *A Study in Anti-Gnostic Polemics: Irenaeus, Hippolytus, and Epiphanius*. Canadian Corporation for Studies in Religion. SCJud 1. Waterloo, Ont: Wilfrid Laurier University Press, 1981.

Van den Broek, R. "The Present State of Gnostic Studies," *VigChr* 37 (1983), 41–71.

Van den Broek, R., and M. J. Vermaseren, eds. *Studies in Gnosticism and Hellenistic Religions Presented to Gilles Quispel on the Occasion of his 65th Birthday*. Leiden: Brill, 1981.

Van den Eynde, Damien. "Eucharistia ex duabus rebus constans: S. Irénée, Adv. Haer. IV, 18, 5" *Ant.* 15 (1940) 13–28.

Van der Straeten, J. "Saint Irénée fut-il martyr?" in *Les Martyrs de Lyon (177)*. Paris: Éditions du Centre national de la Recherche scientifique, 1978, 145–153.

Van Unnik, W. C. "Theological Speculation and Its Limits," in *Early Christian Literature and the Classical Tradition. In Honorem R.M. Grant*. ThH 53. Paris: Beauchesne, 1979, 33–43.

Welch, John W., ed. *Chiasmus in Antiquity: Structures, Analyses, Exegesis*. Hildesheim: Gerstenberg, 1981.

Widmann, M. *Der Begriff Oikonomia im Werke des Irenäus und seine Vorgeschichte*. Theol. Diss. Tübingen, 1956.

_____. "Irenäus und seine theologischen Väter," *ZThK* 54 (1957) 156–173.

Williams, Rowan. "Does It Make Sense to Speak of pre-Nicene Orthodoxy?" in Rowan Williams, ed., *The Making of Orthodoxy: Essays in Honour of Henry Chadwick*. New York: Cambridge University Press, 1989, 1–23.

Wingrin, Gustaf. *Man and the Incarnation: A Study in the Biblical Theology of Irenaeus*. Translated by Ross McKenzie. Philadelphia: Muhlenberg, 1959.

Wisse, Frederik. "The Nag Hammadi Library and the Heresiologists" *VigChr* 25 (1971) 205–223.

_____. "The Use of Early Christian Literature as Evidence for Inner Diversity and Conflict," in Hedrick and Hodgson, eds., *Nag Hammadi, Gnosticism, and Early Christianity,* 177–190.

Wright, Addison G. *The Literary Genre Midrash*. New York: Alba House, 1967.

Yamauchi, E. M. "Pre-Christian Gnosticism in the Nag Hammadi Texts," *ChH* 48 (1979) 129–141.

Index of Biblical References

Boldface denotes quotation; *italics* denotes extended treatment.

Index, *Adversus haereses*

Boldface indicates principal treatment.

General Index